SOCIAL POLICY

An Introduction

Third Edition

John R. Graham
University of Calgary

Karen J. Swift
York University

Roger Delaney
Lakehead University

PEARSON

Prentice
Hall

Toronto

This book is lovingly dedicated to Russell and Jean Graham;
to Peter, Julian, and Evan Holland; and to the late
Dr. John Gandy, academic mentor and friend.

Library and Archives Canada Cataloguing in Publication

Graham, John R. (John Russell), 1964–
      Canadian social policy : an introduction / John R. Graham, Karen J. Swift, Roger
Delaney. — 3rd ed.

Includes bibliographical references and index.
ISBN 978-0-13-240238-5

1. Canada—Social policy—Textbooks. I. Swift, Karen II. Delaney, Roger III. Title.

HV108.G735 2008   361.6'10971   C2007-905585-0

ISBN-13: 978-0-13-240238-5
ISBN-10: 0-13-240238-6

Vice-President, Editorial Director: Gary Bennett
Senior Acquisitions Editor: Laura Forbes
Marketing Manager: Sally Aspinall
Associate Editor: Brian Simons
Production Editor: Söğüt Y. Güleç
Copy Editor: Nancy Mucklow
Proofreaders: Laurel Sparrow, Laura Neves
Production Coordinator: Andrea Falkenberg
Composition: Laserwords
Art Director: Julia Hall
Cover Design: Brett Miller
Cover Image: Photodisc

Statistics Canada information is used with the permission of the Minister of Industry, as Minister responsible for Statistics Canada. Information on the availability of the wide range of data
from Statistics Canada can be obtained from Statistics Canada's Regional Offices, its World
Wide Web site at http://www.statcan.ca, and its toll-free access number 1-800-263-1136.

1 2 3 4 5   12 11 10 09 08

Printed and bound in the USA.

Contents

Preface

There are numerous books on social policy in the United Kingdom and United States. *Canadian Social Policy: An Introduction* is a response to the need for a Canadian perspective. It is a single-volume introduction to a highly diversified field, one that provides a framework for analyzing social policies. The book stresses concepts and policies as parallel and equal means to a framework. Our thinking owes much to recent forces in social policy practice and scholarship, particularly as they relate to feminist, postmodern, and social diversity writings, widely construed, and to the concerns of social justice raised by this scholarship.

Social policy is a fundamental component of social work practice and should never be seen as an ethereal or aloof add-on to the curriculum. It is important in other ways, perhaps more so than at any other time either in our country's history or in the history of the social work profession. The now prolonged assault on universal programs, the ever more limited scope of policies, the ascendancy of neo-conservative ideology, the growth of globalization, the imperative of diversity—these, among other phenomena, will greatly influence social work practice and social policy analysis in future years. It is essential, therefore, that students introduced to Canadian social policy understand these dynamics and have at their disposal an analytical frame of reference that will make them sensitive to the nuances of policy work and to the diverse needs of society's most marginalized people.

Canadian Social Policy: An Introduction examines major social policy considerations in Canada. It is intended for an audience of graduate, senior undergraduate, and senior community college students in social work, and for professionals who want to update their knowledge of current policy contexts. It is also intended to offer insights to students and practitioners of other disciplines, such as anthropology, business administration, Canadian studies, clinical psychology, development studies, divinity, economics, education, geography, history, nursing, occupational therapy, political science, public administration, rehabilitation studies, and sociology.

We greatly appreciate the supportive and useful advice from reviewers and from readers, which significantly influenced the third edition. The third edition builds upon and updates data from the first and second editions, including two additional stand-alone chapters on welfare state institutions and social policy analysis/implementation, respectively. Some chapters pay greater attention to the demographics of poverty and to policy-making processes, among other areas. The introductory chapter outlines some conceptual ideas that form a foundation for social policy analysis and application. Chapter 2 considers historic influences on Canadian social policies; Chapter 3, some of the country's major social welfare programs; and Chapter 4, significant policy-related ideological, social, and economic facets. Chapter 5 covers globalization, the environment, social inclusion, and social movements. Chapter 6 introduces the key notion of diversity to social policy formation; and Chapter 7 presents how social policies are applied to social work practice and to social service delivery in general. The final two chapters examine the policy-making process in Canada, from stages and structures through to analysis, implementation, and assessment.

This textbook has been a number of years in the making. It started out as a proposal submitted by Roger Delaney. Once a publishing contract was received and the work begun, Roger invited John Graham and Karen Swift to be co-authors. The textbook's initial focus then expanded in order to place greater emphasis on the historical origins of Canadian social policies and on the impact of social diversity on all aspects of policy formation and analysis. The writing process has been truly collaborative, with each author contributing to the others' sentences, paragraphs, references, and ideas, and acting as a sounding board over all matters related to authorship. Roger took the lead in Chapters 1, 8, and 9; John in Chapters 2, 3, 4, and the first part of Chapter 5; and Karen in the latter part of Chapter 5 and in Chapters 6 and 7; but the entire final product has each scholar's imprint.

The authors have been fortunate for so many things, including the kind encouragement of readers and our press. The second edition, released in 2003, expanded beyond the first edition to include greater discussion of Canada's welfare state institutions, social welfare theory, socioeconomic class, social policy practice, globalization, the physical ecology, and social movements. This third edition, released in 2008, considerably updates the analysis and provides further analysis of social policy practice, and social policy development in a market state era of less government and ascendant liberal capitalist ideology. Like previous editions, we pay particular attention to writing clear and precise prose and to trying to present social policy as the relevant, important thing that it is.

Acknowledgments

Many people, too numerous to mention, were extremely influential in the completion of this text. Special thanks are extended to Tanjeem Azad, Helen Boukos, Andreas Breuer, Cathryn Bradshaw, Xiaobei Chen, Stefanie Kaiser, Patricia Bianchini, Susan Graham, Sarah Meagher, Nikoo Najand, Louise Querido, and Micheal Shier in particular, for extremely helpful and timely research assistanceship. John Graham's father, Russell Graham, read the entire first-edition manuscript and provided, as always, exceptionally valuable editorial advice. Staff at Pearson Education Canada were unendingly cooperative and encouraging. In the early 1970s, the late Albert Rose of the Faculty of Social Work, University of Toronto, conceived a social policy chart for teaching purposes. In light of substantial policy changes since then, part of the conceptualization in Chapter 3 is loosely based on Dr. Rose's original chart and is dedicated to his memory. A major contributor to the development of Figures 4.2 and 8.2 is Raika Abdulahad, a Ph.D. student at the University of Calgary. Keith Brownlee, Issam Dawood, Paul DeBakker, M.D., David Este, Gayle Gilchrist-James, Jacqueline Ismael, Margaret McKee, and Bob Luker were among colleagues who provided much-appreciated support and advice. Funding from the University of Calgary Starter Grant for newly recruited faculty provided money for research assistanceship for the first edition; particular thanks are extended to the University of Calgary and the Alberta government for this critical support. Grateful acknowledgment is extended for grant support from SSHRC to the Caring Labour Network and the project on "Risk and risk assessment in child welfare." A Senate Research Grant from Lakehead University was likewise instrumental in moving the manuscript toward completion. Finally, thanks are extended to the Caledon Institute of Social Policy, the Canadian Council on Social Development, Human Resources and Social Development Canada, the National Council of Welfare, Statistics Canada, and those publishing companies that allowed us to cite various research.

The editors and authors would like to thank the following reviewers for their helpful commentary on previous editions: Robert Marino of King's College, University of Western Ontario; Francis Turner of Wilfrid Laurier University; and Brian Wharf of the University of Victoria. The editors and authors would also like to thank the following reviewers for their helpful commentary on the second edition: Michael J. Holosko of the University of Windsor; Lynda E. Turner of Kwantlen University College; and Thérèse Jennissen of Carleton University.

Chapter (1)

Introduction to Canadian Social Policy

Social policy is premised in the past, implemented in the present, and directed toward the future. It is profoundly influenced by societal values and ideologies, by domestic and international factors, and should be sensitive to the diversities that constitute Canadian society. A thorough understanding of social policy is essential to effective social work practice. This text, therefore, presents Canadian social policy from a framework that takes into account the imperatives of history, diversity, and relevance to direct practice in Canada. Likewise, the book consciously affirms the empowerment of all Canadians—particularly those who have historically been marginal within local, regional, national, and international power structures.

For a beginning student, one of the most immediate means of understanding social policy is through terminology. This chapter, therefore, introduces several key concepts and concludes with a look at the relationship of policy to direct practice, a theme that is elaborated in Chapter 5. The student is also encouraged to refer to the glossary at the end of the book, which contains core definitions used in the present chapter and throughout the text.

Human beings believe in a wide range of religions and philosophies, organize around a wide range of political and social principles, and value different human attributes and characteristics. However, there is a common attribute—the fact that each of us is a human being. Moreover, these world views and physical and human attributes *describe* human beings but do not *define* human beings. In other words, gender, religion, skin colour, physical attributes, social norms, ideologies, intelligence, physical fitness, gender preference, age, and other physical and mental attributes describe what is different about people, but not who we are as human beings.

These differences represent our world views. World views are constructed from values drawn from religious, political, social, and physical information about humans and the societies they create. Once accepted by a group of people, these world views become *agreement realities* (Babbie, 1986, 1977). Agreement realities become the *truth* for all those with a similar world view, and this truth is passed down from generation to generation.

If you were born and raised only in Canada after 1970, then the many elements that currently make up Canadian society probably make sense to you. If you live in an organized community (such as a city or town) that elects officials

1

(such as mayors, reeves, and councillors) to govern the community, this process of governance seems normal to you. Other things that would be normal to you would include electing provincial and federal members to provincial, territorial, and federal parliaments to represent you (representative democracy); having your basic health-care costs paid for by government (medicare); having free public education to Grade 12; being free to travel throughout Canada without a passport; working for a salary or profits in a competitive marketplace; and having police forces that are accountable to elected officials.

You would also be acquainted with the rules that govern people's conduct in Canada, such as criminal laws that make such activities as murder, theft, kidnapping, and physical and sexual assault illegal. You would be aware of rules that govern conduct in the workplace, such as those dealing with harassment, exploitation, and injury. You would be aware that there are rules that also protect the vulnerable, such as children and the elderly, from being exploited or injured. Finally, you would also have discovered a number of rules that govern our activities, such as traffic laws, snowmobile and boating laws, and hunting and fishing laws.

You would also be aware that Canada is made up of many different people who speak different languages, believe in different religions, live different lifestyles, and value different things, all of which are protected from discrimination by Canada's Charter of Rights and Freedoms.

More importantly, in addition to these shared world views, how you experience all of the above elements of Canadian society is influenced by such factors as whether you are rich or poor; white or a person of colour; male or female; heterosexual or gay or lesbian; married or single; renting or owning; working, unemployed, or retired; young or old; citizen or immigrant; professional or minimum-wage worker; full-time employed or part-time employed; or healthy, injured, or ill. Most of us will experience life in Canada from perspectives shaped by many combinations of the above attributes over the course of our lives.

Because people experience Canada differently, they can also differ about what they believe is in Canada's best interest. If people are rich, powerful, and respected, they may very well want Canada to remain as it is or to change only in ways that benefit them. Philosopher Karl Mannheim (1936) calls this *ideological thinking*. On the other hand, if people are poor, unemployed, and living in slum conditions, they may very well want Canada to change drastically and in ways that benefit them. Mannheim (1936) called this *utopian thinking*.

The study of social policy helps us to understand how world views influence the way in which members of social arrangements (i.e., societies, communities, families, or clubs) feel about such things as:

➤ social power, including personal powers and freedoms;

➤ social justice, including social equality, social status, roles, and prerogatives;

➤ human, civil, and social rights;

➤ human and social diversity;

➤ the nature of society;

➤ the relationship between people and society; and

➤ the nature of human relationships.

These are all very big issues; because they are so big, social policies can affect human beings in every aspect of their lives. Social workers and other human service professionals support the notion that society is about people, and that when properly resourced physically, emotionally, and spiritually, human beings will strive to become more fully human, whether that be by achieving higher order needs (see Chapter 4) or by fulfilling a human ontological vocation (Freire, 1994) to become more fully human. This view is not shared by some people in our industrialized societies, who offer a view of society governed by economic or human attribute supremacy. For example, Payne (1998) argues that social work failed when the profession accepted the position that environment (unemployment/underemployment, racism, ageism, ghettos, poverty) significantly affects human behaviour because social work then created a society of expectant giving with no personal responsibility. In his view, the Charity Organization Society had it right: poverty and social alienation are a result of personal failure and inadequate character. Should this view become the social policy basis for societal public policies on welfare, then the poor would be blamed as the cause of their own poverty. Simply put, if you cause your own problems, why should society be responsible for you? When society refuses to take responsibility, the poor are made black against the night; they simply disappear from public consciousness. The views expressed by Payne have been embraced by the political right, who hold increasingly greater power in Canada and other industrialized countries (including Great Britain and France).

Social policy is about making decisions that are—in the perception of those making them—in the best interests of Canada and Canadians. Because these perceptions are very subjective, it is essential to ask certain questions in order to understand what impact social policies will have on society. Specifically, who has the power to make social policy decisions? Whose views of life in Canada are driving the policy-making process? Who is benefiting from these policies? Who is not benefiting from these policies? How consistent are these policies with societal norms?

One of the most important aspects of social policy for beginning students is the multitude of approaches available to study it. Among the many approaches that will be explored throughout the book are the contrasting perceptions of social policy as comprehensive versus incremental, global versus local, and value-driven versus scientifically derived. These variations in approach reflect the social work profession's and society's confusion about just what social policy is.

What Are Social Policies?

The late British scholar Richard Titmuss (1974) examined social policy by first exploring the meaning of the terms *social* and *policy*. To him, *social* referred to all of the non-economic factors that affect people in society and relate to people as social beings. *Policy*, Titmuss insisted, is about enduring the dilemmas of choice created when one objective must be selected over others.

Exploring various definitions and perceptions about social policy can be a frustrating journey into subtle abstract differences or esoteric debates. Moreover, many social workers and human service workers often confuse just what social policy is. For example, it is not uncommon to hear social workers talk about their agency's *social policy* rather than the correct term, *agency policy* or *public policy*.

The following social policy definition is intended to provide you with a framework to ground your study of social policy. Throughout the book, you will be able to use this definition to analyze social policy debates.

Social policy describes societal visions—that is, values and beliefs that people hold about what a society should look like, based upon a notion about human beings, the nature of society, and the way society and humans interact. For example, different political parties talk about programs and policies that they believe will benefit society. Different interest and advocacy groups also have visions about what a society should look like. This makes it possible to identify social policy positions related to different competing groups in a society. We can also assume that groups of like-minded people will support a common vision and will disagree with the different visions of other groups. If all people agreed on one societal vision, then society would have only one social policy position.

However, those elected to form a government are in a unique position. They can translate their social policy vision into law, thus creating new public policies that reflect their vision, revising existing public policies and repealing others. Public policies guide public programs and laws and are binding to all citizens. Therefore, if you gain power, you can implement your social policies and require all citizens to live under the societal vision reflected in your social policies. People who disagree with the new laws are left with limited options, such as supporting a party with an opposing policy vision to help it win the next election, using social and/or economic power to prevent or discourage an elected government from implementing policies, or revolting against the existing government and taking power through force.

Public policies inform social programs and define both the nature of the programs and the citizens whom the programs serve. Agencies, government departments, and ministries (the formal social organizations) are empowered and financed to provide these social programs within the framework provided by the enabling act and subsequent regulations. In turn, agencies and government services have organizational cultures that influence how services are delivered even within their guiding legislation.

In summary, social policy positions influence legislation, which in turn influences programs, which in turn influence services. Whoever has the power to implement his or her social policy position or to prevent others from implementing their positions determines the quality, range, and availability of social programs.

Definitions of Social Policy

Richard Titmuss—Models of Social Policy

Richard Titmuss (1974) argued that social policy is basically about "choices between conflicting political objectives and goals and how they are formulated" (49). These choices are influenced by views of what constitutes a good society, based on that which "culturally distinguishes between the needs and aspirations of social man [sic] in contradiction to the needs and aspirations of economic man [sic]" (49). Titmuss argues that social policy can best be understood in terms of the following three models or functions:

1. *The Residual Welfare Model of Social Policy:* This model argues that the private market and the family are responsible for meeting an individual's needs. Only when these break down should social welfare institutions intervene. As discussed in Chapter 3, proponents of neo-conservative and liberal ideologies favour this model.
2. *The Industrial Achievement-Performance Model of Social Policy:* This model argues that social needs should be met on the basis of merit, work performance, and productivity. Known as the "Handmaiden Model," it is favoured by positivists (Federico, 1983) and other economic and psychological theorists who advocate incentives, effort, and reward.
3. *The Institutional Redistributive Model of Social Policy:* This model argues that social welfare should be a major integrated institution in society, providing universal services outside the market, based on the principle of need.

Policy can emerge from these approaches only in areas of life where choices exist. Without choices, there is no policy; rather, there is a law, either natural or legislated. For example, since people cannot control the weather, societies have no policies concerning weather control. However, should science ever learn how to control weather, then societies would have to make choices about how to control the weather. Tension might arise between people who want warm sunshine and farmers who want rain (*preferential choices*). Further, controlling the weather might cause well-known ecological effects, such as sterilizing some insects or wildlife (*anticipated consequences*). Finally, controlling the weather might even have detrimental effects that are not even known (*unanticipated consequences*). In this example, the choice to control weather would result in an anticipated consequence for insects and wildlife, some potential unanticipated consequences, and a decision about whether the farmer gets rain or the public gets sunshine.

Martin Rein—Value-Driven Policy

The weather example shows that values and beliefs are important to decisions in social policy. The American scholar Martin Rein (1974) suggested that "social policy is, above all, concerned with choice among competing values" (298). From Rein's perspective, society consists of people holding diverse values (world views) who are in competition with each other and each other's values, in an effort to achieve maximum power. So ingrained are values in every aspect of social, economic, and public policies that many social policy theorists—such as Rein, Gil (1998), and Wharf and MacKenzie (1998)—warn that a major role of policy-makers is to learn how to control their own values and prejudices. This warning is further discussed in Chapter 8.

Rein suggests that values influence social policy in five major ways:

1. Values influence the definition of the purpose of the policy, especially policies dealing with "moral" decisions. An example would be a policy addressing abortion.

2. Values influence priorities by assigning greater "value" to some courses of action over others. An economic example would be the decision to reduce the rate of inflation by increasing interest rates. This decision assigns higher value to the protection of business interests and lower value to the maintenance of employment levels.

3. Values demand change when they are formally and legally articulated. Once a position is articulated and the means to bring it about are put in place, people will assign it importance (which is value-derived) simply because it exists (has form). As a result, society may have to change in order to allow that form to exist. For example, the North American Free Trade Agreement has caused significant changes to the Canadian economy, leading to the closure of some industries, the increase in some markets, the decrease in others, and so on.

4. Values focus on usefulness and feasibility. Policy-makers can become preoccupied with usefulness and political feasibility rather than societal need. A current example is the federal government's Axworthy social policy reform document of 1994, which is seen by many to have done little to change many social policies, since few of the proposals were ever implemented.

5. Values influence the interpretation and evaluation of outcomes. One example is the claim that certain poverty lines do not really describe poverty. As discussed in Chapter 3, Canada has many different poverty lines, each with its own threshold below which a person's annual income is declared "in poverty"; ultimately the threshold level is determined by some value of what is seen to be fair (adapted from Rein, 1974, 298).

Since social policy is often articulated as public policy, public policy documents reflect values that gain dominance. Public policies are legislated acts, regulations, and by-laws (including all associated policies in the ministerial, agency, and public arenas) at the federal, provincial, and municipal levels of government (Doern & Aucoin, 1971). As such, public policies are *social statements* reflecting the values and ideology of the political party or parties sponsoring them. Because public policies are encased in law, they have three distinct attributes:

1. Public policies are *legitimate*. Although an issue may be heavily debated—gun control, for example—once a policy is legislated, it is the law and is right or legitimate. Those who opposed the issue must now accept it as law, even if they are working to change it.

2. Public policies apply to everyone.
3. Because government *controls* (much, but not all) *coercion* in society, public policies can be enforced. Governments control enforcement agencies, such as the police, government investigators (e.g., income tax and welfare fraud investigators), and, in the case of the federal government, the army. These enforcement agencies ensure that the government can enforce the law.

Public policies provide boundaries and controls to regulate citizen behaviour, either directly (e.g., game and fishing policy, housing policy, taxation policy) or indirectly (e.g., foreign policy). As such, public policies play an instrumental part in all aspects of societal life.

David Gil—Social Justice

David Gil (1970), who, along with Rein, and Wharf and MacKenzie, is discussed in greater length in Chapter 6, suggested that social policies are concerned not only with the life-sustaining activities that ensure minimum basic needs, but also with those that stimulate our human potential. But the range of possibilities for these activities is as great as the range of world views that influence them. From a *polycentric perspective*, variation in views allows a more complete world view to emerge. A polycentric perspective, first articulated by McPherson and Rabb (1994), argues that

radically different world views not only reveal something about culture and language, but about reality itself and the ways different people have come to know it. Therefore, each world view reveals something about the total picture, which can never be fully known. An accurate picture of reality is only possible by attempting to accommodate and reconcile as many world views as possible (Delaney, 1995, 13).

Moreover, Gil (1998) saw a need for social transformation. Systemic inequalities based on world views supporting "inequality, individualism, selfishness, domination, competition, and disregard for community (from local to global)" (35) need to be replaced by world views "affirming equality, individuality, liberty, cooperation, community and global solidarity" (35). Fundamental to this perspective is the view that human beings have physical, emotional, and spiritual dimensions and that human social functioning is impeded without the resources that meet these physical, emotional, and spiritual dimensions. The result would be humans whose potential is limited or constrained. Should one group of people attempt to ensure that their physical, emotional, and spiritual dimensions are satisfied at the expense of another group, then this would be an act of oppression.

Other approaches to social policy tend to reflect the comprehensive–incremental continuum.

Braybrooke and Lindbloom—Incrementalism

Braybrooke and Lindblom (1963) identified *incrementalism* as a key feature of social policy. They suggested that the world is just too complex and organic to allow for comprehensive policy and planning. For one thing, comprehensive policy-makers themselves have to fill in variables about society and people about which they do not have valid and reliable information, thus allowing their own values to influence the design of social policies. Instead, these authors suggested that throughout history, people have simply corrected problems as they arose, and, over time, made substantive changes.

This incrementalist approach to social policy analysis is limited to considerations of alternative policies that are only incrementally different from the status quo. Because incrementalist theory has no major framework, the overall policy approach tends to be disjointed. Because different people are preparing policies for different problems independently, the term *disjointed incrementalism* is often applied to examples of this approach, which displays the following characteristics:

1. Analysis is limited to a few familiar alternatives.
2. Analysis of policy goals is intertwined with empirical aspects of the problem.
3. Analysis is concerned with remedying ills rather than with seeking positive goals.
4. Policies undergo a sequence of trials, errors, and revised trials.
5. Analysis of only some of the important consequences of those alternatives is considered.
6. Analytical work is fragmented among many partisan participants in policy making (Hogwood & Gunn, 1984).

Some observers argue that incrementalism closely approximates *functionalism*. Functionalism suggests that every social system must meet four functional prerequisites in order to persist. These four prerequisites apply to all social systems:

1. *Adaptation:* The policy is adapted to the external environment;
2. *Goal attainment:* The policy co-ordinates collective activities to reach certain goals;
3. *Integration:* The policy integrates members of society to maintain solidarity and harmony; and
4. *Pattern maintenance (or latency):* The policy ensures that the activities required by members are performed with optimum compliance.

Functionalists view social welfare activities as a means of helping to create harmony among social institutions and individuals and hence maintain communal solidarity. The essential framework of functionalism is to value stability and continuity above social change. In other words, society as it currently exists is considered to be good; therefore, only when something goes wrong should it be changed.

Critics of functionalism, such as Mishra (1981), suggest that the increase in poverty, privilege, and exploitation in the United States and the universal problems of racism and sexism have served to undermine the validity of the functionalist model. Mishra and other scholars argue that the dominant metaphor for social organization is conflict between groups in society, rather than social stability, as functionalist theory implies.

But more important than incrementalist and functionalist approaches is the question of who determines the priorities, the structure, and the method of implementation of social welfare programs.

Turner and Yelaja—Group Goals and Objectives

Canadian scholar Francis Turner views social policy as statements of the social goals and objectives to which various groups—professional, governmental, or private—are committed. "They are the mission statements of various groups, and . . . vary widely in a country such as ours. . . . [A]s responsible citizens in a democratic country, we have a responsibility to understand this important component of our lives. This responsibility exists whether our goal is to become a social worker, a member of other related professions, a better-informed recipient of services, an advocate for social change, or a fully participating member of society" (1995, 10).

While reflecting the competition among values held by various groups for domination, Turner's view also states that social policy is culturally relevant— that is, Canadian social policies are not the same as those of other countries.

Another rather comprehensive definition of social policy comes from Canadian scholars Shankar Yelaja (1987), Ann Westhues (2003), and Rosalie Chappell (2006), whose definitions of social welfare reflect a social administration approach. For Yelaja et al., social policy is concerned with

the public administration of welfare services, that is, the formulation, development and management of specific services of government at all levels, such as health, education, income maintenance, and welfare services. Social policy is formulated not only by government, but also by institutions such as voluntary organizations, business, labour, industry, professional groups, public interest groups, and churches. Furthermore, social policy is to be understood within the framework of societal ends and means, which are interdependent (1987, 2).

Westhues (2003) furthers Yelaja's position by viewing social policies as courses of "action or inaction chosen by public authorities to address a given problem or interrelated set of problems" (8). Public authorities include decision-makers in government, social service organizations, and collective agreements. Chappell (2006) views social policies as sets of guidelines that provide structure and direction to Canada's social welfare programs. According to this perspective, social policy reflects social reality within a cultural context.

Gilbert and Specht, Marshall, Mishra, and Lightman— Social Action

American scholars Gilbert and Specht (1974) tried to teach social workers how policies affect the populations they work with. They define the institution of social welfare as "that patterning of relationships which develops in society to carry out mutual support functions" (5). A British social policy theorist with a similar social administration orientation is T.H. Marshall (1965), who notes that *social policy* is not a technical term with an exact meaning; instead, it refers to

the policy of governments with regard to action having a direct impact on the welfare of the citizens by providing them with service or income. The central core consists, there-fore, of social insurance, public (or national) assistance, the health and welfare services, [and] housing policy (7).

Marshall argues that the best way to ensure the welfare of citizens is to culti-vate a sense of the right (or entitlement) to the following three things:

1. civil rights, which guarantee individual liberty and equality before the law;
2. political rights, which ensure the right to vote and seek political office; and
3. social rights, which ensure equal access and opportunities to all social institutions.

To ensure these rights, social policy advocates rely on the legal system to mon-itor and correct any abuses of these rights. However, Drover (2000) warns that globalization requires a redefinition of Marshall's notion of social citizenship, because nations now have restricted ability to respond to the rights of their citizens.

Rice and Prince (2000) envision a cooperative union between the forces driving economic policies and social policies, where social policy is treated as a partner of economic policy rather than as a drain of national and international economies.

Mishra (1981) defines social policy as referring "to the aims and objectives of social action concerning needs as well as to the structural patterns or arrange-ments through which needs are met" (x). For Mishra, social policy is concerned with deliberately and rationally matching ends and means through social institu-tions designed for that purpose.

Lightman (2003) views Canadian social policy as a spectrum. At one end is a set of values, programs, and practices designed to (theoretically) bring Canadians together as a community by relating to shared experiences and mutual interde-pendence. At the other end of the spectrum, social policies are sets of programs designed for Canada's poor and vulnerable populations. Lightman views social policies as the choices made with respect to a group, community, or collective, and these choices have real consequences and costs for people and society.

In a similar argument, Lafitte (1962) claimed that social policy is "an attempt to steer the life of society along lines it would not follow if left to itself" (9).

Freeman and Sherwood (1970) view social policy as consisting of "con-clusions reached by persons concerned with the betterment of community conditions and social life, and with the amelioration of deviance and social disorganization" (13).

Quality-of-Life Approach

Another perspective that allows comparisons of the impact of social policies is the *quality-of-life approach*. This approach is used by the United Nations, which makes statements about the social health of nations on the basis of data collected on quality-of-life indicators. Quality-of-life indicators include the following:

- physical and mental health;
- education and occupational achievements;
- development in the arts and science;
- production and consumption;
- wealth and income (including child poverty);
- conditions of the natural environment;
- patterns of recreation;
- patterns of social participation;
- patterns of social morality; and
- social deviance and alienation.

Quality-of-life indicators allow social workers to compare their country's social welfare programs internationally. In recent years, the amount of money Canada spends on social programs has slipped considerably and the number of poor children and families has increased.

The social policy theories described above all seek to explore the following questions: Is society organized around the needs of human beings? Are human beings organized around the needs of society? Are the needs of human beings and the needs of society interdependent? While these questions may sound rather simplistic, their resolution is not simplistic: ideologies and world views seek to make certain questions central to all social policy statements. For example, the current dominant social policy approach in Canada is based on the economic model of people, which advocates that human beings be organized around the economic needs of society. To challenge this view is also to challenge the power establishment, not just in Canada but internationally. As globalization creates more treaties among nations giving substantial power to economic interests, national governments have less say in the quality-of-life and social program issues that affect their people.

Social Policy in a Time of Mistrust and Cynicism

One of the unfortunate consequences of the replacement of the Canada Assistance Plan (CAP) with Canada Health and Social Transfer (CHST) in the 1990s was that it unleashed the *ideology of mistrust*. CAP, which was hailed by many countries as positive and progressive social welfare legislation, provided a standard of social assistance across Canada for people in need or likely to be in need. Originally designed to share welfare costs with the provinces on a fifty–fifty basis, CAP had slowly begun to decrease cost sharing with the provinces during the late 1980s and early 1990s. With the passing of CHST, responsibility for the funding of social services devolved from the federal government to the provinces and even down to local communities in some of these provinces. Moreover, the removal of

CAP increased the privatization of social services across Canada. This will be discussed further in Chapter 3.

The ideology of mistrust suggests that poor people are "guided by an 'acquisitive instinct,' that is, they are out to get all they can by any means" (Macarov, 1995b, 147). Mistrust has existed for centuries. The Law of Less Eligibility (also referred to as *wage stop*) is one example. Passed in 1834, this law required all people receiving charity to be given less money or goods than the lowest paid worker in the parish. This law was designed to starve those who were "lazy" or "immoral" back to work. The nineteenth-century English workhouses, which encouraged brutal and cruel treatment of unemployed workers, are another example of social policy being driven by the ideology of mistrust. Similarly, the "ideology of the elite" argues that while most people are deserving and trustworthy, people receiving charity or social assistance are not trustworthy or deserving because they lack moral character and cannot plan and think for themselves. This view also supports "the politics of conduct," which argues that a person's conduct should determine both the quality and quantity of services provided.

The resulting mistrust of poor people can lead to public announcements that welfare cheats are being hunted down and will be punished. Certainly, the news media are more attracted to welfare cheaters being caught than to the many stories of those who are trying to both subsist and exist as people on social assistance. Consider how often you have heard people who are not poor speak knowingly about youth who are abusing Employment Insurance, women who are having babies in order to live off the public purse, immigrants who are sending their welfare money to support terrorists, youth who are committing horrible crimes and getting away with it, homeless people who are all mentally ill or lazy, unions who are trying to destroy business, gays who want extra rights, or children of the poor who are so much like their parents—just no good.

As the ideology of mistrust becomes more pervasive in Canadian society, that society becomes more cynical. It quickly becomes evident that people who are rich demand and have opportunities that those who are not rich do not have. For example, while medicare attends to the health needs of the general population, those with sufficient money can go to the United States and receive medical attention and procedures more quickly.

Political and Social Consequences

Lerner (1997) believes that the current ethos of cynicism and selfishness has led to an economy-first attitude. People feel more and more insecure if they are not among those who are "winning" in today's economic marketplace. Lerner envisions an alliance of the shrinking middle class with the poor to work on combating the selfishness, materialism, and corporatism (Saul, 1995) espoused by the rich and by multinational conglomerates. For Lerner, the *politics of meaning* is a political process aimed at achieving the following five goals:

1. to create a society that "encourages and supports love and intimacy, friendship and community, ethnic sensitivity, and spiritual awareness" (55);

2. to redefine production and profit in terms of practices that foster spiritual harmony, loving relationships, mutual recognition, and work that promotes the common good;

3. to construct social conditions that promote the material, emotional, and spiritual uniqueness, sanctity, and infinite preciousness of every human being;

4. to design a society that recognizes the need and provides for the opportunity to develop our inner lives; and

5. to create a society that instils awe and joy in how we relate to the world and each other.

For social workers whose value and ethical base is grounded in principles of social justice, social equality, and respect for the inner being of all humans, these goals, while seemingly idealistic, speak to the very heart of their profession. Many other twentieth-century writers, such as Fromm (1967, 1955), Teilhard de Chardin (1955), Freire (1994, 1985, 1968), Frankl (1969), Gil (1998, 1992, 1970), and Titmuss (1970) have all supported aspects of Lerner's five goals.

Titmuss studied the effects of encouraging altruism (1970) and noted that the donation of blood in countries such as Britain and Canada is done voluntarily and without financial payment, while in other countries, such as the United States, donors are paid for their blood. Titmuss examined whether the altruistic act of donating blood created different results from the market mechanism of purchasing blood. Titmuss concludes that the selling of blood

represses . . . altruism, erodes the sense of community, lowers scientific standards, sanctions . . . the profits in hospitals and clinical laboratories, legalizes hostility between doctor and patient, subjects . . . medicine to the laws of the marketplace, places immense social costs on those least able to bear them . . . [and] increases the danger of unethical behaviour (245–246).

In effect, blood systems that purchase blood may create a situation in which blood and blood products are transferred from the poor to the rich. Moreover, where blood is given voluntarily, supplies and the quality of these supplies of blood are expected to be superior to those within systems where blood is purchased.

As elaborated in Chapters 5 and 9, there are profound implications to the current ethos of cynicism, as it relates to the environmental movement, global economic and political structures, and the decrease of social service programs.

Social Policy and Social Welfare Policy

Many beginning students of social policy are confused about the terms *social policy* and *social welfare policy*. What is apparent from the various approaches to social policy that we have discussed is the lack of consensus about how *social policy* ought to be defined. The generally prevailing view of social policy is that it is concerned with the "big picture" of society and with the big issues in society, such as social justice, social equality, human rights and freedoms, empowerment and human authenticity, progressive distribution of wealth, full employment, medicare, criminal justice, and mutual aid (Mullaly, 1993).

Because social policy deals with major social issues, it is concerned with the espoused visions and social remedies articulated by groups such as political communities, business communities, professional communities, labour communities, multicultural communities, interest groups, and special-needs communities representing people who are poor, physically challenged, and homeless.

Issues of social power and social control are also important concerns for social policy. In a very real way, social workers who work in the area of social policy become monitors of social conditions and public policies. In this capacity, they play an important role in educating the social work profession and society-at-large regarding anticipated or unanticipated consequences of new or revised public policies or of changes in government and business practices in Canada.

Social policy is also concerned with "politics," trade agreements, environmental issues, hiring practices, taxation, racism, gender and sexual preference discrimination, economics, and other related subjects. Advocates for social justice often use the social policy forum to promote political solutions for social problems (Gil, 1998; Carniol, 1995; Mullaly, 1993); they view the role of the social worker as one of promoting social justice and social equality not only in the service community but also in the population-at-large. Social change based on humanistic values drives this agenda for change and promotes a collaborative partnership in Canadian policy-making.

Social welfare policy, on the other hand, is concerned with welfare programs and the relationship between public and business policies and welfare programs. As such, it is less abstract and global than social policy and deals with very concrete issues, such as the quality and effectiveness of social service programs, citizen participation in policy and service issues, the role of community, and the actual impact of public policies on people. By studying social welfare policy, social workers directly observe the impact of public policies on the lives of people. As a result, social welfare policy advocates deconstruct the social myths that drive current social programs and encourage direct involvement of people in finding solutions to their life problems.

Social welfare policy advocates are very concerned with the role of the community in the lives of its members (Delaney, Brownlee, & Sellick, 1999; Wharf & McKenzie, 1998; Cassidy, 1991). Wharf and McKenzie (2004) describe community governance using the metaphor of a three-runged ladder. The first rung represents community programs essentially under community control, such as water and sewage, garbage, parking, and recreation programs. The second rung represents programs mandated by provincial, territorial, or federal government levels but operated by the community. This level includes programs such as child welfare and health services. The third rung is concerned with principles of equity and requires a collaborative partnership between government and the community. Included on this rung are programs such as Social Assistance and Employment Insurance. Wharf and McKenzie (2004) conclude that community governance models provide "an opportunity to reform the policy process and policy outcomes by involving people who are significantly affected by these outcomes" (125).

It is in the area of citizen participation that social welfare policy excels. While social policy tends to deal comprehensively in the political and societal arenas, social welfare policy lends itself to involving people in policy development and renewal. The issues that social welfare policy addresses are issues that people know about and that affect everyday living. People can more readily see the cause–effect relationship between how programs operate and how these programs affect them. It is much easier to involve people in actions that are clear, local, and achievable. On the other hand, advocacy in social policy tends to be national, provincial, or territorial; it also tends to be ideological, value-based, and complex. This makes it much harder to involve people. For example, in a university or college setting, it is always much easier to get students to participate in a march against rising tuition fees than it is to get students to join a political party to influence its educational policies in favour of lowering tuition fees.

A final consideration is the distinction between policy-making and policy advocacy. Jansson (1990) suggests that policy advocates must have analytical skills (for policy evaluation and development), political skills (for development and implementation of political strategies), interactional skills (for development of collaborative partnerships), and values-clarification or ethical-reasoning skills. Both policy advocates and policy-makers must be able to perform six policy tasks: setting agendas, analyzing problems, making proposals, enacting policy, implementing policy, and assessing policy. As Jansson notes:

When presenting problems to agency, community, and legislative decision makers, the [policy practitioners and policy advocates] engage in agenda-setting tasks. When they use social science research . . . practitioners use problem-analyzing tasks. They also analyze social problems, such as homelessness, in classifying homeless persons, gauging the problem's prevalence in various communities, and seeking its causes (13).

Social Work and Social Policy

All schools of social work have at least one course that deals with social policy. One reason is that social policy and social welfare policy govern the environment in which most social workers work. Another is that the quality of services available and the attitudes of those who rely on these services for their well-being depend on social policy. As the following section discusses, there are still other reasons why social policy is important to social work.

As subsequent chapters will explain, every social work intervention—be it with an individual, a family, a group, an organization, or a community—is somehow referenced to a social policy. Assisting a family to seek adequate housing invariably relates to social housing policies; assisting an individual to re-enter the community after a prolonged period of incarceration may relate to vocational policies. These considerations therefore influence the nature of Canadian social work education.

From a curriculum perspective, the Educational Policy Statements of *The Manual of Standards and Procedures for the Accreditation of Canadian Programs of Social Work Education* (1996), approved by the Canadian Association of Schools of Social Work (CASSW), state that the social work curriculum at the first university level (HBSW) shall ensure that social work students learn "critical analysis of social work and social welfare history, and social policy as socially constructed institutions and their implications for social work practice" (CASSW, 1996, 3). Accreditation Standard Article 5.8 (d) states that social work students in the first university level shall have "transferable analysis of the multiple and intersecting bases of oppression and related practice skills" (CASSW, 1996, 6).

Although this explains why schools of social work teach social policy, it does not explain why you should study social policy. Perhaps the following narrative will help.

While driving home from work one day in 1979, I heard on the radio that the city was going to increase swimming pool rates from 10 cents per child to 25 cents per child. I thought to myself that inflation is striking everywhere and, while annoyed, gave this no further thought. After all, a 15-cent raise is not the end of the world.

Three days later, I was listening to the same station's call-in show, and I heard a mother relate the following. She was a single mother with five children, living on social assistance. Each summer, she saved money to allow her children to go swimming three times a week at a cost of $1.50. However, with the new rates, this would now cost her $1.25 per day or $3.75 for the three days. She could not afford this and would have to cut back the time her children could go swimming.

She was greatly distressed, as swimming was one of the few activities to which she could afford to send her children. Now her children would become even more isolated from other children, and she was helpless to do anything about it. When asked why she could not just save more money, the mother replied that she was giving up meals for herself in order for the children to go swimming under the old rates.

I was embarrassed as I listened to this mother and angry that she even had to tell such a story. As a social worker, I should have been more sensitive to the price hike. Worse, since I could afford to pay the extra 15 cents, I did not even consider that there were those who could not. This is one policy I vowed to fight and one new awareness that allows me to assess policies better. I just hope I did learn.

The study of social policy can increase our sensitivity to the people we serve. Because we know the circumstances under which many of our clients live, we can become proponents for policies that will enhance their well-being and advocates against policies that negatively impact them.

The study of social policy also allows you to learn how social inequalities, disempowerment, marginalization, and oppression can seep into political agendas and affect those least able to fight against them. Bishop (1994) sees these elements as part of a "power-over" agenda. A power-over agenda seeks to create a world of systems designed to keep people unequal. It uses four types of power over people. The first type, *political power*, concentrates power in the hands of fewer and fewer people because those making decisions build up the power of their own group. The second type, *economic power*, occurs when one group has access to more economic resources than others. The third type, *physical force*, uses the army and the police to back up economic and political power. The fourth type, *ideological power*, allows one group to influence thought and shape popular ideas of what is possible, desirable, and valuable (36–37).

Understanding how groups gain social, economic, and political power through social policy is important for social workers. Wharf (1990) suggests that social work insufficiently oriented to social change fails in four ways. First, it makes the assumption that once a problem is identified, change will occur and the problem will be solved. This is rarely the case in real practice. Second, it ignores power and its distribution in Canada. Third, because social workers are not assigned responsibility by society for bringing about change, some agencies may become the problem and not the solution. Fourth, the issue of auspices is not addressed: because social workers are employed in agencies that receive their mandates from those holding political power, the social worker's efforts to change the system are limited by each agency's political and social agendas (Wharf, 1990, 23–25).

By understanding the policy-making process, social workers can learn to advocate for social changes that benefit those in society least able to fend for themselves. Many current beliefs about leadership, privilege, hierarchy, power, and wealth have developed over long periods of history and have created patterned inequalities of status and rights (Gil, 1992, 1970). By exposing these historical inequalities and confronting the metaphors that support social inequality, social workers can participate in the policy debate. In fact, both the American and Canadian Social Work Codes of Ethics make the study of social justice a practice requirement.

It is important for social workers to understand and be sensitive to the different life experiences of Canadians. Moreover, understanding social policies' impact on issues of human diversity is critical for social workers who live in a pluralist society. Social workers are asked to play a variety of practice roles— teacher, enabler, facilitator, mediator, organizer, advocate, case manager, and administrator, among others. Social policy gives an added contextual dimension to these roles because it places the client situation within the social arena—an arena that too often has little or no regard for the client or the client's situation.

The following story outlines one of the authors' experiences with social policy and its direct impact on people.

One day, I reported to my Deputy Minister, who informed me that a prominent author was coming to the province to assist us with reforms to our institutions for children. A major presentation involving the premier, several provincial and federal ministers, and the prominent author was being planned, and I was asked to be the spokesperson for the province. Flattered but anxious, I read every article and book written by this prominent author until I had prepared a speech that I believed would reflect both the province's and the author's position on reform.

On the day of the presentation, which was being held in the province's largest children's institution, I arrived in a very nervous state. As I walked down the rather dingy corridor leading to the elevator, I could not help but notice the children wandering in the corridor. As I looked at each child, I told myself that I was giving this speech for this child. I kept repeating this thought child by child, and I began to feel energized and confident. After all, I had a cause.

Just as I approached the elevator, I saw a young girl stretched out in a wheelchair. The child had no recognizable face. Her skin was pale and wrinkled, and her nose was two holes on her face. Mucus was running from her nose into a gaping mouth.

As I was giving my speech, I noticed the smiles from the officials on the stage, including the author. I was pleased. After the speeches were finished, the moderator asked if there were any questions. Among the several hundred people in the audience was a woman who, after a few polite and complimentary questions had been asked by others, said, "This is all well and good, but these children need someone to love them, to hold them, to comfort them. How are your changes going to achieve this if you don't give us more staff?" Politely brushed off, she repeated the same question in many ways until those sitting near her began to physically indicate by their body positions that they were not with her.

I was really angry with this woman because I sensed she had taken the edge off the presentations and, after all, I had been one of the presenters. However, the Deputy Minister came over to me, shook my hand, congratulated me on an excellent speech, and invited me to join the dignitaries for lunch. Flattered, I said I would be along shortly but I wanted to help package our equipment first. Actually, I just needed to work off energy.

Eventually I went into the elevator and upon leaving had this overwhelming urge to turn around. When I did, I saw the woman who had irritated me holding the little girl who had been in the wheelchair in her arms while she was feeding her. I saw the love on this woman's face as she gazed into the girl's eyes and I sensed the love this little girl returned. I stood transfixed, totally shattered, shamed, and humbled.

This is one of those events in my life that was a gift, albeit a very painful one. Before my eyes was a reminder to me that I chose to be a social worker and I had unconsciously drifted from my own values and belief in human beings. I told myself over and over that social and public policies are about people, and policy and people cannot be compartmentalized. As a policy analyst, I use this moment to understand the human face in policy and the beauty that this rugged woman taught me. I wish every policy analyst and social planner had a moment like mine when the intellect is awakened to human potential and the power of love.

I did not go to lunch. I did not give another speech for five years. But I did learn a beautiful but painful lesson about the human spirit and about the purpose of social policy.

This story is a reminder that policy is about people, not just facts, statistics, laws, rules, manuals, power, and politics. Social workers whose values put people first and promote the human imperative to become more fully human (Freire, 1968) are positioned to play a vital role in the development of Canada's social policy and social welfare policy.

Finally, social policy provides a wealth of information on such issues as how our current social structures came to be; who is benefiting from these structures; who has the real power to make social changes; what the most effective approaches to citizen participation are; who is being oppressed, isolated, or ignored in society; and what array of ideological powers exist to maintain the current social agenda regarding the distribution of wealth, powers, and privilege.

Conclusion

Social policy helps social workers to better understand people. It does this by describing both the social context in which people live and the forces that created this context. It allows us to appreciate that the world in which we live did not just happen. Rather, it was created on the basis of decisions people made about what this society would look like and what values and beliefs would drive the development of this society. The inequalities that exist in Canada are not accidental. Moreover, as this chapter points out, there are different ways of conceptualizing social policy, differences between social policies and social welfare policies, considerable interface between all levels and fields of social work practice and social policies, and profound significance of such social values as cynicism and ideology in how social policies are created and carried out. The next chapter discusses how understanding the historic origins of social policies means appreciating how social policies evolved, what the major factors in this evolution were, and what might be a reasonable basis for thinking about their present and future development.

Discussion

To help you explore the issue of equality and its importance to social policy, the following exercise is intended to provide a source of discussion.

Are You a Number One?

Issues of equality are of enormous concern to advocates of progressive social welfare in Canada. However, for beginning (and sometimes advanced) students of social policy, this concept can be deceptive, simply because a "living" society is enormously difficult to understand.

Equality does not view human beings as "the same," which is what the political right attempts to say. In fact, it is just the opposite. Equality recognizes that every human being is unique and capable of human development. In essence, equality promotes the notion that every person is entitled to the same chance to develop and evolve her/his human potential.

This exercise uses the number 1.0 to illustrate just how complex this concept of inequality is. Assume that a society assigns every human being in that society the value of 1.0. In a democracy, every eligible citizen has one vote and therefore a 1.0 value. But the term "eligible citizen" suggests that there must be people who are not eligible to vote and who politically are assigned a value of less than 1.0, or in this case, 0. At the turn of the twentieth century, Canada did not allow the mentally ill, criminals, women, children, immigrants, refugees, Aboriginals, and others the right to vote. Advocacy groups fought to gain the value of 1.0 for some of these people but not for all. At the turn of the twenty-first century, some of those listed here are still assigned the value of 0 (for example, immigrants and the mentally ill). In other words, they have no voice in the Canadian political election system.

Now, let's examine power and privilege assigned to people in political office—the very people who can highly influence policy decisions. People who hold political office are given a value greater than 1.0. Canadian political traditions and laws give the prime minister greater powers and prerogatives than an ordinary citizen, and he or she may therefore be viewed as a 2.5. A major cabinet minister may have a rating somewhere around 2.0, and an elected official might be 1.4. However, when these people leave office, they return to 1.0 (at least in theory). In a dictatorship, leaders assign themselves values even higher than 2.5, and most citizens in that society have a value of 0. In a feudal system, the king may be a 5.0 or 10.0, the nobility somewhere between 1.1 and the king's value; and freepersons may have a value of 1.0, but serfs are 0s.

For policy made in Canada, who influences the policy-making process and what value do they have? For example, the National Business Council currently exerts greater influence than the National Anti-Poverty Organization. Northern communities have complained that the views of southern communities dominate policy decisions and disempower and disrespect northern realities and people. Even within social movements that espouse equality, inequality can exist among those who have influence and those whose voices are not heard. Inequalities and injustices can occur within and between different social, political, and economic arrangements in society.

Another perspective from which to consider the issue of equality involves everyday life situations. For example, consider something as simple as applying for a job. If my mother owns the company and I apply for a job, my value may be a 10.0. Other applicants may be 1.0s because they are well qualified and some, equally qualified, may even be less than 1.0 if colour, religion, gender, or other variables are being used to select candidates. In a like manner, some people try to assign their status, job, wealth, family name, religion, race, or other attribute a value greater than 1.0 in order to achieve superiority and advantage over others. Can you think who these people might be and provide some examples that illustrate this?

Let us examine yet another dimension. As a college or university student, what value is being assigned to you, to your professors, or to the school's administrators? Are different academic units viewed as having greater value than 1.0? For example, is medicine viewed as equal to social work? Is law viewed as equal to psychology? Is psychology equal to social work?

Now, let's examine one more level of complexity. One person may have several different values for different social situations. For example, an unemployed white male who lives in a home with a family of three and who is a star hockey player may be viewed by a right-wing society as a 0.4 because he is unemployed, a 1.0 because he is a white male, a 1.5 because he has a family, and a 2.0 for his hockey skills.

However, one's perception of one's own social worth is also an issue. For example, a son in a rich family with a social status of 3.0 may view himself as being only a 0.5. On the other hand, the daughter of a poor family with a social value of 0.1 may view herself as a 1.0. It is obviously a difficult chore for the rich son to understand that others will see him as a 3.0, regardless of how he sees himself, and he may very well believe that he is underprivileged. The same is true for the poor daughter. Perception can blind one's view of justice and equality. A millionaire who is the poorest in her neighbourhood may believe she is only a 0.8.

You can apply the number 1.0 to assess how any situation values participants. The above examples deal with individual value, social value, organizational value, and human value at political, civil, and social levels of societal interactions. Obviously, this type of analysis can become very complex very quickly. Experiment by using the number 1.0 to analyze family situations, relationships, social groups, and others. You may wish to read Gil (1998), Saul (1995), Swift (1995), and/or Bishop (1994) for more information on equality.

Chapter 2

Historical Influences

Social policies are in a constant state of change, but their roots may be traced back to the earliest stages of human evolution. Familiarity with history therefore provides you with tools for thinking about how social policies could be constructed for today and tomorrow. Rather than being constrained by the present-day circumstances of time or place, your imagination can be free to consider possibilities. You can readily challenge prevailing assumptions, rather than benignly accepting them. You can also use creative approaches, rather than overlooking them or assuming that they are untenable.

This chapter examines several areas of English Canadian social welfare history; further elaboration of the experiences of Aboriginal peoples and of French-speaking Canada appears in Chapter 6. Although this chapter also presents data in chronological order, the following 12 themes are evident throughout:

1. Policies are in a constant state of evolution—they have taken on different forms during different periods of history.
2. Social policies are "cultural constructs"—they are profoundly influenced by myriad cultures, values, and ideologies in a society.
3. Social policies sometimes represent the highest aspects of being human. At their very best, they reflect a basic concern for other people, a recognition of our interdependence, and an impulse to act upon this recognition.
4. Social policies have a contradictory nature. Among recipients, some aspects have been beneficial, while others, as will be seen, have not. Motivations among proponents of social policies, whether conscious or not, have been just as variable. As a result, social policies may reflect motivations and/or have consequences that are troubling: the drive to contain social unrest, to maintain social control, or to reproduce social inequalities with respect to gender, ethnicity, race, range of mental or physical ability, or other areas of diversity.
5. Social policies have different impacts on different groups in society. Recipients of a particular policy, for instance, may have an experience disparate from that of the person who is paid to carry out the policy.

6. Various concepts in the history of policy development remain with us to the present day, such as the distinction between deserving and undeserving poor, or the local responsibility for social welfare.

7. In contemporary times, social policies have mirrored the growing social and economic complexity of modern life: the increasing mobility of people, the spread of urbanization, the deep impact of industrial capitalist development, and the gradual appreciation of human diversity. Corresponding also with industrial capitalist development has been the increasingly atomized, stratified nature of society, and the rise of bureaucratic structures, of which social work has been an important part.

8. The arrangements of capitalism during the past several decades have eroded the range of social policies and their comprehensiveness. Across the globe, more flexible forms of capital accumulation, labour market organization, and consumption patterns have prevailed. These, in turn, are seen by many observers to have compromised the range of social policy choices available to political leaders. International industrial capitalism and its multinational corporations have been increasingly freed from earlier notions of national responsibility. Environmental policy, workplace conditions, job security, wages, and social policies may well be determined less by national policy and more by the market-driven, lowest-bidder ethos of an increasingly international and competitive industrializing world.

9. The state has increasingly relinquished social service delivery to the private realm, a process often called the privatization of social services. This development reflects current national and international trends that emphasize the private marketplace over the direct role of government.

10. More and more, the economy requires a flexible workforce made up of part-time jobs, underemployment, and limited employment in the form of contract jobs of short duration. Social workers, like their clients, will be expected to respond to this new workplace environment, where, among other things, lifelong learning and vocational flexibility prevail.

11. Reflecting the inherently political nature of social policies, the Constitution of Canada is significant in determining which level of government has a particular administrative or financing authority. At the beginning of the twentieth century, local or municipal governments funded and administered most social services. But over the course of the century social welfare responsibilities gradually emerged among provincial and, in particular, federal jurisdictions.

12. The conceptualization of social welfare has transformed from a "residual" to an "institutional" (Wilensky & Lebeaux, 1958) and finally to a "market-state" perspective (Bobbitt, 2002).

It is this final theme that provides a framework for exploring the preceding ones, as these terms—*residual*, *institutional*, and *market-state*—describe approaches that represent the three major periods in which Canadian social welfare history occurred from European contact to the present time.

The Residual Approach

In Canada, the residual concept of social welfare predominated until the twentieth century. During times of sickness, unemployment, or interrupted or insufficient income, the family and the economic marketplace were considered the "normal" channels of help. For example, if sickness made it impossible for a family member to go to work, alternative sources of income—credit, a loan, or a different family member taking on additional employment—were sought. Alternatively, the family could turn to relatives for temporary assistance. Only after these sources were exhausted would other parties intervene, including members of the immediate community, religious institutions, or, later, charities (Emery & Emery, 1999). This residual model of social welfare is contrasted by the institutional approach. The institutional model emphasizes the role of government in responding to social needs, and is elaborated later in this chapter.

Classical Civilizations

The impulse to come to another's assistance is a fundamental part of what it is to be human. Indeed, anthropologists have observed that sharing is an essential characteristic of some of the earliest forms of human organization (Berman, 2000). Among early hunting–gathering societies, when food became scarce and hunger acute, generosity and sharing prevailed over hoarding. This is more than a simple matter of etiquette, because the maintenance of social bonds was essential to determining a group's fertility and rate of survival (Dolgoff & Feldstein, 1984, 16, 26). Given the threat of raids from other tribes or species, and the hazards of eking out an existence amidst a harsh physical climate, an individual could not survive without belonging to the collective. In a very real life and death context, people were aware of the symbiotic benefits of doing good unto their neighbours.

The present discussion of hunting–gathering societies indicates how the responses we make to those in our identified group differ from those we make to people who are considered outsiders. Traditional societies often differentiate their treatment of members inside their own group from those outside it. In the same manner, contemporary social policies provide benefits for members of Canadian society, yet not to members of other societies. Social welfare assistance is an example of a program that only applies to Canadians living in Canada. Canadian social policies have other subtle ways of distinguishing between insiders and outsiders. As will be seen, particularly in Chapter 6, various areas of diversity—such as race, ethnicity, gender, range of ability, sexual orientation, and others—influence social policies.

Many ancient cultures throughout the world expressed social responsibilities in religious terms. As early as 2000 BC, Sumerian society placed a divine value on the protection of widows, orphans, and the poor. In fourth-century-BC China, Confucian ideals of humane and righteous leadership compelled rulers to target public funds toward the care of the aged, the poor, orphans, or those affected by natural disasters, as well as toward the creation of public lands for the gathering of wood and herbs (Dolgoff & Feldstein, 1984, 28–30). Aboriginal societies in present-day North America continue to use such symbols as the Medicine Wheel to express the sacred bond between humanity and the physical and spiritual planes of existence (Feehan & Hannis, eds., 1993; Bopp et al., 1985). In the Judeo-Christian tradition, several Old Testament injunctions compel part of an annual harvest to be donated to the poor (Leviticus 19:9–10) and to the widowed and strangers (Deuteronomy 24:19–22). The New Testament instructs Christians to care for the disadvantaged (Matthew 25:31–46) and to forsake the love of material possessions (Luke 6:20–38). Muslims also have a strong tradition of concern for the poor. In fact, one of the Five Pillars of Islam, alms-giving, is described not as a tax or a charity, but as a religious duty (Sura 9:60).

Such widespread religious ideals were manifest in tangible forms. Ancient Grecian temples served as medical centres and care stations for the poor. In Roman society, a system of public charity was so advanced that, during the second century AD, as much as half of Rome's population relied on some form of public assistance. In the Byzantine East, a complex system of maternity hospitals, medical facilities, and food rationing was provided from the revenues of the Orthodox Christian patriarchs (Dolgoff & Feldstein, 1984, 31–40). In our own time, social legislation has been the bedrock of the welfare state and is far from a historical aberration or a peculiarity of our own time. Indeed, one of the earliest explicit social policies occurred in medieval England, the 1349 Statute of Labourers, which, in the aftermath of the Black Plague, froze workers' wages to their pre-plague levels and limited the mobility of labour outside of one's home parish (de Schweinitz, 1943, 1–2).

The Medieval and Elizabethan European Heritage

Many of the direct roots of Canadian social policy are derived from a European heritage. Three non-governmental forms of European institutionalized charity gradually developed and were particularly significant. The first of these were the medieval guilds, representing various merchant classes and artisans. Acting as mutual aid societies and charitable organizations for their members, the guilds built and maintained hospitals, distributed food to the needy, provided lodgings for the travelling poor, and gave other forms of incidental help. The second form of charity, the private foundations were established by affluent benefactors and devoted to the construction and maintenance of hospitals, almshouses, and other such institutions. By the early sixteenth century, there were 460 such foundations in England alone. The third source of charity was the Church, providing assistance through various monastic orders among the thousands of local parishes across the continent. In Western Europe, among other parts of Christendom, tithing to the Church was compulsory, and one-third of all collections went to the poor (Dolgoff & Feldstein, 1984, 39–44). The tithe may be seen as an early precursor to the contemporary income tax system, which helps finance the modern welfare state.

This elaborate system of medieval charity was turned upside down by the sixteenth-century Protestant Reformation. In England, as in other parts of Europe, Protestant sects emerged, and Roman Catholic monasteries were dissolved. A new system of English social welfare was established and enshrined in the Elizabethan Poor Laws of 1601. Earlier voluntary modes of charity now fell to the local (parish) governments on a national scale, with accompanying punishments for non-compliance. Each parish was required to appoint an overseer of the poor, who, in consultation with church wardens, dispensed relief to the poor. The significance to the present day is twofold. First, the overseer was an obvious precursor to the modern-day social worker. The role of overseer also had an obvious social control function. Indeed, the fact of Elizabethan overseers provides an excellent reminder that not all of social work's roots have been altruistic. Secondly, these changes meant that for the first time in history, social welfare responsibility became, in practice and in legislation, a formalized, local arrangement. Voluntary forms of charity, including orphanages, hospitals, and almshouses for the old, remained alongside other local arrangements (Leiby, 1978, 38–41). The establishment of a comprehensive state role, a concept that emerged in its complete form in the twentieth century, saw its beginnings, therefore, in the sixteenth century. Up to the present time, this strong presence of local jurisdictions in social service delivery has persisted.

Other aspects of the Elizabethan Poor Laws remain with us today. The principle of local residency was legislated, requiring that an individual receiving alms (or, in contemporary usage, welfare) within a particular parish had to be a resident of that parish. In our own time, local governments as well as provinces have legislated that recipients must live within a particular province or municipality for a certain length of time before being entitled to receive social assistance.

A final feature of Elizabethan welfare was the differentiation made between deserving and undeserving poor, an aspect that had been part of previous forms of charity but which was now outlined in legislation. While present-day terminology and practices may be different, this compulsion to distinguish between those who are worthy and those who are not has endured. In Elizabethan times, the classification was threefold: the impotent poor—that is, those who could not work (pregnant women, extremely sick men or women, those over the age of 60)—were allowed to live in what became known as poorhouses; any able-bodied people who could not seek employment or were temporarily unemployed were consigned to workhouses; and "unregenerate idlers" were placed in houses of correction (Bruce, 1961, 26; Dolgoff & Feldstein, 1984, 46). Today, income security programs differentiate between classes of eligibility. Able-bodied individuals who temporarily cannot work due to work-related illness or injury may apply for Workers' Compensation. Able-bodied individuals who are capable of work but are between jobs may be eligible to receive Employment Insurance (EI), or if EI entitlements run out, provincially/locally administered social assistance pro-grams under various names, including Ontario Works. Those who cannot work due to physical or psychiatric incapacity may receive Workers' Compensation long-term disability, Canada Pension Plan long-term disability, or provincially administered income security programs. Those who cannot work due to the responsibilities of single parenthood may receive benefits from provincially administered income security programs (Graham, 2008a).

The Elizabethan Poor Laws also distinguished between men and women. For example, women were classed in the impotent poor category. In our own time, as will be seen, social policies have continued to be constructed differentially for men and women.

In the 1600s, as in previous centuries, the plight of the poor was deplorable. Hospitals, poorhouses, workhouses, and other such institutions were invariably overcrowded, lacked public health standards familiar to the contemporary reader, and were the loci of such deadly diseases as cholera, tuberculosis, and typhoid (Desert, 1976; Gonthier, 1978). Marginalized members of society—vagrants and those who were sick or disabled, among others—were forced into poorhouses that were as wretched as—and were sometimes one and the same as—local jails. Levels of alms were deliberately minimal. To seek assistance beyond the residual bounds of one's immediate family or the economic market-place could be the source of frequent and intense public derision. Idle men refus-ing work were whipped, sent to prison, or both. Others were permanently maimed in an effort to rid them of their idleness. For these and other reasons, people were known to turn to prostitution, theft, or other crimes to avoid the disgrace and hardships of receiving alms (de Schweinitz, 1943, 20–22; Dolgoff & Feldstein, 1984, 49).

Before leaving the Elizabethan period in England, one final point should be emphasized: the Reformation Protestant theology of Calvin, Luther, and other thinkers influenced virtually all aspects of society, social welfare included. This thinking, moreover, continues to resonate in those twenty-first-century coun-tries, such as Canada, where the historic influence of a Protestant theology remains strong. In Calvinist terms, work was a divine vocation and therefore a religious activity; idleness and worldly temptations interfered with the glory of God. Personal responsibility, discipline, and intense individualism were all revered (Weber, 1930, trans. 1958). As for social welfare, a legacy of punitive and repressive approaches found new rationalization. In this Protestant worldview, pauperism was thought to result from the character defects of an individual or the flaws of a family. For moral and religious reasons, indiscriminate alms-giving was condemned, and the poor were visited by Poor Law overseers or by other community representatives, such as clergy, to root out the drunk, the idle, and other undesirables (Dolgoff & Feldstein, 1984, 46–7).

The Nineteenth-Century European Heritage

For several centuries, the principles established during the Elizabethan era pre-dominated. But in the early nineteenth century, changes came about due to two issues of public concern: the rising costs of British poor relief, and the rising numbers of relief recipients. A three-year royal commission was struck, resulting in the Poor Law Reforms of 1834. These reforms established several new principles. The first was the "less eligibility" principle, which stated that the basic provisions one received while on relief were to be *less* than the lowest-paying available job. The rationale was to dissuade people from receiving relief and to encourage self-reliance via the economic marketplace. This less eligibility principle continues to dominate social welfare thinking in our own time. Throughout the 1990s, economists and other analysts referred to and supported the development of policies to encourage swift return to work, rather than reliance on income security programs (Burns, Batavia, & DeJong, 1994; Lewin & Hasenfeld, 1995; Shah & Smith, 1995; Schansberg, 1996; Smith, 1993). Beginning in the mid-1990s, social assistance programs in Canada, as in the United States, increasingly tied benefits entitlement to job skill development, job search, and, in some jurisdictions, welfare for work. In the provinces of Alberta and Ontario, for example, social assistance programs have been renamed to "Alberta Works" and "Ontario Works," respectively, to reflect this greater emphasis on job retention. Furthermore, over the last decade, some politicians and policy analysts have called for further reductions in social welfare entitlements, described in the next chapter.

The second 1834 principle was a delineation between outdoor and indoor relief, the forerunner of the current Canadian system of provincially/municipally administered social assistance. Outdoor relief provided material assistance to a select category of recipients who were allowed to live at home: the sick, the aged, the orphaned, or the widowed. Indoor relief, in contrast, was limited to able-bodied men who were deemed employable. Indoor relief could not be received at home. Recipients were obliged to live in workhouses and to undertake hard, manual labour—for example, breaking piles of large stones—in compensation for work. The intention was to punish and to limit the appeal of relief so as to encourage the able-bodied to fend for themselves.

This distinction in legislation between outdoor and indoor relief spelled out different categories of the poor and was reminiscent of comparable Elizabethan notions. Also present were various assumptions anchored to the Protestant Reformation: that those poor who had been responsible for their own poverty were morally at fault, but, at the same time, were capable of "uplift"—to use a term from the Victorian era—through discipline, thrift, hard work, and righteous living.

Three prominent thinkers of the nineteenth century also reinforced Poor Law thinking. The first was the Reverend Thomas Malthus who, in the late eighteenth century, wrote that the human population was increasing at a greater rate than such means of subsistence as the food supply. This, to many, was a clarion call to limit the appeal of relief: if the dependent classes were "coddled," or so the thinking went, they would multiply too quickly and start to exert undue pressure on society's limited material wealth. The second was the economist Adam Smith, who saw a natural harmony between the self-seeking of an individual and the well-being of society. His view was typical of the strongly individualist outlook of the eighteenth and nineteenth centuries, which encouraged minimal standards of relief. The third thinker was philosopher Jeremy Bentham, who introduced the utilitarian notion that society should promote the greatest possible good for the greatest possible numbers (Bruce, 1961, 46–7, 78): a form of collectivism, but one that tended to promote the views of the majority and to minimize the benefits for those who were poor or in other ways disempowered.

A final historical experience bears emphasis. The Speenhamland experiment of 1795 was a remarkable example of a social policy that challenged prevailing assumptions. Due to a short harvest and a severe winter, local justices of the peace of the Speenhamland area of England decided to pay subsidies to low-income employed individuals who had families to support—setting a minimum based on the price of bread and scaled according to family size. The Speenhamland experiment, as it later became known, spread to other parts of England. Following its implementation, familiar criticisms led to its abolition. Some argued that individual initiative would cease, the numbers of dependent people would grow, productivity would drop, and costs of relief would rise inordinately. Others argued, in hindsight, that its major problems were the maintenance of artificially low market wages, and the creation of artificial barriers to labour mobility (Bruce, 1961, 41, 76–7; de Schweinitz, 1943, 72–3; Dolgoff & Feldstein, 1984, 55). While historically brief, the Speenhamland experiment highlights the issue of wage supplementation for low-income citizens, which contemporary governments continue to debate. Some Canadian provinces have provisions in their welfare programs to defray additional expenses that recipients face when they start working, such as daycare, transportation, work clothing, and tools. Others have considered programs that ease the transition from welfare to work via a "top-up" income supplementation program during the initial re-entry into the workforce (National Council of Welfare, 2006b). The Speenhamland experiment demonstrates that wage supplementation has historical roots.

Canada Up to 1945

The European heritage blended with a North American context to create a distinctly Canadian approach to social welfare. One of the most significant and tragic aspects of North American history is the colonization of Aboriginal peoples. Sporadic attempts at tenth-century Viking habitation along the northeast coast were followed by the permanent settlement of French habitants in the sixteenth century. This occurred largely along the St. Lawrence River, in a land they named New France. The French—and, after the 1759 conquest of New France, the British—forever changed North America. The continent's Aboriginal peoples, decimated by disease and war, were forced onto reserves of land in the late nineteenth and early twentieth centuries, where they were further marginalized—economically, politically, and socially. As elaborated in Chapter 6, the resolutely Eurocentric orientation of Canadian social policies contributed much to the tragedy of colonization of Aboriginal peoples.

New France and, later, British North America possessed an isolating geography, tormenting physical elements, and numerous forms of social misfortune: poverty, vagrancy, alcoholism, illegitimate births, and debtor classes, among others. Long-standing models of European social organization, however, could only be adapted haphazardly to the patterns of sparse inhabitation of frontier settlement. In Nova Scotia and New Brunswick, locally financed overseers of the poor administered Poor Laws. Present-day Quebec, like Newfoundland, relied upon the Roman Catholic Church to administer and dispense a complex system of social welfare, in addition to public education and health services. In Ontario, the absence of either Poor Law legislation or a strong Roman Catholic influence meant that spontaneous forms of community concern had to prevail (Boychuk, 1998; Graham, 1995; Splane, 1965).

These machineries of social welfare carried on into the seventeenth, eighteenth, and early nineteenth centuries. But they were later transformed, mirroring the ferment of economic, social, and political changes of the day. Throughout this period, a series of primary economic staples dominated the economy. The cod fisheries of present-day Newfoundland became important in the sixteenth century, and they were supplemented in the sixteenth to nineteenth centuries by the fur trade, corresponding with the slow but persistent westward pattern of human settlement. The latter gave way to a timber trade in the nineteenth century, and then to a wheat staple, first in present-day Central Canada, and then, after the 1880s, in Western Canada. Over the last quarter of the nineteenth century and into the twentieth, Canada experienced an industrial revolution, making Montreal and Toronto the leading urban centres of a growing network of national cities (Easterbrook & Aitken, 1956).

During this time, there were several waves of immigration, highlighted by Loyalist settlement from south of the border following the American Revolution, significant British immigration during the middle of the nineteenth century, followed by a more diverse European settlement, much of it westward bound, during and after the 1880s (Lower, 1958, 187). From a scattered population of 70 000 in 1759, there appeared significant demographic growth. In 1851, present-day Ontario, Quebec, and the Maritime provinces had combined populations of 2.5 million people. In 1901, Canada's population had risen to 5.37 million, and in 1921, to 9 million (Easterbrook & Aitken, 1956, 395, 400; Prentice, Bourne, Cuthbert, Brandt, Light, Mitchinson, & Black, 1988, 108). Meanwhile, the percentage of Canadians living in urban centres steadily climbed from 13 percent in 1851, to 35 percent in 1901, to 47 percent in 1921, and to 52.5 percent by 1931 (Artibese & Stelter, 1985, 1887).

In 1867, the former colonies of British North America united to form Canada. Equally significant, the effects of industrialization, urbanization, and demographic growth transformed Canada from a small, resource-based mercantilist economy into an industrializing nation. As society became increasingly complex, social welfare had to adapt accordingly. Houses of Industry—in effect, workhouses for the poor—emerged in Canada in the 1830s, through the influence of the British Poor Law Reforms of that decade. These tended to be administered on a local basis and alongside local and provincial hospitals, with the latter signalling governments' growing responsibility for social welfare. The voluntary sector at the same time remained vital, and a profusion of publicly and privately founded specialized charities were established over the next 80 years, among them, Houses of Providence, Boys' and Girls' Homes, city missions, Protestant and Roman Catholic orphanages, Jewish philanthropic organizations, hospitals for the sick, and refuges for the old. A distinct form of charity also came into being in the late nineteenth century—the settlement house, wherein the well-to-do, often university students, lived among and sought to help a city's poor. These were often significant loci of community social change (Irving, Parsons, & Bellamy, 1995).

Nineteenth-century social welfare institutions and social movements were inextricably linked. For example, religious organizations provided tangible services and a moral rationale for expanded activities, and proved to be a political force compelling greater state intervention into the country's social milieu. The Social Gospel Movement, a loose coalition of Protestant denominations influenced by British and American counterparts, emerged in Canada in the 1890s, applying Christian principles to prevailing social and economic issues. Similar forces were evident in twentieth-century Quebec, where, through the *Semaines sociales*, Roman Catholic clergy and laity discussed social issues. The Social Service Council of Canada, so named in 1913, was a public education and advocacy organization; originally created in 1907, it included representatives from the Anglican, Methodist, Presbyterian, and Baptist churches, as well as the Trades and Labour Congress of Canada (Guest, 1997, 34). Protestant clergymen had been particularly important in the creation, leadership, and perpetuation of the Cooperative Commonwealth Federation (renamed the New Democratic Party in 1961), a social democratic political party elected to national and provincial legislatures and advocating a more comprehensive welfare state (Allen, 1971).

In the late 1880s, what has become known as an **urban reform movement** emerged—a loose coalition of journalists, clergy, charity workers, government officials, and other interested parties. It pursued a broad array of public causes: public control of utilities, including public transit; better public health provisions, including the expansion of public health nursing services, improved sanitation, improved housing standards, and improved standards of meat processing and water quality; and the establishment of more green spaces in urban areas—parks and playgrounds; and improved standards of relief, child welfare, and other social programs (Stelter & Artibese, eds., 1977). A leading proponent was Toronto *Globe* journalist J.J. Kelso, founder of the Toronto Humane Society in 1887, later renamed the Children's Aid Society (Fingard, 1989, 171; Jones & Rutman, 1981). Another was Herbert B. Ames, a well-to-do Montreal manufacturer who published an 1897 study entitled *City on the Hill,* documenting the deplorable living conditions endured by Montreal's working class (Copp, 1974).

The working class itself did much to assist the working poor: nineteenth-century workers organized fraternal societies, with each member contributing a small regular amount to a fund from which they could draw if sickness or an accident interfered with work. Canadian trade unions helped to raise standards of living, protect workers' wages, and improve workplace conditions (Kealey, 1980; Palmer, 1979). Women were responsible for fundraising and service provision within many local charities. By the end of the nineteenth century, these women's activities had expanded to include a number of reform organizations, many now national in scope. The National Council of Women (established in 1893), the Woman's Christian Temperance Union (1874), and the Young Women's Christian Association (established nationally in 1895), to name three, sought numerous social improvements, including women's right to vote (obtained federally in 1918 and provincially shortly before and afterwards), and social policies that would assist women and children (Kealey, 1979; Strong-Boag, 1976).

One of the most important social effects of industrialization was the segregation of people according to gender. In earlier economies, a family's income would often focus on agricultural production and take place at home, relying on the work of men, women, and children within families. But in an industrial economy, a family's livelihood depended more and more on men's employment outside the home; some literature refers to this as the phenomenon of the "breadwinner male." Increasingly, women in the industrial economy remained at home, and focused their attention increasingly on domestic work such as raising children, cooking, laundering, and sewing, and less on producing goods for trade or barter; certain literature refers to this phenomenon as "women's domesticity," or "the domestication of women." In an industrial society, there emerged a gendered split between the public realm outside the home, dominated by men, and the domestic realm of women and children. However, women's social advocacy and charitable activities, it should be stressed, did take women outside the home. And they were important precedents to the growing presence of women employed outside the home during the post-1960s period.

Patriarchy was and still is a major theme of social welfare history. The political franchise had been extended in the nineteenth century to include men who did not hold property. But only in the post-World War I period did women achieve the right to vote in federal elections—a right that was established in the West during the war and that spread to other provinces until 1940, when Quebec women got the right to vote. Another landmark was the 1929 Famous Five court challenge in which five Canadian women successfully sought legal recognition as persons under the British North America Act.

The Industrial Revolution of the nineteenth century ushered in massive disparities in health and standards of living between those who worked in factories and those of greater means. It also created large concentrations of urban poverty (Ball & Gready, 2006). Unions were at the fore of the charge to change these inequalities, always against concerted opposition. After much effort, a nine-hour day was successfully obtained in 1872, and the Canadian Labour Union was created but then abolished that same decade. The Royal Commission on the Relations of Labour and Capital (1887) ultimately recognized the social value of unions. By the 1890s, there were 240 unions nationwide, and with a growing urban reform and women's movement, positive change was occurring. By 1894, labour had become so respectable that the first Monday in September became a national holiday (now known as Labour Day). In 1900, the federal government established the Department of Labour to mediate disputes between workers and owners.

The nineteenth and twentieth centuries also covered the tragic story of oppression of Aboriginal peoples—first by the experience of European contact, disease, and economic exploitation; and then, during the development of New France, British North America, and Canada, by the taking over of an entire continent by colonizers. A series of land treaties were negotiated between successive colonizing governments, and the 1876 Indian Act enshrined this colonial orientation—defining what was meant by "Indian," extending power to the Canadian government to regulate Aboriginal peoples, providing federal government guardianship over Aboriginal lands, and restricting the political franchise to those who assimilated. An infrastructure of assimilation emerged during the post-Confederation period, during which some Christian churches and government officials collaborated to provide residential schooling for Aboriginal children. The legacy of residential schooling has traumatized generations of Aboriginal peoples and continues to have massive negative repercussions to this day. Also during the post-Confederation period, Aboriginal peoples were relegated to reserves of land, many of which remain chronically underserviced for basic urban infrastructures and became places of high unemployment and high despair. Chapter 6 elaborates.

Chapter 6 also discusses the impact of racism upon Canadian society—a major theme in the history of Canadian social policy, as in Canadian history in general. Prior to the early 1960s, Canadian immigration policy was overtly racist, stating preferences for immigration to certain preferred ethnic and racial backgrounds. The state promoted racist policies. It interned Ukrainian Canadians during World War I and Japanese Canadians during World War II; in 1885, it imposed a head tax upon people of Chinese background to reduce immigration, and in 1923, it excluded Chinese immigration entirely (rescinded in 1947).

The Canadian social work profession in its early years therefore was largely white. It also had strong roots in national organizations that represented women, churches, and trade unions, as discussed above. It was likewise influenced by the Charity Organization movement, which was preceded by American and British counterparts and which sought to rationalize charity, to make it more efficient, more humane, and more proficient in its techniques. The world's oldest schools of social work opened in Great Britain in 1890 and the United States in 1903, and Canada's first school appeared soon afterwards, at the University of Toronto in 1914. It was followed by similar schools at McGill University (1918), the University of British Columbia (1928), the Université de Montréal (1939), and at an independent institution that ultimately became affiliated with Dalhousie University in Halifax, Nova Scotia (1941). The Canadian Council on Child Welfare was founded in 1920 (renamed the Canadian Welfare Council in 1935 and the Canadian Council on Social Development in 1969). The Canadian Association of Social Workers was founded in 1926, and two years later, the First International Conference of Social Work was convened, spawning the International Association of Schools of Social Work. These were among the myriad organizations that sought more comprehensive social policies at the provincial, national, and international levels (Graham, 1996b).

Social Policies

Among the most significant pieces of social policy legislation before World War II was the Workmen's Compensation Act of 1914, first established in Ontario but soon imitated by other provinces. It provided injured workers with regular cash income as a right, rather than as something that followed often lengthy litigation against an employer. As early as 1919, the federal government was pledging to create national systems of health insurance and unemployment insurance (UI, now named Employment Insurance or EI). But a national system of health insurance did not come into being until 1966. Unemployment Insurance finally came into force in 1940, several decades after the establishment of comparable programs in Britain and other advanced industrialized nations. Its introduction had been delayed for decades because of the federal government's reluctance to amend the Canadian Constitution, allowing the federal government jurisdiction in this area. Meanwhile, in 1916, Manitoba became the first province to introduce Mother's Pensions, a selective program providing a small, means-tested income to widows and divorced or deserted wives and their children (Guest, 1997). The next major piece of legislation—also selective—was the 1927 Old Age Pensions Act, the cost of which was shared on a fifty–fifty basis by the federal and provincial governments.

Under section 92 of the Canadian Constitution (the British North America Act, 1867, renamed in 1982 as the Constitution Act, 1867), the areas of education, health, and welfare were (and remain to this day) provincial prerogatives. But by strength of precedent, local governments continued to take on funding and administrative responsibilities for many social programs. As creatures of the provinces with no constitutionally prescribed autonomy of their own, municipalities could be created and disbanded by provincial writ and tended to have a limited tax base. But because of the unprecedented extent and duration of unemployment during the 1930s, local governments could not withstand the financial and administrative commitments of unemployment relief, among other social programs for which they had always been held responsible. Over the course of that decade, higher levels of government consequently took on greater financial responsibility (Graham, 1995). In the process, social welfare was massively transformed.

The Institutional Approach

Canada, 1945–1973

Canada changed dramatically after World War II. Immigration levels increased significantly. New immigration selection practices came into effect in 1962, intending to introduce principles that were universal and non-discriminatory; in 1967, further selection practice changes led to the introduction of what was intended to be a more objective points system. This is not to suggest, however, that Canadian immigration practices became entirely objective. Indeed, as several scholars point out, there remain discriminatory standards, sometimes less obvious and sometimes different from earlier practices. Excellent current examples relate to the rules and procedures that categorize immigrants in three main groups (family class, economic class, and refugee class), that set the number of individuals to admit in each of these categories, and that emphasize integration into Canadian society in relation to societal barriers for immigrants in each of these categories (Beach, Green, & Reitz, 2004).

The country's growing racial and ethnic diversity, discussed in Chapter 6, was further reinforced by the federal government's introduction of an official policy of multiculturalism (1971), the Charter of Rights and Freedoms (1982), and the Canadian Multiculturalism Act (1987). In addition to being significantly more diverse, the country's population was also more numerous. In 1971, Canada consisted of 21.6 million people, nearly a twofold increase from 1941. In the same year, 1971, the percentage of Canadians living in urban centres had increased to 76.1 percent.

Social work grew proportionately. In 1941, the census reported 1767 social workers in Canada. By 1981, there were more than 27 590 (Drover, 1988, 2034). An earlier reliance on a two-year, post-BA diploma (and before this a one-year, post-BA certificate) gave way, in the post-war era, to the dominance of the Bachelor of Social Work/Master of Social Work sequence.

The country's first Doctor of Social Work program was inaugurated at the University of Toronto in 1952. Moreover, by 1949, there were eight Canadian social work schools—nearly a threefold increase over a ten-year period—and by 1970, there were twelve (Graham, 1996a, 129). Numerous social workers forever changed the face of Canadian society. Harry Cassidy (1900–1951), an economist at the University of Toronto School of Social Work, wrote numerous studies on Canadian social security programs. Charlotte Whitton (1896–1975), director and driving force behind the Canadian Welfare Council (later named the Canadian Council on Social Development), was responsible for several aspects of the profession's history. Yet although she crusaded for improved standards of child welfare and for changes in social policies, she also advocated harsh welfare assistance eligibility requirements for single mothers, among other practices that might be considered less than progressive by today's standards (Rooke & Schnell, 1987). Bessie Touzel (1904–1997) was trained in the 1920s at the University of Toronto and held a succession of appointments of increasing responsibility, such as Chief of the Ottawa Public Welfare Department, Executive Secretary of the Toronto Welfare Council, and Executive Director of the Ontario Welfare Council. A staunch advocate of improved casework practices, she wrote numerous policy studies, was an adviser to the Marsh Commission (see below), and served with the United Nations in Tanzania (Obituaries, *The Globe and Mail*, April 26, 1997).

Social Policies

Everything changed after the 1943 *Report on Social Security for Canada* (the Marsh Report), written by economist Leonard Marsh, who taught social work at McGill University. The Marsh Report echoed the famous 1942 Beveridge Report in Great Britain. Both were blueprints for a comprehensive and largely universal welfare state in their respective countries, and both provided a rationale for what scholars describe as an institutional model of social policy. In contrast to the residual approach, the institutional approach saw the welfare services as normal, "first line" functions of modern industrial society, a proper, legitimate function of modern industrial society in helping individuals achieve self-fulfillment (Wilensky & Lebeaux, 1958, 138). The tendency to construct stigmatizing programs was much reduced, and means testing, under a universal program, was no longer the primary requirement for eligibility. Under universal programs, a sense of entitlement, or right of citizenship, prevailed (Graham, 2008a).

As noted in Figure 2.1, spending for social programs increased markedly over the following several decades. Following the introduction of UI, the next major Marsh Report proposal, a universal Family Allowances (FA) program, came into being in 1944: regardless of family income, *all* Canadian mothers of children under the age of 16 would receive a monthly allowance. The next major development after that was the 1951 conversion of the Old Age Security (OAS) program from a selective to a universal program. As of that year, all seniors over the age of 70 would receive a pension, regardless of their level of income.

A universal system of health insurance first appeared in Saskatchewan, under the political leadership of the first social democratic government elected in North America: the Cooperative Commonwealth Federation. In 1945, Premier Tommy Douglas set up a social assistance medical care plan covering old age pensioners, recipients of mothers' allowances, blind pensioners, and wards of the state. This selective program was supplemented in 1947 by the introduction of universal, state-administered hospital insurance, and in 1959, by universal, provincewide medical insurance. Meanwhile, in 1956, the federal government initiated the Hospital Insurance and Diagnostic Services Act, a negotiated cost-sharing agreement between Ottawa and the provinces, covering a basic range of in-patient hospital services. Again, following the lead of Saskatchewan, the federal government installed a universal health-care system in 1966; and by 1972, every province and territory was administering its own health services. The story of social policy has been one of intense competition between groups in society, and health care was no exception. Companies that had provided private health insurance resisted what some perceived to be the intrusion of the state. So, too, did many physicians acting individually and through professional associations,

FIGURE 2.1   Total Social Spending in Canada, 1945–46 to 1992–93

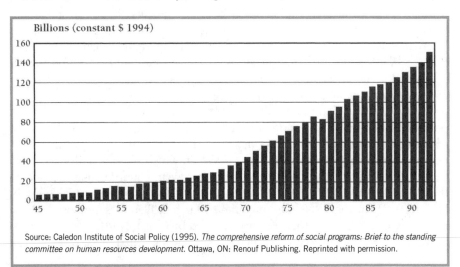

Source: Caledon Institute of Social Policy (1995). *The comprehensive reform of social programs: Brief to the standing committee on human resources development*. Ottawa, ON: Renouf Publishing. Reprinted with permission.

claiming that physicians' autonomy would be compromised, and that access to comprehensive health-care services would be reduced (Naylor, 1986).

As the legislation described it, "programs for the provision of assistance and welfare services to and in respect of persons in need" were cost-shared equally, on a fifty–fifty basis, by the federal government and each province under the Canada Assistance Plan (CAP). The Medical Care Act (1966) was another cost-sharing plan. Under the CAP, provinces also set up and administered such social services as child welfare protection, rehabilitation, home support for the elderly and people who were disabled, employment programs, child care, and social assistance. The federal government, with massive revenue sources from the income tax system, corporate taxes, and tariffs, was expected to provide otherwise vulnerable programs with a solid basis of funding.

As early as 1966, the federal government had introduced the Canada Pension Plan (CPP), providing social insurance protection for retirement and disability, as well as survivors' benefits. A national program (with the exception of Quebec, which legislated the equivalent in the Quebec Pension Plan), this compulsory plan was tied to workplace earnings and was portable if the individual moved or took on a different job within Canada. The CPP and OAS were supplemented in 1966 by an income-tested pension plan for low-income earners, the Guaranteed Income Supplement.

But as Andrew Jackson and Matthew Sanger point out, "from the 1950s through to the mid-1970s, even as state provision of direct care expanded, the voluntary social services sector" increased in like proportion. In Canada, voluntary sectors were not ipso facto replaced by an increasingly robust government responsibility for social well being: "It is wrong to see a process of one-dimensional evolution from voluntaristic charity provision" of the residual era to the formal, state structures of institutionalism. "As the welfare state grew, so did the non-profit sector" (2003, 30).

On the international scene, the seeds of an emerging globalization of the market state era had already been sown. Post-World War II economic arrangements were concluded by the Bretton Woods Agreements (1944), which culminated in the development of the International Monetary Fund (IMF), the International Bank of Reconstruction and Development (later renamed the World Bank, or WB), and a proposal for an international trading organization (developed in 1947 as the General Agreement on Tariffs and Trade—GATT—later, in 1994, developing into the World Trade Organization, or WTO). These new international economic institutions were driven by American economic and foreign policy (Hobsbawm, 1995) and coincided with the emergence of more powerful transnational corporations (Ellwood, 2006). Europe in the post-World War II period experienced the Marshall Plan (1947), in which billions of dollars of aid and technical assistance poured into those European countries that had joined the Organization for Economic Cooperation and Development (OECD, established 1948). In the 1960s, a comparable Marshall Plan was proposed for an emerging, post-colonial Africa, but was rejected by Global North policy elites—a move that development economist Jeffrey Sachs has labelled racist (2005, 190).

Several important international institutions had emerged after World War I, including the precursor to the United Nations: the League of Nations (1919); its member agency, the International Labor Organization (1919), which intended to promote the rights of labour worldwide; and the International Council on Social Welfare (1928). In the aftermath of World War II, the United Nations was established in 1945, and with it came the emergence of a battery of social welfare institutions at the international level, including the World Health Organization (1948), the United Nations Children's Fund (UNICEF) (1946), and the United Nations Development Program (1965). The 1948 Universal Declaration of Human Rights is an exemplary international covenant adopted by the UN and a succession of other policies followed: the International Covenant on Economic, Social, and Cultural Rights (1966); the International Covenant on Civil and Political Rights (1966); and the Convention on the Rights of the Child (1984), among others (Ball & Gready, 2006).

The Market-State Approach

By the late 1960s and early 1970s, it seemed as though many of the basic programs had been established, and continued policy initiatives would simply fill in the gaps that had been overlooked or had developed. The Unemployment Insurance program was considerably expanded in 1971 by increasing benefit rates, widening the program's compulsory coverage to include nearly all employees, and easing qualifying conditions. During the same decade, the Canada Pension Plan benefit rates were also elevated, and OAS benefits were extended to recipients' widows (Guest, 1997, 173, 188). A growing awareness of female poverty led to the 1975 introduction of the Spouse's Allowance, a means-tested supplement paid to old age pensioners' spouses. Several studies in the late 1960s and 1970s, including a Senate Committee report, *Poverty in Canada* (1971), revealed as many as one in five Canadians living in poverty (Guest, 1997, 156). The report called for a Guaranteed Annual Income (GAI), which would have provided, had it been adopted, a minimum threshold of income below which no individual would fall. There also emerged a gradual recognition of poverty and inequality as a reflection of such social diversities as gender, ethnicity, race, Aboriginal status, range of ability, and geography. These, given their critical significance, are examined in greater depth in Chapter 6.

Historian Philip Bobbitt considers the rise of the twentieth century welfare state period in a broad historical context, from the mid-fifteenth–century emergence of the European princely state (which was founded when people rallied around a prince for mutual protection) through to the late nineteenth-century nation-state, when the twentieth-century welfare state began to unfold (Bobbitt, 2002). The post-welfare state period of the mid 1970s to the present is manifestly different, a cataclysmic shift from the nation-state structure to a market-state structure (Bobbitt, 2002).

Just as many countries of the previous period, Canada included, could be described as nation-states, so too are many countries in addition to Canada now market-states. The market-state is characterized by a number of factors, including computer technology and communication on a global scale, the decentralization of governments, the reduced scope and sanction of government, the increased significance of liberal ideology (as elaborated in the next chapter), and the increasing importance of the private sector. The "market" has become a defining metaphor, the benchmark by which government and non-government sectors operate. In a market-state, the old era of governments funding and delivering a welfare state has been replaced by the growing authority of the private and voluntary sectors. The state's primary purpose, far limited in scope, is to support private-sector goals and the economic growth and accumulation that represent them. As Bobbitt (2002) points out, governments within the market-state are no longer mandated to provide for the welfare of the nation. The social welfare responsibilities of government are entirely reduced in scope from that which Marsh and Beverage envisioned in the mid-1940s. In the institutional period, Canadians were citizens; in the market-state era, Canadians are now consumers. As Chapter 1 describes, this can be aptly viewed as an age of cynicism.

Social Policies

As the market-state emerged in the mid-1970s, several factors conspired to gradually erode Canadian social policies, and this erosion marks the underlying difference between the institutional and market-state models of social policy. Seven aspects relating to the market-state period are of particular significance. The first is that government funding for social programs, when adjusted for inflation, has remained largely the same since the mid-1970s (see Figures 2.2 to 2.7). But, overall,

FIGURE 2.2   Total Social Spending in Canada, 1978–79 to 2002–03

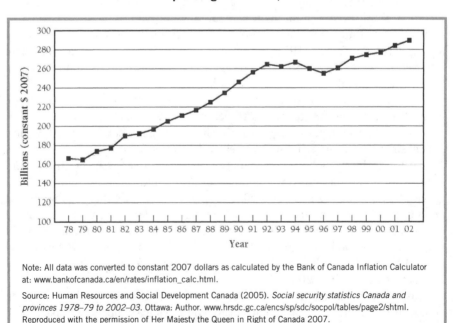

Note: All data was converted to constant 2007 dollars as calculated by the Bank of Canada Inflation Calculator at: www.bankofcanada.ca/en/rates/inflation_calc.html.

Source: Human Resources and Social Development Canada (2005). *Social security statistics Canada and provinces 1978–79 to 2002–03*. Ottawa: Author. www.hrsdc.gc.ca/encs/sp/sdc/socpol/tables/page2/shtml. Reproduced with the permission of Her Majesty the Queen in Right of Canada 2007.

FIGURE 2.3   Total Social Spending in Canada Per Capita, 1978–79 to 2002–03

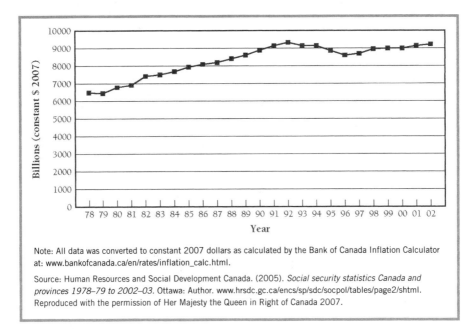

Note: All data was converted to constant 2007 dollars as calculated by the Bank of Canada Inflation Calculator at: www.bankofcanada.ca/en/rates/inflation_calc.html.

Source: Human Resources and Social Development Canada. (2005). *Social security statistics Canada and provinces 1978–79 to 2002–03*. Ottawa: Author. www.hrsdc.gc.ca/encs/sp/sdc/socpol/tables/page2/shtml. Reproduced with the permission of Her Majesty the Queen in Right of Canada 2007.

FIGURE 2.4   Total Social Spending in Canada as Percentage of GDP, 1978–79 to 2002–03

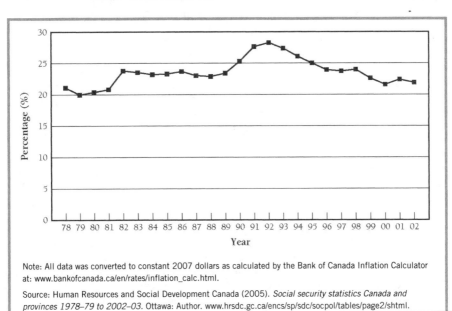

Note: All data was converted to constant 2007 dollars as calculated by the Bank of Canada Inflation Calculator at: www.bankofcanada.ca/en/rates/inflation_calc.html.

Source: Human Resources and Social Development Canada (2005). *Social security statistics Canada and provinces 1978–79 to 2002–03*. Ottawa: Author. www.hrsdc.gc.ca/encs/sp/sdc/socpol/tables/page2/shtml. Reproduced with the permission of Her Majesty the Queen in Right of Canada 2007.

FIGURE 2.5 Total Government (Federal, Provincial, and Municipal) Income Security Expenditures, 1978–79 to 2002–03

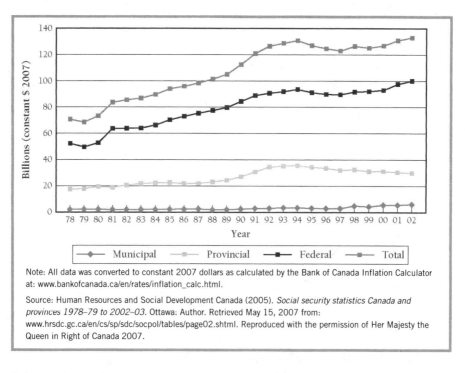

Note: All data was converted to constant 2007 dollars as calculated by the Bank of Canada Inflation Calculator at: www.bankofcanada.ca/en/rates/inflation_calc.html.

Source: Human Resources and Social Development Canada (2005). *Social security statistics Canada and provinces 1978–79 to 2002–03*. Ottawa: Author. Retrieved May 15, 2007 from: www.hrsdc.gc.ca/en/cs/sp/sdc/socpol/tables/page02.shtml. Reproduced with the permission of Her Majesty the Queen in Right of Canada 2007.

FIGURE 2.6 Total Government (Federal, Provincial, and Municipal) Income Security Expenditures Per Capita, 1978–79 to 2002–03

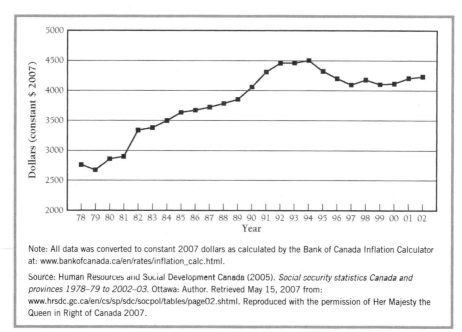

Note: All data was converted to constant 2007 dollars as calculated by the Bank of Canada Inflation Calculator at: www.bankofcanada.ca/en/rates/inflation_calc.html.

Source: Human Resources and Social Development Canada (2005). *Social security statistics Canada and provinces 1978–79 to 2002–03*. Ottawa: Author. Retrieved May 15, 2007 from: www.hrsdc.gc.ca/en/cs/sp/sdc/socpol/tables/page02.shtml. Reproduced with the permission of Her Majesty the Queen in Right of Canada 2007.

FIGURE 2.7   **Total Government (Federal, Provincial, and Municipal) Income Security Expenditures as Percent of GDP, Total Social Security Spending, and Total Spending, 1978–79 to 2002–03**

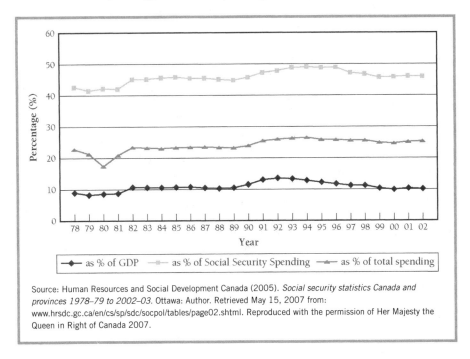

Source: Human Resources and Social Development Canada (2005). *Social security statistics Canada and provinces 1978–79 to 2002–03*. Ottawa: Author. Retrieved May 15, 2007 from: www.hrsdc.gc.ca/en/cs/sp/sdc/socpol/tables/page02.shtml. Reproduced with the permission of Her Majesty the Queen in Right of Canada 2007.

the amount of social spending compared to the percentage of Gross Domestic Product (GDP) has dropped several points since the early 1990s, essentially demonstrating the reduced spending in this budgetary sector. The turning point in the history of social spending in Canada occurred in the early 1990s. These figures show income security expenditures and demonstrate increases into the early 1990s for all levels of government and for per capita spending, followed by a decade-long period of marginal decreases in spending relative to total GDP, total spending, and total social spending. The latter category of comparison is significant because it signifies the changing trajectory of social policy and program financing. For example, social spending has remained relatively consistent, but the proportion that funds income security programs has diminished. Greater analysis is needed to determine precisely what is considered social policy amidst the decreases in traditional programs developed during the welfare-state period.

Several factors have influenced the erosion of these traditional social policies. A primary factor is the decline of federal government transfer payments to provinces, which began under CAP in the 1970s and accelerated up to 1992–93, when the federal share of CAP transfers to the country's three wealthiest provinces was down to 28 percent in Ontario and 36 percent in British Columbia and Alberta (National Council of Welfare, 1995, 7). The CAP itself was replaced in 1996 by a Canada Health and Social Transfer (CHST), which reduced federal government contributions to education, health care, and social welfare by another 15 percent during the first two years of its implementation (Graham, 2008a). The CHST also reduced the federal government's ability to enforce standards as to how the money would be spent and to which of the three major block areas money would be allocated (National Council of Welfare, 1995). Following the CHST, in 2004, two separate transfer programs were created: the Canada Health Transfer and the Canada Social Transfer. Changes in the 2007 federal government budget sought to improve the transparency of how transfer money is spent. Provincial governments, meanwhile, have tended to reduce transfers to local governments for the delivery of programs administered and partially financed by municipalities. These programs vary from province to province but, depending on the province, may include child welfare, general welfare assistance, home-making, rehabilitation services, and other forms.

At the same time, the contributions of individuals and their employers to various programs such as UI/EI (see below) and CPP have increased steadily. Funding reductions of CAP and of social programs not associated with CAP (e.g., UI, FA, CPP, OAS) have helped to create a second feature of the market-state era: the persistent and definite shrinkage in the comprehensiveness and extent of social programs. For example, after 50 years of funding the UI program, the federal government removed its financial support in 1990, making the program fully funded by employer and worker contributions. In the same year, more restrictive eligibility criteria were introduced, alongside shortened benefit periods, higher premiums, and more severe penalties to claimants quitting their jobs without "just cause" (Human Resources and Social Development Canada, 2007; Chappell, 1997, 49). In 1996, UI was changed to Employment Insurance (EI), and various reforms, intended to produce further savings of $1.9 billion, sought to reduce the maximum stay on insurance, penalize repeat users, and take back a proportion of payments from wealthier recipients (Battle, 2001).

While health care has undergone significant erosion in its funding base, the federal government released an important 1984 policy document, the Canada Health Act (CHA), widely viewed as an instrument to maintain federal standards. The document reaffirms five principles of our universal health-care system: its universality, comprehensiveness, accessibility (minimal barriers to services), portability (transferability of services from province to province), and public administration. In the 2007 federal government budget, the government reaffirmed its commitment to these principles; but its ability to enforce these standards may be impaired. One recent provincial document, the Alberta government's 2002 report, *A Framework for Reform: Report of the Premier's Advisory Council on Health*, intends to lead to policy decisions "on what health services are publicly insured in addition to those required under the Canada Health Act." Also in the Alberta report is a mandate to examine how to "diversify the revenue stream" for health-care delivery: "Instead of rationing health services, we need to find better ways of paying for the health services Albertans want and need" (Government of Alberta, 2002).

A third and related aspect of welfare-state retrenchment is the replacement of universal programs with selective programs. An excellent example is the 1992 replacement of the universal Family Allowances (FA) with the Child Tax Benefit, which combines the former FA and child tax credits into one refundable, income-tested child tax credit. In addition, the 1989 introduction of a claw-back on OAS payments to upper-income Canadians essentially abolished the universal basis of this program. As one policy document observes, the de-indexing against inflation of the threshold beyond which the OAS is taxed back means that an increasing number of Canadians will receive partial or no benefits (Battle & Torjman, 1993a, 4). These are but two examples of the trend to move away from universal programs.

A fourth aspect underlying many of the above changes is the growth of government debt. The debt is a cumulative, multi-year calculation based on the total amount of money that the government owes. It is different from a deficit, which is a yearly calculation of annual operating costs where spending exceeds revenue. While all levels of government experience debts and deficits, the present analysis, for sake of illustration, considers only the federal scene. In 2007, the federal government's total debt was $588 billion, or $17 939 for every Canadian. This is a considerable increase from 1965, when the deficit was $17 billion, or roughly $860 per person. Between 1965 and 1975, the federal government deficits were still below 2 percent of Gross Domestic Product (GDP, the value of goods and services produced in the economy based on earnings inside the country), and the debt was a low 18 percent. A combination of circumstances—a recession, accelerated borrowing, and an inability to match revenues with expenses—increased the debt to 48 percent of GDP by 1982, and by 1994 it was 71 percent (*Globe and Mail*, February 13, 1995). Since then, through a combination of circumstances, including reduced interest rates on the debt and reduced program expenditures, the 2001 debt ratio was down to 53 percent (Little, 2001). And in 2006, the debt ratio had fallen further to 35 percent (Department of Finance Canada, 2006). It is not debt in itself that matters, however, but rather how policy analysts, politicians, and others interpret the causes and significance of debt. When social programs are considered the cause of debt, then these programs get cut.

A fifth theme is the gradual recognition—through federal and provincial human rights legislation, the 1982 Charter of Rights and Freedoms, and other policy initiatives—of the rights of historically disempowered peoples, such as Aboriginal peoples, members of ethnoracial and religious minority communities, women, gays and lesbians, and people with disabilities, among others. Yet some of the institutions that had sought these rights in the past are disappearing. In 2004, 31 percent of Canadian workers belonged to a union, down from 38 percent in 1981; and younger workers, particularly under age 35, experienced more pronounced declines in union membership than older workers (Morissette, Schellenberg, & Johnson, 2005). In addition, as Chapter 5 points out, new conceptions of community and individual rights are developing. This is a sea change in social policy: moving from an institutional era of justice as distribution and redistribution, to a market era of justice as the politics of recognition and individual rights (Bakan, 1997; Fraser, 1995).

Likewise, a sixth theme, as elaborated in Chapter 4, is the rise of a neo-liberal ideology. This includes the primacy of financial markets, where even public pension funds, traditional instruments of the institutional state era, are now heavily invested in financial markets (Blackburn, 2002). For example, since 1999, state investors have moved the Canada Pension Plan from the relatively safe purview of bonds and have been increasingly investing these funds in far more volatile financial markets (Cooke, 2003).

A seventh and final theme, also elaborated in Chapter 5, is the impact of globalization on social policy and of new relationships between civil society and the state (Rice & Prince, 2000). The "third sector," or "civil society," is becoming increasingly important. In 2003, Canadians took out 139 million memberships in non-profit organizations (Hall, de Wit, Lasby, McIver, Evers, Johnston, et al., 2004); the country's first study on the topic concluded that non-profits contributed 8.6 percent of GDP (Hamdad, Joyal, & Van Rompaey, 2004). Since non-profits rely on private donations for their survival, 5.5 million tax-filers donated $5.8 billion to charity in 2002 (Statistics Canada, October 29, 2003). Yet a 2006 study points out that businesses ranked at the bottom of those who give money to non-profit organizations, donating less than half as much as individuals (Waldie, 2006). So too, as elaborated in Chapter 6, do human rights take on growing importance.

Conclusion

As this chapter demonstrates, the historical experience is profoundly important in shaping the current nature of social policies. To best understand the present, social work students need to learn about the past and to have some commensurate appreciation of the future prospects of social policies. The next chapter, which emphasizes ideological, political, social, and economic aspects of Canadian social policies, will help you better appreciate the contexts in which social policies are conceived, carried out, and changed.

Chapter 3

Contemporary Welfare State Institutions

This chapter examines major welfare state institutions in Canada. The welfare state refers to those governments that commit themselves to the development of social policies for the collective well-being of all. Welfare institutions form an important part of social service delivery in Canada. Welfare state institutions include, but are not limited to, income security, health, and education. Armitage (2003) outlines seven types of programs and services:

1. Cash programs, such as Old Age Security, Canada Child Tax Benefit, Canada Pension Plan, and postsecondary student loans.
2. Fiscal measures, including tuition-fee deductions, child-care expense deductions, and RRSP exemptions.
3. Goods and services measures, such as hospital insurance, legal aid, and education.
4. Measures related to employment, including minimum wage legislation and employment equity programs.
5. Occupational welfare measures, such as pension and insurance plans, and sports and recreational facilities.
6. Family care and dependency programs, such as home-care provisions.
7. Voluntary/charitable programs, such as shelters, soup kitchens, and food banks.

This chapter and the next touch on many of these components, particularly income security. The chapter first introduces the political and fiscal arrangements in Canada that make contemporary welfare state institutions possible. It then focuses on income security programs and concludes by discussing several related emerging social policy issues in Canada.

Fiscal and Political Arrangements

The Context

Most of the world's countries are unitary; that is, political power is centralized in one central or national level of government. Canada is among the world's approximately 20 countries that are federal states; political power in Canada is divided between a central or national level of government and several provincial levels of government. Canada has 10 provinces, as well as three territories: the Northwest Territories, Yukon Territory, and Nunavut. The provinces have clearly defined jurisdiction areas and tend to have large governments. The territories do not have the constitutionally prescribed autonomy that provinces have; each is governed by the federal government and by territorial governments that have been delegated authority. Since the 1970s, the federal government, through the minister of Indian and Northern Affairs Canada, has increasingly devolved responsibilities to territorial legislatures. Similarly, Aboriginal peoples have assumed either delegated or inherent powers to raise revenues and deliver services to people living on reserves, as elaborated in Chapter 6.

The Canadian Constitution defines the framework for working out social policy within the federal political system by giving both the national and the provincial governments sovereign yet interdependent jurisdictions. As a pre-welfare state document, the Constitution (known as the British North America Act in 1867) was not entirely clear whether the federal or provincial governments were responsible for social welfare. Sections 91 through 95 of the Constitution outline the main division of powers and responsibilities; powers not expressly given to the provinces were to remain the domain of the federal government (Irving, 1987). Only a few social issues are mentioned at all. Under Section 91, the federal government has jurisdiction over quarantine and marine hospitals, penitentiaries, and Aboriginal peoples; Section 92 makes provincial governments responsible for building and maintaining hospitals, asylums, charities, and public or reformatory prisons (Chappell, 1997, 80).

Over several decades, major legal decisions tended to place social welfare under provincial jurisdiction, rather than federal jurisdiction (Irving, 1987; Thomlison & Bradshaw, 1999). Irving (1987) suggests two reasons for these decisions. First, the Great Depression highlighted the imbalance between community-based social welfare initiatives and the ability of local communities to pay for these; for this reason, responsibility for social welfare moved to the provinces. Second, the courts began to interpret the provinces' property and civil rights responsibilities as a mandate to deal with social problems; and the federal government, in contrast, was mandated responsibility for those issues not directly associated with social problems, namely "peace, order, and good government." Thus, responsibility for social welfare, health care, and employment services became principally under provincial control.

Many social policies, such as Unemployment Relief in the 1930s, were historically delivered at the municipal or local level of government. In some regions, local governments continue to be responsible or co-responsible for the funding and delivery of social assistance, supported housing, home care, day care, and other services. Types of Canadian local governments include cities, towns, villages, and municipalities (which range from rural municipalities to regional and metropolitan governments that serve major urban areas). Under the Constitution, local governments are creations of the provinces; they can be created or disbanded by a provincial government, as recent amalgamations of major urban centres such as Toronto, Ottawa, and Montreal illustrate. Municipal powers are set out by provincial legislation often known as the Municipal Act, the Local Government Act, the Cities and Towns Act, or a similar name. Local governments, like their provincial and federal counterparts, are democratically accountable; legislation determines cycles of municipal elections of mayors, councillors, or their equivalents. Local councils make and carry out policies and receive revenue, principally through municipal taxes on real property and grants from provincial governments.

In addition to receiving transfers from provincial governments, local governments also receive specific-purpose transfers from the federal government, usually for infrastructure and transportation services. In both cases, the higher level of government tends simply to impose specific rates and amounts, rather than negotiating, in the way that federal and provincial governments negotiate federal–provincial transfers. Just as the federal government has been criticized for offloading responsibilities for funding major social programs to provincial governments, provincial and federal governments—particularly provincial governments—have been criticized for offloading to local governments, without comparable increases in cash transfers (Graham, 1995). Municipal budgets for social services have become constrained. In 1988, transfers from federal, provincial, and territorial governments accounted for 23 percent of the total revenue collected by municipal governments. This figure decreased to 16 percent by 2001; and in 2005, it rose slightly to 17 percent (Statistics Canada, 2006). As a result, municipalities have been forced to endure larger deficits. In 1988, the total municipal deficit was $800 million; by 2005, this figure had grown to $2.2 billion (Statistics Canada, 2006). Downloading from higher to lower levels of government is occurring in many advanced industrial countries, not just Canada, with commensurate impacts upon the social and economic well-being of communities worldwide (Kahn & Kamerman, 1998).

Higher levels of government became involved more extensively in the Canadian welfare state over the course of the early twentieth century, with accelerated presence in the aftermath of the Great Depression of the 1930s. As the need for health and welfare services increased across Canada during that calamitous decade, the financial burden became too heavy for the provinces and their municipal counterparts to carry (Graham, 1995). Most taxation powers resided with the federal government. A constitutional dilemma ensued: how to develop strategies for securing federal monies without violating the provincial jurisdictions of social welfare delivery. After World War II, in particular, with the rise of a more comprehensive welfare state, the federal government developed cost-sharing programs as a means of providing financial assistance for the delivery of social programs by the provinces and territories. These arrangements facilitated the development of our current welfare state. Federal powers such as the responsibility for public debt and property and the ability to raise monies by taxation were important for supporting social policies. Through the spending power of the federal parliament, social welfare transfer monies became available to the provinces and territories without changing much of the original constitutional jurisdiction.

Note that not all social programs are cost shared and provincially delivered, as the following pages will show. Several, such as Employment Insurance, are federally administered and employer–employee funded.

The Fiscal Context

Intergovernmental finance refers to the web of financial flows that link governments in a federal system. Since the federal government has especially comprehensive tax-raising capacities, a considerable portion of intergovernmental finance involves federal-to-provincial transfers; provincial-to-municipal transfers and federal-to-municipal transfers also occur.

The literature often refers to seven types of transfers (also noted in the glossary at the end of this book). Some intergovernmental grants are *block grants* (or general-purpose grants), while others are *specific-purpose grants*. A block grant is a cash transfer provided by one level of government to another, the amount of the transfer being fixed independently of the purpose to which the funds are put. Its opposite is a specific-purpose grant, the amount of which is tied to its intended purpose. An example would be a matched or shared-cost program.

Thirdly, there are unconditional grants, or *equalization payments*, which require no particular commitment by the recipient government to tie the grant to an expected type of expenditure. Equalization payments are intended to address two types of imbalances. The first is a *horizontal imbalance* between provinces—differences in fiscal capacity between "richer" and "poorer" provinces. The second is a *vertical imbalance*—differences in fiscal capacity between the federal government and a particular province. *Fiscal capacity* refers to a particular level of government's ability to change the total or composition of its revenues (e.g., taxes) or expenditures (e.g., social programs). The final type of transfer is a *conditional grant*, which is tied directly to an expected type of service delivery. An example of a conditional grant is the Canada Assistance Plan (1966–96), which provided federal transfers to provincial governments to cover the provincial delivery of health, education, and social services.

Horizontal imbalances between provinces can be addressed in two ways. First, the federal government can take over a particular responsibility. For example, Unemployment Insurance was inaugurated in 1941 as a federal, rather than a provincial, social program. A second way of addressing a horizontal imbalance is the direct transfer of federal monies to a province, via either an unconditional grant (equalization payment) or a conditional grant. Vertical imbalances are usually addressed through equalization payments from the federal government to "poorer" provinces.

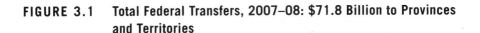

FIGURE 3.1   Total Federal Transfers, 2007–08: $71.8 Billion to Provinces and Territories

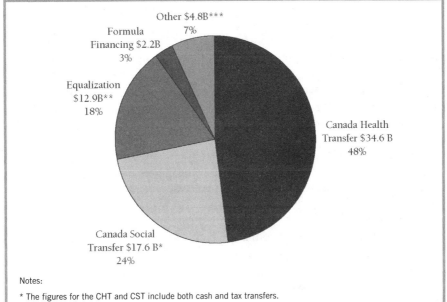

Notes:

* The figures for the CHT and CST include both cash and tax transfers.

** Equalization associated with the tax transfers and paid through the CHT and CST accounts for $1.6 billion of the total equalization figure.

*** The federal government provides assistance to provinces and territories under other programs, such as infrastructure and environmental/air pollution (the latter being the Canada Eco Trust for Clean Air and Climate Change, a three-year funded program expiring after the 2009/10 fiscal year).

Sources: Department of Finance Canada. *Federal transfer payments to provinces and territories* (March 2007a). Website: www.fin.gc.ca/FEDPROV/mtpe.html.

Department of Finance Canada. *Restoring fiscal balance for a stronger federation* (March 2007b). Website: www.budget.gc.ca/2007/bp/bpc4e.html#equalization. Reproduced with the permission of the Minister of Public Works and Government Services, 2007.

As indicated in Figure 3.1, in the 2007–08 fiscal year, the federal government transferred roughly $71.8 billion to provincial and territorial governments, which included $34.6 billion for the Canada Health Transfer (CHT), $17.6 billion for the Canada Social Transfer (CST), $12.9 billion for equalization payments, a further $4.8 billion for other expenditures, and $2.2 billion for territorial funding for various programs (Department of Finance Canada, 2007a; 2007b). These transfers account for about 27 percent of aggregate provincial and territorial estimated revenues for 2007. Precise values vary by province and are more significant for less financially wealthy provinces than more prosperous provinces. For example, according to the 2007 provincial budgetary estimates, federal payments represented 36 percent of revenue in Nova Scotia (Nova Scotia Finance, 2007), compared to just 10.5 percent in Alberta (Government of Alberta, 2007a).

Equalization Payments

Initial arrangements for Canada's system of intergovernmental finance were set out in the Canadian Constitution and have been revised periodically as federal–provincial relations and governmental services became more complex. The first formal equalization program was introduced in 1957 as a cost-shared program, in order to ensure that per capita revenues of all provinces—personal income taxes, corporate taxes, and succession duties—matched those of the country's wealthiest provinces, which were British Columbia and Ontario at the time. In the first of the required five-year revisions to these arrangements, the level to which these transfers were equalized became the all-province average, rather than the wealthiest two provinces. Also in this first revision, recipient provinces were guaranteed revenues equal to 50 percent of the all-province per-capita resource revenues. The system evolved during the 1960s until the present time, with changes to actuarial formulas for determining how to measure a fair transfer of revenue. Such changes were generally determined via conferences of federal and provincial first ministers. The last five-year arrangement was introduced in 2004 but was scrapped in 2007 for a formula that attempts to be more responsive to several concerns regarding the inequality within the entire system of equalization. But a 2005 critique describes it as a program with "reasonable origins" that has become "a self-propelling monster based on obscure calculations" and that discriminates against certain provinces (Naylor & Martin, 2005).

At the time of writing this chapter, one of the more contentious equalization issues is a perceived disincentive for equalization-receiving provinces to develop revenue capacities. For example, Ottawa would "claw back" in equalization payments the amount that a province such as Newfoundland or Nova Scotia collected in offshore oil or onshore mineral production projects. Adjustments outlined in the 2007 Federal Budget, which were built upon the findings of the O'Brien Report, planned to respond to this issue by excluding non-renewable resource revenues from the formula of determining the amount of equalization allotted to a particular province (Department of Finance Canada, 2007c). Other reports demonstrate the inflated cost of delivering public services in provinces that receive equalization payments. One report found that Newfoundland was spending $2351 more for each person on public service than that which was being spent on a resident of Ontario (*The Globe and Mail*, July 4, 2006, A12). Other reports have complained that wealthy provinces end up transferring considerable funds to Ottawa that are then distributed to poorer provinces. In 2002, Alberta's contribution to Ottawa amounted to more than $2560 per capita, the highest per-capita contributor, followed by Ontario and British Columbia. (*The Globe and Mail*, February 10, 2005, A23). Yet the Constitution is clear that Ottawa is responsible for ensuring delivery of reasonably comparable levels of public services at reasonably comparable levels of taxation to all Canadians, regardless of where they live. This, to many, is the rationale for continuing equalization, in the face of calls for its modification.

The Canada Health Transfer (CHT) and the Canada Social Transfer (CST), 2004

Perhaps the apex of the creation of a universal welfare state in Canada occurred after the 1966 introduction of the Canada Assistance Plan (CAP, 1966–1996). The CAP was a funding agreement that enabled the federal government to cost-share with the provinces for the delivery of education, health, and social service commitments. The CAP was a landmark social policy, allowing the federal government to ensure minimum standards of service delivery and relatively equal standards of services across the provinces.

The CAP started to unravel in the mid-1970s, as reductions in cost-sharing arrangements eroded the amount of money transferred to provinces. By 1992–93, the federal share of CAP transfers to the country's three wealthiest provinces was down to 28 percent in Ontario and 36 percent in British Columbia and Alberta (National Council of Welfare, 1995, 7). The CAP had ceased to be a fifty–fifty cost-shared relationship. Many provinces, in turn, downloaded significant financial responsibility to local governments, such as social assistance, supported housing, home care, daycare, and other services.

The Canada Health and Social Transfer (CHST) replaced the CAP in 1996 and resulted in a 15 percent decrease in federal transfers intended for health, postsecondary education, and social services over the following two years (Scott, 1998, xv). In response, provinces reduced benefit rates for social assistance and other programs. The CHST therefore eroded enforceable federal government standards, leaving provinces free to allocate the funds however they wished—even if this meant substantial reductions in program entitlements, and restrictions on eligibility and access. One of the country's foremost social policy think-tanks, the Caledon Institute of Social Policy (CISP), contended that this change in enforceability "constitute[d] one of the worst mistakes in the history of our social security system." In fact, they argue, it turns back "the social policy clock" to a period of minimal standards and far greater risks for society's most vulnerable (Torjman & Battle, 1995a, 5). A second CISP document warns: "There will be no guarantee of a safety net in the country" (Torjman & Battle, 1995b, 2).

This one piece of legislation—passed in the federal House of Commons in 1995—highlighted the extent to which social policy directs social work practice and affects the lives of many social work clients. For example, the federal government's CHST cutbacks to provincial governments for the cost-shared funding of health services, social services, and education had an impact on provincial government delivery of services, as well as on the relative role of each level of government (federal, provincial, and local) in social policy. One observer insists that the "relative power of the provinces over social policy" increased as a result of these cutbacks, as well as its devolution of labour market social programs, such as employment training, to the provinces (Battle, 2001, 16). Yet Ottawa "dominates income security policy," and the provinces deliver "most welfare, social service, and health care" policies, depending on cost-sharing arrangements with the federal government (16). As a result of new imbalances, federal–provincial fiscal and administrative relations are in "full evolutionary flight." Another expert points out: "There is no status quo" (Courchene, 1996, cited in Inwood, 2000, 128), in effect, the federal government had erased the norms of the previous system. But the funding of health and social programs continued to evolve. In 2004, the CHST was divided into two separate block transfer programs: the Canada Health Transfer (CHT, 2004) and the Canada Social Transfer (CST, 2004).

The CHT governs the main transfer of federal money to the provinces in support of health care, and the CST governs the funding arrangements in support of education, social services and social assistance, and child development programs. One goal of these two transfer programs is to provide greater spending accountability. First, it clarifies how much federal transfer money was spent specifically on each program area. Secondly, and of greater significance, the block transfer nature of these grants makes clear what proportions of the transfers are to be spent on each program area. While the new funding arrangements do not replace the restrictions and levels of accountability on provincial spending and program delivery that were present during the time of the CAP, they provide a greater check on government spending and program funding than was present during the period of the CHST.

Public discontent about accountability and transparency led to further revisions to the CST, this time identifying specific amounts of federal support for education, social programs, and children's programs, compared with present provincial and territorial spending in these areas (Department of Finance Canada, 2007b). The 2007–08 Federal Budget outlined that of the $9.5 billion in transfers that year: $850 million was provided for children's programs, $2.4 billion for postsecondary education, and $6.2 billion for other social programs (Department of Finance Canada, 2007b). Data reporting the actual spending of the $8.1 billion tax portion of the CST was not available at the time of writing. The relative balance of participation of the provincial and federal governments, and the dynamics that create these ever-shifting arrangements, are examined in greater detail in the next section.

Federal–Provincial Relations

Canadian federalism has never been static. With the increased scope of the post-World War II Canadian welfare state, and with federal and provincial responsibilities for social welfare becoming more complex, federal–provincial relationships have become increasingly important to government and to the country's policy-making processes. Indeed, most of the important areas of contemporary social policy cut across loosely defined boundaries of federal and provincial jurisdiction. National policies can often only be carried out with some degree of provincial cooperation; and most provincial responsibilities rely on some degree of federal cooperation—in social policy, this often means the transfer of federal monies to provinces.

The Political Context

Federal–provincial relations take place in many arenas. They range from informal, sometimes daily, contact between federal and provincial civil servants, to formal contact that includes large-scale conferences of provincial and federal first ministers (i.e., the prime minister and provincial premiers). Contact itself covers the widest gamut of jurisdictions—from international trade to fiscal arrangements to economic development. Each year, formal contacts usually number in the hundreds, while less formal contacts are far more numerous. Joint federal–provincial agreements are essential to many types of social policies, particularly in relation to joint funding arrangements.

The tone and nature of federal–provincial relations have changed significantly through history. Some scholars argue that the end of World War II until the early 1960s was an era of "cooperative federalism," where federal–provincial relations were relatively cordial. During the late 1960s and 1970s, an era of "executive federalism"—as one scholar describes it—emerged: federal–provincial relations became more acrimonious (Smiley, 1976, 54). Several factors may have precipitated this changing dynamic. Provincial responsibilities had grown in scope and magnitude since the cooperative federalism era. In addition, during the 1960s, a Quiet Revolution was occurring in Quebec: a renewed sense of nationality was propelling the Quebec government to assert its right to withdraw from certain federal social welfare programs, such as the CPP (and to create its Quebec counterpart, the QPP), and its right to modernize Quebec social and political affairs (Trofimenkoff, 1983). During the 1970s and afterward, Western provinces were likewise increasingly asserting their rights (Inwood, 2000, 129). Moreover, federal–provincial constitutional struggles became increasingly visible, with more elaborate and formal federal–provincial "diplomacy": institutionalized first ministers' conferences, and the creation of entire specialist bureaucracies to support these exchanges (Inwood, 2000, 129).

Several major attempts at re-establishing a Canadian constitutional framework over the past 30 years have had a significant, incremental impact upon federal–provincial relations. In 1976, the Parti Québécois was elected in Quebec; and in 1980, it held a provincial referendum on sovereignty association with Canada. Sovereignty association referred to the political sovereignty of Quebec, with economic and other types of ties with Canada, including a common currency, a free trade zone, a common tariff, and a court of justice composed of equal numbers of Canadians and Québécois to oversee this associative arrangement. The referendum was defeated by a 60 percent No to 40 percent Yes return. During that referendum, during which Prime Minister Trudeau campaigned for the No side, Trudeau promised to repatriate Canada's Constitution— then called the British North America Act, which was still held in London, England. In 1982, the federal government repatriated the Canadian Constitution and added to it the Charter of Rights and Freedoms. However, the government of Quebec had never agreed to the repatriation process and refused to sign the new constitution; and its premier, Réné Lévésque (whose government had lost the 1980 referendum), publicly expressed a feeling of betrayal of Quebec by the other premiers and Prime Minister Trudeau.

In 1987, a new federal government under Brian Mulroney sought to induce the government of Quebec to officially accept repatriation of the Constitution through the Meech Lake Accord, a set of new constitutional reforms. The Accord's five basic points, proposed by Quebec Premier Robert Bourassa, included a guarantee of Quebec's special status as a "distinct society" and a commitment to Canada's linguistic duality; increased provincial powers over immigration; provincial input in appointing Supreme Court judges; restricted federal spending power; and restoration of the provincial right to constitutional veto. Prime Minister Brian Mulroney and all the provincial premiers agreed to the Accord on April 30, 1987, although the premiers of Ontario and Manitoba, several women's groups, and Native groups expressed strong objections. The Accord died on June 22, 1990, when the legislatures of Newfoundland and Manitoba failed to approve it before the deadline. This led to a national referendum in 1992 over a proposed constitutional renewal (the Charlottetown Accord), which contained several provisions, including Quebec's special status within the Canadian federation. The Charlottetown national referendum of 1992 was defeated nationally by 54 percent of votes cast. It did, however, receive approval in New Brunswick, Newfoundland, Prince Edward Island, the Northwest Territories, and, by the narrowest of margins, Ontario. Three years later, in 1995, the sovereigntist government in Quebec held a referendum on whether or not Quebec should become sovereign, after having made a formal offer to Canada for a new economic and political partnership. This referendum narrowly lost by a vote of 50.6 percent against and 49.4 percent for.

Since then, federal–provincial relations have been relatively cordial, but Quebec has remained on the periphery of some federal–provincial agreements. One example is the 1999 social union agreement struck between the federal government and all provinces except Quebec. Its goal was to improve transparency, accountability, and mutual collaboration in social policy and remains an important benchmark for current federal–provincial relations in this area (Inwood, 2000, 128; Federal/Provincial/Territorial Ministerial Council on Social Policy Renewal, 2003).

An excellent example of the spirit of intergovernmental cooperation is the Canada Child Tax Benefit (CCTB) program. The CCTB consists of the Canada Child Tax Benefit, which provides federal income support to all low- and middle-income families with children; the Child Disability Benefit, a benefit provided to families caring for a child with a mental and/or physical disability; and the National Child Benefit (NCB) supplement for low-income families (National Council of Welfare, 2001, 43). The CCTB is the culmination of a much simplified federal approach to child poverty, blending several older programs (Family Allowances, children's tax exemption, and the refundable child tax credit) into one federal benefit. Moreover, it also introduced new provincial income-tested child benefits to be administered on behalf of the provinces by the federal government through the income tax system (Battle, 2001, 40). Because of the joint nature of the CCTB, federal and provincial governments shared administrative data in these areas.

Some analysts assert that at the best of times, Canada's federal system creates a form of "institutional fragmentation" that limits the state's capacity to create social policies (Banting, 1985, 49). This is precisely what the CCTB attempted to overcome. But there is a long historical legacy of fragmentation, as the following section on income security illustrates. The federal government is responsible for such programs as Employment Insurance, Old Age Security, and the Canada Pension Plan.

Provinces have jurisdiction over social assistance and Workers' Compensation. These different federal and provincial roles, as pointed out in Chapter 2, evolved for historically specific reasons.

Income Security Programs

Canadian social policies cover a wide range of health, education, and income security measures. The present chapter, for purposes of brevity, concentrates on income security programs—that is, those social programs that provide cash payments to recipients. As Chapter 2 emphasizes, prior to the development of a comprehensive welfare state in the 1940s and 1950s, Canadians living in poverty had few avenues of assistance. They were expected to be self-reliant. If, however, they had no options but to seek help from others, they would ordinarily go first to family, then to friends, and then to community sources such as the church or a charity (Graham, 1992; Splane, 1965). When these were exhausted, "unemployment relief"—the precursor to contemporary social assistance—was accessed (Graham, 1996c; Struthers, 1983).

In today's world, a far more elaborate system of income security exists, encompassing all three levels of government (and hence different offices with which a social worker might be in contact) and falling under a wide spectrum of categories. Different income security programs have been designed for, among other categories:

➤ lone-parent families (income support programs—the exact name varies by province);

➤ families with children (Canada Child Tax Benefit; Universal Child Care Benefit);

➤ individuals experiencing lengthy periods of unemployment (income support programs—the exact name varies by province);

➤ individuals experiencing a short period of unemployment (Employment Insurance);

➤ youth without guardian support (income support programs—the exact name varies by province);

➤ individuals who are injured at work (Workers' Compensation);

➤ people with a disability (income and health benefits programs, the exact name varies by province; or Canada Pension Plan; or Workers' Compensation);

➤ the elderly (Canada Pension Plan, International Benefits, and Old Age Security—which includes the Guaranteed Income Supplement and Spousal Allowance programs; some provinces have top-up programs for the elderly poor);

➤ refugees new to Canada receiving Government of Canada assistance (Resettlement Assistance Program); and

➤ veterans of wars (War Veterans' Allowance).

Social workers need to be fully familiar with this system in order to help clients identify the programs for which they are eligible and to ensure prompt and full access to these programs. The social worker's success may be of crucial significance to the client. It may make the difference, for example, between a client's going hungry or having food, being homeless or being able to secure accommodations, being in despair or feeling hopeful, being trapped in poverty or having the means to better their standard of living.

Some Key Terms and Concepts

There are two major forms of income security programs in Canada: selective and universal. Each has its own assumptions.

Selective Programs

Selective programs have a long history, extending to Elizabethan poor relief in England, and were brought to Canada with European colonization. "Unemployment Relief" was a selective program, as is its contemporary successor, general welfare assistance, also called "social assistance," "social allowance," or more recently, "income support" or "social benefit." The usual form of a selective payment involves a transfer of money from a level of government to an individual. Eligibility for selective programs is based on a means test. Means tests are carried out to evaluate, first, a person's financial resources—such as income, assets, debts, and other obligations—and second, other criteria, such as number of dependants or health status of the applicant.

Selective programs are subject to several criticisms. One criticism is that they personalize problems of poverty, rather than focusing attention on broader societal structures that create the conditions for poverty. The economy is one example of a societal structure. Say, for instance, that a weak economy leads to the closure of a pulp and paper mill in a one-industry town. This external condition would cause job losses, leading individuals to apply for assistance.

Moreover, selective programs, critics contend, may stigmatize people who, through factors outside their immediate control, experience temporary or permanent loss of income. Selective programs devote considerable administrative resources to monitoring the lives of individual clients, rather than focusing on broader community and societal changes that might improve the opportunities of a client. Proponents, on the other hand, believe that selective programs are the most efficient means of targeting money to those in need. As well, some believe means tests may motivate recipients to return to the workforce.

Universal Programs

Universal programs provide cash benefits to *all* individuals in a society who fall into a certain category. They differ from selective programs in that eligibility is a right of citizenship, rather than an entitlement that has to be proven through a means test. The implications are several-fold. A recipient's level of specific needs, or economic status, is not taken into account when determining eligibility.

Where selective programs focus attention on an individual claimant's worthiness to receive benefits, universal programs operate under manifestly different assumptions. The state expresses responsibility to provide income security for all citizens, and society implicitly recognizes the presence of conditions beyond an individual's control that may impede economic well-being. Stigma has little place in a universal program, since all people, regardless of level of need, may have access to benefits as long as they fulfill eligibility conditions (such as age for Old Age Security, or children under the age of 6 in the case of the Universal Child Care Benefit).

While universal programs may target money to a greater number of people, including the well-to-do, many argue that the income tax system can be used to counterbalance payments to the rich—and not the social program itself. In a progressive income tax system, the proportion of taxes paid increases with earnings; those with a greater ability to pay end up paying more taxes. In contrast, in a regressive tax system, taxes are not collected on an ability-to-pay basis. The most extreme instance of a regressive tax—such as a sales tax—is one that is levied equally. How so? Whether a person paying a sales tax is below the poverty line or the president of a major bank, the sales tax charged remains the same, even though the poor person has much less ability to pay this tax. Canada's tax system is somewhat—although far from completely—progressive. Thus, higher income earners pay a greater proportion of their money on income tax than do those in lower income categories. Governments try to offset the regressive nature of sales taxes through refund cheques to people who qualify. Some people might argue that universal programs do *not* wrongfully direct money to the better-off, given the existence (or potential existence) of a progressive income tax system and refund programs (Muszynski, 1987). But some argue that with everyone receiving benefits from a universal program, the middle and upper classes are politically co-opted into supporting the program. This means that benefits are less likely to be reduced in scope or eligibility than in a selective program that is geared only toward the less politically powerful poor (Titmuss, 1958; 1987).

Universal programs came to the fore during the World War II period. But they have eroded over the past 25 years, as selective programs have found new favour. The reasons for these changes are elaborated in Chapter 2.

Demogrant, Social Assistance, Social Insurance

Several other terms are used to describe income security programs. Familiarity with them is essential to social work practice. A *demogrant* is a cash payment to an individual or family based on a demographic characteristic (usually age), as opposed to need; an example is Old Age Security. *Social assistance* refers to selective income security programs that use a means or needs test to determine eligibility; these are often administered at the provincial or local governmental level, depending on the province. *Social insurance* refers to income security programs in which eligibility for benefits is determined by a previous record of contribution and on the occurrence of a particular contingency, such as unemployment, retirement, injury, or widowhood; examples include the Canada Pension Plan and Employment Insurance (Armitage, 1996, 190–195).

Major Income Security Programs in Canada

Several levels of government deliver income security programs. These programs constitute part of, but not the entirety of, transfers to persons and transfers to governments. The following programmatic descriptions are deliberately succinct and simplified, covering major aspects of eligibility and benefits but omitting minor details that are too numerous to discuss. Many programs are not discussed, due to the need for brevity. Greater elaboration is found in Graham (2008a), Guest (1997), and McGilly (1998).

Federal Government Programs

Employment Insurance (EI, 1996–)

Employment Insurance (EI) was previously known as Unemployment Insurance (1940–1996). There are three ways to obtain EI: loss of job due to termination, temporary disruption of work due to illness, and application for maternity/parental benefits. EI is based on hours worked, rather than weeks worked—which is a fairer practice for part-time and multiple-job-holding workers. The entrance requirements have become more stringent over the past 15 years but continue to vary depending on job type and rate of unemployment in the region where the claimant lives. For example, in areas with high unemployment (above 13 percent), a minimum of 420 hours are needed, whereas in places of low unemployment (below 6 percent), 700 hours are needed (Human Resources and Social Development Canada, 2007a). Furthermore, if a worker happened to be unemployed for a period greater than two years, or was entering the labour market for the first time, they would have to prove 910 worked hours prior to qualifying for Employment Insurance benefits (Service Canada, 2007). These restrictions have resulted in a large percentage of jobless people not qualifying for benefits. In 2004, 42 percent of jobless individuals in Canada did not qualify for Employment Insurance benefits (Human Resources and Skills Development Canada, 2004). Most recipients receive up to 55 percent of their average weekly insured earnings (up to a particular ceiling); however, during the 1970s, entitlement was as high as 64 percent of working wages (Battle, 2002). As of May 1, 2007, the maximum benefits payment is $423 per week. The program used to be funded by the federal government and employer–employee contributions; it is now funded only by employer and employee contributions. Furthermore, the length of time an individual can receive employment insurance benefits is restricted, based on where an individual resides. The maximum time ranges between 36 and 45 weeks (Human Resources and Social Development Canada, 2007a).

Canada Pension Plan/Quebec Pension Plan (CPP/QPP, 1966–)

Canada and Quebec Pension Plans are insurance plans to which people must contribute during their working years. Both were created the same year and are similar in design; the QPP is administered by the Quebec provincial government and is solely for people working in that province; the CPP is administered by the federal government and is for those in all provinces and territories other than Quebec. CPP and QPP also comprise survivor's pensions for the spouses of deceased pensioners, disability pensions, children's benefits, and death benefits. Eligibility is based on past contributions to the plan. In instances of retirement (as distinct from disability or spousal death), it is paid to contributing claimants over the age of 60 and is intended to replace about 25 percent of the income the claimant was earning while paying into the plan. As of May 1, 2007, the maximum benefits are $863.75 per month for retirement payments; $1053.77 for disability payments; $518.25 for spousal survivors' payments (age 65 or over); and $204.68 for children's survivor payments. The program is funded by employer and employee contributions. The program is considered social insurance.

Old Age Security (OAS, 1952–)

The Old Age Security pension is a monthly benefit for people 65 years of age or over. It originated in 1927 as a selective, means-tested program but was transformed into a universal program in 1951. Because it is a universal program, employment history does not play a part in eligibility, and a claimant need not be retired. Those on an OAS pension pay both federal and provincial income tax on the money they receive. Those with higher incomes repay part or all of their benefit through the tax system. As such, some argue that OAS ceases to be a universal program, due to this "claw back" of benefits from higher-income-earning Canadians. As a result, it excludes many people from full entitlement and a substantial number from ever receiving any compensation. Moreover, claw-back amounts have systematically increased since the late 1980s. As of May 1, 2007, the maximum benefits were $436.55 per month. The program is financed from federal government general tax revenues and is considered a demogrant.

Guaranteed Income Supplement (GIS, 1966–)

The GIS was established to supplement the earnings of low-income OAS recipients and is administered under the OAS program. Eligibility is determined by need and may increase or decrease according to a claimant's overall yearly income. As of October 1, 2007, the maximum benefits are $620.91 per month for a single applicant, and $410.04 for individual applicants who are married. The program is funded through federal government general tax revenues and is considered social insurance.

Spouse's Allowance (SPA, 1976–)

The SPA was established to provide income to the spouse of an OAS pensioner, or to a widow or widower. Like the GIS, eligibility is based on need, and the SPA is only provided to those within certain income limits. The SPA stops when the recipient turns 65 and becomes eligible for the OAS, or if the recipient leaves the country or dies. As of May 1, 2007, the maximum benefits were $901.97 per month for a beneficiary married to an OAS pensioner, and $999.81 for a widow or widower of a former OAS pensioner. The program is funded from federal government general tax revenues and is considered social insurance.

Veterans' Pensions (VP, 1919–)

Those members of the armed forces who incur a disability during wartime (Active Force), peacetime (Special Duty Area), or other military service are eligible for the VP. The amount of pension is determined by degree of disability and varies accordingly; maximum rates as of May 1, 2007, were $2221.08 for the pensioner and $555.27 for spousal recipients. The program is funded from federal government general tax revenues and is considered a demogrant.

War Veterans Allowances (WVA, 1930–)

This income-related program ensures a minimum annual income for wartime/peacetime service veterans who served in World Wars I or II or the Korean War. Eligibility is based on need and a minimum qualifying age of 60 for a man and 55 for a woman. Survivors' allowances are also available. As of May 1, 2007, the maximum benefits were $1176.50 per month for single claimants and $1787.95 for those living with a spouse and/or a child. This program is funded from federal government general tax revenues and is considered a form of social assistance.

Resettlement Assistance Program (RAP, 1998–)

Administered by Citizenship and Immigration Canada (CIC), the Resettlement Assistance Program (RAP) provides financial assistance for up to one year after arrival to government-assisted refugees arriving to Canada. In many instances, funding may also be provided via cost-sharing sponsorship agreements between CIC and sponsorship agreement holders at the local, regional, and national levels.

Almost all newcomers to Canada are independent-class immigrants or are sponsored by others, such as Canadian family members. A small proportion of immigrants are refugees, defined as having "a well-founded fear of persecution in his or her country of origin because of race, religion, nationality, membership in a social group, or political opinion" (Government of Canada, 2007). RAP is only for refugee-class immigrants. Benefit levels are consistent with provincial social assistance programs and are intended to provide the necessary financial resources for food, shelter, and clothing. The program also seeks to provide opportunities for new Canadians to enroll in English or French language classes and develop the means to secure employment. It is parallel to the Immigrant Loans Program, also intended to assist the resettlement process. Local, regional, and national immigration-service organizations provide hands-on transition assistance to help a refugee secure housing, education, employment, and other services, and RAP is delivered in collaboration with these organizations. The program is funded through federal government general tax revenues and is considered a form of social assistance.

Canada Child Tax Benefit (CCTB, 1998–)

The CCTB (formerly the Child Tax Benefit, 1993–98) replaced the following three benefits: the Family Allowance (1944–1992) and refundable and non-refundable tax credits. Under the CCTB, the federal government provides payments to parents or guardians on behalf of children under the age of 18. It is usually paid to the mother of the child if the child lives with her. The amount is different according to the family income, the number of children, and the children's ages. This program also coincides with comparable programs at the provincial and territorial levels; eligibility for those programs is determined by information provided for the CCTB application. The three main components of the CCTB are the base benefit, the National Child Benefit (NCB) supplement, and the Child Disability Benefit. The CCTB is tax free; and as of May 1, 2007, in all the provinces except Alberta, the benefits can be as much as $3199.92 per child per year. The NCB supplement, an important component of the system, is a federal, provincial, and territorial initiative designed to tackle child poverty and is available to low-income families. In May 2007, the supplement provides $162.08 per month for the first child and $143.33 for the second child in families with an annual income of less than $20 435. The CCTB is an example of a formerly universal program (the Family Allowance) that has been replaced by a selective/income-tested program (the CCTB). Some commentators criticize the program for providing inadequate benefits in light of pervasive child poverty (Freiler & Cerny, 1998; National Council of Welfare, 2001).

Provincial Programs

Workers' Compensation (WC, 1914–)

Workers' Compensation is designed to make payments to and cover rehabilitation and medical costs for workers who have been injured on the job. In the case of workplace death, it also provides payments to an employee's survivors. It was first introduced in Ontario and subsequently spread to other provinces. Assistance levels vary from province to province. Eligibility criteria are stricter now than in the past, and benefits have been reduced in scope. In Alberta, for example, benefits as of 2007 are 90 percent of net income up to $62 600 (Government of Alberta, 2007b), and in Ontario, 85 percent of net income up to $71 800 (Government of Ontario, 2007a). The program is funded by worker and employee contributions and is considered a form of social insurance.

Social Assistance (SA, various years)

Social assistance, often called welfare or public assistance, helps people in need who are not eligible for other benefits and is one of the most important income security programs with which a social worker should be familiar. It is typically delivered to three broad categories of people: families with dependent children in need (often this is long-term need), individuals with disabilities (often this is long-term need), and individuals or families in short-term need. These three categories may have different names and may be administered out of different offices. The last category—short-term assistance—is seen as an income program of last resort. Benefit payments help pay for food, shelter, fuel, clothing, prescription drugs, and other health services. Since its introduction in 1998, CCTB has covered some of the cost of welfare for families with children.

Eligibility rules and amounts of payment differ from province to province and from municipality to municipality in provinces where municipalities administer and/or partially fund programs. Especially for short-term need assistance, means tests are common. Applicants must be of a certain age, usually between 18 and 65, but some provinces have provisions for minors under the age of 18 not living with a legal parent or guardian. Under certain circumstances, full-time students in postsecondary education may be eligible for assistance in some provinces but not in others. Single parents seeking assistance must have already tried to secure court-ordered maintenance and child support from the other spouse if they were entitled to it. Workers on strike are usually not eligible for assistance, nor are sponsored refugees or sponsored family-class immigrants during their period of sponsorship. In general, social assistance is granted if a household's net assets are less than the cost of regularly recurring basic needs for food, shelter, and other necessities.

Fixed and liquid assets are usually assessed in the application process. Most provinces exempt the value of a car, a principal residence, furniture, clothing, Retirement Savings Plans that are locked in, and Registered Education Savings Plans. Other allowable assets—cash, bonds, securities that are readily convertible to cash, the value of life insurance—are limited by household size and employability. Applicants are usually required to convert non-exempt fixed assets into liquid assets and deplete those assets before qualifying for welfare (National Council of Welfare, 2006b).

Benefit rates fall well below low-income cut-off (LICO) poverty lines, as indicated in Table 3.1. (The calculation of poverty lines is elaborated in Chapter 4.) Benefit rates and definitions of eligibility have also tightened in recent years. For example, in 1995, during its first term in administration, the Ontario Conservative government slashed social assistance by a remarkable 21 percent. Due to tightened eligibility requirements nationwide, one million Canadians who would have qualified for benefits in 1994 no longer qualified in 2004 (Greenaway, 2004). One major cause of this shrinkage in numbers is the relative prosperity in the 2000s in Canada; another is the new restrictions placed on those qualifying to receive benefits. Some provinces have also introduced workfare. Workfare requires recipients to undergo training programs and/or other forms of work-related activities in return for benefits. The program is funded by federal and provincial monies under the CST, and in some instances, partially by municipal governments.

The Caledon Institute of Social Policy points out that it may be wiser to approach social assistance as a human resource strategy issue rather than as workfare (Torjman, 1996a). Workfare implies compulsory labour and mandatory participation in designated activities. A human resource strategy, on the other hand, is voluntary. Both, ideally, are collaborative with numerous stakeholders—industries, educators, social welfare, and justice. Both are also supposed to provide a range of opportunities, including job search, academic upgrading and skills training, and employment creation; but some argue that workfare emphasizes these less. A human resource strategy also ensures "that appropriate supports are in place—notably, high-quality, affordable childcare and transportation subsidies—so that recipients can move off welfare" (Torjman, 1996a, 1). Finally,

TABLE 3.1 Social Assistance Nationwide, 2005

	Total Income	Poverty Line	Poverty Gap	Total Welfare Income As % of Poverty Line
Newfoundland				
Single Employable	$ 8 198	$17 895	−$ 9 697	46%
Person with a Disability	$ 9 728	$17 895	−$ 8 167	54%
Lone Parent, One Child	$16 181	$22 276	−$ 6 095	73%
Couple, Two Children	$19 578	$33 251	−$13 673	59%
Prince Edward Island				
Single Employable	$ 6 214	$17 184	−$11 570	35%
Person with a Disability	$ 8 084	$17 184	−$ 9 700	45%
Lone Parent, One Child	$13 707	$22 139	−$ 8 432	62%
Couple, Two Children	$21 213	$33 046	−$11 833	64%
Nova Scotia				
Single Employable	$ 5 422	$17 895	−$12 473	30%
Person with a Disability	$ 8 897	$17 895	−$ 8 998	50%
Lone Parent, One Child	$12 917	$22 276	−$ 9 359	58%
Couple, Two Children	$19 032	$33 251	−$14 219	57%
New Brunswick				
Single Employable	$ 3 427	$17 895	−$14 468	19%
Person with a Disability	$ 7 995	$17 895	−$ 9 900	45%
Lone Parent, One Child	$13 656	$22 276	−$ 8 620	61%
Couple, Two Children	$17 567	$33 251	−$15 684	53%
Quebec				
Single Employable	$ 6 947	$20 778	−$13 831	33%
Person with a Disability	$10 063	$20 778	−$10 715	48%
Lone Parent, One Child	$15 395	$25 867	−$10 472	60%
Couple, Two Children	$20 704	$38 610	−$17 906	54%
Ontario				
Single Employable	$ 7 007	$20 778	−$13 771	34%
Person with a Disability	$12 057	$20 778	−$ 8 721	58%
Lone Parent, One Child	$14 451	$25 867	−$11 416	56%
Couple, Two Children	$19 302	$38 610	−$19 308	50%
Manitoba				
Single Employable	$ 5 818	$20 778	−$14 960	28%
Person with a Disability	$ 8 601	$20 778	−$12 177	41%
Lone Parent, One Child	$13 282	$25 867	−$12 585	51%
Couple, Two Children	$20 357	$38 610	−$18 253	53%
Saskatchewan				
Single Employable	$ 6 663	$17 895	−$11 232	37%
Person with a Disability	$ 8 893	$17 895	−$ 9 002	50%
Lone Parent, One Child	$13 235	$22 276	−$ 9 041	59%
Couple, Two Children	$19 327	$33 251	−$13 924	58%

TABLE 3.1   Social Assistance Nationwide, 2005 (continued)

	Total Income	Poverty Line	Poverty Gap	Total Welfare Income As % of Poverty Line
Alberta				
Single Employable	$ 5 050	$20 778	−$15 728	24%
Person with a Disability	$ 7 851	$20 778	−$12 927	38%
Lone Parent, One Child	$12 326	$25 867	−$13 541	48%
Couple, Two Children	$19 497	$38 610	−$19 113	50%
British Columbia				
Single Employable	$ 6 456	$20 778	−$14 322	31%
Person with a Disability	$10 656	$20 778	−$10 122	51%
Lone Parent, One Child	$13 948	$25 867	−$11 919	54%
Couple, Two Children	$18 466	$38 610	−$20 144	48%

Sources: Adapted from National Council of Welfare (2006). *Welfare incomes 2005*. Volume Number 125. Website: www.ncwcnbes.net/en/research/welfare-bienetre.html. Reproduced with the permission of the Minister of Public Works and Government Services Canada, 2007.

and perhaps most importantly, a human resource strategy promotes, rather than destroys, human dignity and well-being.

Some provincial governments have sought to revise their social assistance programs previously targeted for children and families to align these with the federal CCTB. British Columbia was the first to consider a federal–provincial integrated child benefits system payable to low-income families with children (Battle & Mendelson, 1997, 2). Other provinces have followed suit. Earnings supplement programs for working poor families are also available in several provinces.

Provincial Top-Ups for the Elderly (various years)

The combined OAS + GIS supplements are low enough to qualify most elderly couples in most provinces for social assistance. To avoid having the elderly as SA recipients, some provinces have introduced seniors' income supplemental programs. Benefit rates vary from province to province and are intended to raise incomes of recipients to roughly the income levels of public assistance recipients. Not all provinces have these particular benefits programs. An example of a provincial top-up for the elderly is the Saskatchewan Income Plan, which, as of May 1, 2007, provided a maximum of $90 per month to single claimants and $72.50 to married claimants (Government of Saskatchewan, 2007). Another program, the Ontario Guaranteed Annual Income System (GAINS), as of May 1, 2007, provided a maximum of $83 per month for a single claimant (Government of Ontario, 2007b). Provincial top-ups for the elderly are selective social assistance programs, funded jointly by federal and provincial monies under the CST.

Conclusion

Income security policies work best when they are integrated with other social and economic policies and when they successfully address categories of people who are most in need. The disgraceful incidences of poverty among Aboriginal peoples, children, people with disabilities, and women, among other social groups, ought to compel more comprehensive and successful policy responses. Disability pensions within the CPP, for example, have been criticized for not allowing beneficiaries who can work irregularly or part-time to do so—unless they are willing to forfeit all benefits (Torjman, 1997). Some likewise argue that social assistance programs should be designed to provide income top-ups to low-income labourers, and that social programs should provide special transportation, childcare, and other supports necessary to full and vital functioning in and beyond the workplace (Torjman, 1996a; 1996b; 1997; 1998a; 1998b; 1999).

So, too, might policies be delivered in ways that more sensitively appreciate how age, ethnicity, gender, geography, race, religion, and range of ability, among other parameters, affect need. In 2002, new Canadians during their first year in Canada were 3.5 times more likely to be in a low-income category than Canadian-born citizens, which fell only slightly to 3.2 times greater in 2004 (Picot, Hou, & Coulombe, 2007). Other research also suggests that immigrants who have been in Canada for ten years are at risk of being in, or falling into, poverty (in Picot, Hou, & Coulombe, 2007). The implications are considerable. People new to Canada may have little appreciation of or experience with a welfare state and may require especially skilful and competent social work assistance to gain access to income security programs. Further research is needed to address the often profound and troubling questions regarding immigrant access to labour markets (Galabuzi, 2006).

These issues of diversity are examined in further detail in Chapter 6. But before discussing them, the following two chapters examine some social, economic, and political consequences of social welfare (Chapter 4), as well as some broader contextual issues such as globalization, social movements, social inclusion, and social welfare retrenchment (Chapter 5).

Chapter ④

Ideological, Social, and Economic Influences

Chapter 1 points out that the various definitions of social policy each influence how policies are conceived and carried out. Chapter 2 shows that history is important in determining how policies developed into their current state (Chapter 3) and in determining their future prospects. This chapter builds further on the preceding three chapters. It considers the ideological, social, and economic factors that influence social policy development. After reading the chapter, you will have a better understanding of how such dynamics influence social policies—and hence how they affect the lives of social work clients. In addition, this chapter will help you appreciate why social workers who are genuinely concerned about the people they work with are interested in such forces; and why, as a result, social workers and their professional associations ought to be continuously engaged in social advocacy leading toward social change.

Ideology and the Political Spectrum

Ideology refers to a shared way of thinking based upon a set of ideas that reflect the values, beliefs, attitudes, and experience of a particular person or group. Ideological beliefs focus on the nature of the ideal political system, the ideal economic order, and the ideal social goals. Political ideology places a special emphasis on the role government should play in economic and social matters.

Ideology provides a way of interpreting problems and designing appropriate solutions. Ideological considerations are not the only factors that influence political decisions about social policy and social problems; but political parties attempt to shape social policy decisions from their ideological base. Individuals such as social workers also embrace particular ideologies because all social policy decisions influence the work social workers perform. Social policy decisions affect the funding and delivery of social services, as well as who will receive what services.

This section very briefly explores different ideological approaches to social policy and then relates these approaches to the way the major Canadian political parties think about social policy. But before beginning either, we will cover a few

FIGURE 4.1   Major Political Ideologies: The Political Spectrum

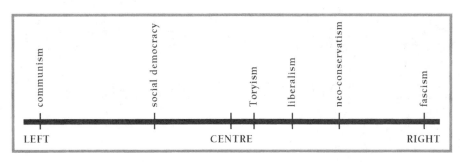

core definitions that are key to ideology: communism, socialism, liberalism, Toryism, neo-conservatism, and fascism (see Figure 4.1). Note that there is tremendous diversity of views within each term; as a result, consider the following to be a short and necessarily non-comprehensive paraphrase of major attributes within each.

The six political ideologies presented in Figure 4.1 are ordered along a continuum from communism on the extreme political left to fascism on the extreme political right. It is important to remember, as you read about these political ideologies, that they do not necessarily represent the Canadian political parties that may bear the same name. The Liberal Party of Canada, as an example, has some aspects that are liberal in ideology and others that are not. Though political parties may have their foundations in certain ideological positions, each party has been uniquely shaped by historical, economic, and social forces as much as by ideological values and beliefs. Those to the left of the spectrum have tended to emphasize an institutional perspective to social welfare, as discussed in Chapter 2. The neo-conservative ideology on the right end of the spectrum tends to emphasize the market-state. Tory and liberal ideologies have emphasized both institutional and market-state perspectives, depending on the moment in history.

Because most political ideologies have something to say about the social unit of attention—the collective (society) or the individual—the following concepts are often used in ideological descriptions: individualism and collectivism, and egalitarianism and elitism:

> *Individualism* emphasizes the individual's freedom, worth, and self-determination in the political, social, and economic spheres.

> *Collectivism*, by way of contrast, places the rights and welfare of the group or society above those of any and all individuals.

> *Egalitarianism* is the belief that all people should have equal political, social, and economic rights.

> *Elitism* is the organization of society around interrelated but unequal functional groups, usually with those in the political or economic leadership group referred to as the *elite*. Elitism is a hierarchical rather than an egalitarian organizational view.

The central organizing principles of each political ideology will be discussed according to its stance on such dimensions as liberty or regulation, equality or hierarchical organization, and individualism or collectivism.

Communism

Distinguishing between Marxist, radical, and communist perspectives is important; since each of these ideologies is based on particular assumptions, they should not be used interchangeably. As one author points out, "whereas Marxist social work is certainly radical, the reverse is not necessarily true" (Webb, 1981, 145). As elaborated in Chapter 7, *radical social work* emerged from a variety of theoretical traditions that included labelling theory and new criminology (Webb, 1981, 145). Marxism, for purposes of this chapter, represents a variety of approaches based on the writings of Karl Marx; as such, Marxism is one part of the broader rubric of communist political ideology.

Although the term *communism* has roots extending back centuries, as a contemporary ideology, it owes much to the contributions of such nineteenth- and early twentieth-century thinkers as Karl Marx, Vladimir Ilyich Lenin, and Friedrich Engels. Communism often brings to mind the twentieth-century communist regimes of the Soviet Union, China, and Cuba (Krieger, 1993) and is a distinct version of socialism. Communism has become associated with a political movement directed by the working class to establish an alternative to capitalist societies and also with a societal ideal of egalitarianism.

The focus of communism is collectivism—that is, social ownership and control of lands as well as the *means of production* (the land, labour, and capital used by a society to produce material goods). State ownership and production is directed toward meeting human need rather than for profit, as in a capitalist state. Communism assumes that citizens will regard themselves as co-owners of the means of production, acknowledge their true needs and the needs of fellow citizens, and work diligently to produce what is necessary to accomplish these ends (Krieger, 1993; Marchak, 1988). According to some communists, these goals have to be organized under a dictatorship of the proletariat: for example, during the Russian Revolution, the Communist Party assumed political control in Russia without democratic elections and created a classless, communist society. In summary, the core ideological principles of communism are a highly communal and egalitarian social and economic order (Chappell, 1997).

The Communist Party of Canada was founded in 1921, preceded by various activities within trade unions, collectives, and former political organizations, such as the Socialist Party of Canada (British Columbia, founded 1904). Until 1937, the Communist Party was illegal under the Canadian criminal code, and its members were persecuted. Party members took leadership positions in some trade unions and were elected to the federal legislature (Fred Rose, 1943) and provincial legislature (W.A. Kardash, Manitoba, 1941; A.A. MacLeod and J.B. Salsberg, Ontario, 1943), as well as to many municipal councils. One of the party's founders, Jacob Penner, served on Winnipeg City Council between 1931 and 1960; his son Roland became the province's attorney general in 1981. The

Communist Party (Marxist-Leninist), founded in 1970, espouses similar ideology to the Communist Party of Canada (Penner, 1992).

Social Democracy

Contemporary social democracy finds its roots in nineteenth-century Europe, which was strongly associated with labour activism and criticism of both capitalism and an unbridled free-market economy (Krieger, 1993). Social democrats believe that free-market economies cannot ensure the efficient and effective allocation of economic resources to meet the needs of all citizens. Most support the market economy model, but with some important state interventions; the degree of support for either may vary from one social democrat to the next. Social democrats often focus on economic issues, such as the ownership and regulation of basic or key economic resources. From this perspective, the state is responsible for planning, directing, and regulating economic sectors as well as providing social welfare services for those in need. In the Western world, socialism has most often become associated with social democrats as opposed to communists. Social democrats advocate free elections and democracy.

Unlike communism, in which a dictatorship of the proletariat without recourse to democratic elections may exist, social democrats limit the extent of state control to that determined by a democratic election process, and temper capitalism with egalitarianism through government legislation and regulation (Chappell, 1997; Krieger, 1993). Texts often cite Sweden and other Scandinavian countries as quintessential examples of social democracy (although there have been shifts to the political right in these countries); to some extent the province of Quebec retains some social democratic traditions more obviously than other parts of Canada. In summary, social democracy seeks collective and egalitarian means to moderate the effects of capitalist, free-market economic forces.

It is important to reiterate that these definitions are "ideal types": conceptually precise terms that have divergent applications in real life. While the New Democratic Party (NDP) in Canada is seen as a major locus of our country's social democratic ideas, there are many social democrats who disagree with the NDP's approach to current social, political, and economic issues, perceiving them to be too right-wing. These same criticisms may be applied to social democratic parties in other industrialized countries, such as France, Germany, and Great Britain.

Toryism

In the eighteenth century, conservatism was a movement to counter the liberalization of traditional ideals and the advent of egalitarian ideologies that threatened the status quo (Hoover, 1992). A "Tory" conservative ideology contrasts with American brands of "liberal conservatism" because it retains its British roots (Horowitz, 1970; Mishra, 1995). The traditional Canadian attitude of deference to authority is seen as an expression of Tory elitism (Horowitz, 1970). Toryism also sees itself as collectivist in an organic sense of society, because the ideal of social and economic hierarchies contributes to economic security and social stability (Mishra, 1995). Toryism's social "law and order" orientation contrasts with liberalism's individual liberty and freedom perspective. Marchak (1988) places Toryism as slightly right of centre on the egalitarian–elitist and the individualist–collectivist spectrum, but left of the neo-conservative position on these dimensions. Historically, the term *Tory* has been used to describe members of the former Progressive Conservative Party of Canada. But, as we shall see, political parties change. Although some Conservatives are still Tory, many Conservatives these days are in fact liberal or neo-conservative in ideology.

Liberalism

The ideology of liberalism evolved in the eighteenth and nineteenth centuries as a change-oriented perspective that emphasized individual development in a social, political, and economic order unencumbered by government restraints (Krieger, 1993). Modern liberal doctrine for many liberals acknowledges the constraints of capitalism and the free-market economy in the unequal distribution of wealth and its attendant status and power (Chappell, 1997). This has led to a tempered liberal outlook with stronger humanistic values becoming more prominent. The liberal ideology is strongly individualistic, though its proponents claim it staves off the extremes of the left and the right by developing policies that reduce economic and social inequalities (see Krieger, 1993, for a more extensive historical review). Nineteenth-century liberalism in economic matters was often referred to as *laissez-faire*, which called for no government interference in the marketplace. But liberalism has since moved from a belief that individual differences accounted for economic and social inequalities to a recognition that some government intervention is needed to facilitate equality of opportunity (Marchak, 1988). The extent of this intervention would be less, as a rule, than what a social democrat might advocate. The Liberal Party of Canada should not be confused with the ideology of liberalism described here. The terms *Liberal*, with a capital letter and describing the Canadian political party, and *liberal*, with a lower-case letter and describing the ideology, are not the same. Only *some* Liberals are liberal in ideology; others have social democratic leanings, and others are neo-conservative.

Neo-Conservatism

Conservatism recognizes the inequalities among people but sees differences as more important than similarities (Hoover, 1992). Neo-conservatism refers to the "new right"—the rejection of collectivist values and the return to laissez-faire economics, which advocates less government and a more minimalist position toward social and economic affairs. Hoover (1992) identifies neo-conservatives as "individualist conservatives," sharing much in common with liberals. More traditional Tories and "red Tory" conservatives accept inequality less willingly, whereas neo-conservatives more strongly revere freedom and personal initiative. Many policy scholars use the terms "neo-liberal" and "neo-conservative" interchangeably in the popular media. One can consider the two terms as synonymous.

Fascism

Fascism refers to a government or political philosophy that is typically totalitarian, extreme right-wing, and nationalist. Twentieth-century fascist political parties rose to power between the two world wars in Mussolini's Italy and Hitler's

Germany. Payne (1992) describes fascism as an ideology opposed to almost all other political ideologies of the time—communism, socialism, and liberalism. The strong, radical, nationalist stance of fascism arose out of several forces, among them an intense fear of communist and socialist ideology, and a racist assertion of nationality. Fascism gave rise to a one-party authoritarian state that maintained an active control of the economy, but without socialist ownership of the means of production. Like communism, fascism is inherently undemocratic. Once a fascist government comes to power, it tends to ban open elections. In addition, fascists embrace a radical collectivist stance (i.e., a particular form of nationalism, often racially and/or ethnically based). They place the interest of the nation or groups within a nation ahead of any particular class or individual. They also reject the egalitarian perspective of communism and socialism and maintain an elitist or class structure in society, *but* with the belief that the class structure should be subordinate to the social cohesion of the nation.

Mainstream Canadian Political Parties

There are numerous political parties in Canada, and many that do not have representatives in federal or provincial legislatures represent theoretical concerns of interest. But for purposes of brevity, this section examines four divergent political ideologies as represented in mainstream Canadian political parties: neo-conservatism, Toryism, liberalism, and social democracy. Common to all the major political parties of Canada are some basic values, such as the inherent right of citizens to self-determination, a belief in democracy, and a commitment to varyingly regulated forms of industrial capitalism—depending on the political ideology. But among our major political parties, and indeed within society, principles of egalitarianism appear to be weakening, as liberal tenets of individualism gain greater currency.

It is best, though, to appreciate the complex, sometimes contradictory and divergent ideological base within the same party. Holding each party together and determining its social policy stance is a complex set of interactions between ideological, historical, economic, political, and social forces. For example, some scholars have characterized the Liberal and former Progressive Conservative parties as governing by "brokerage" politics since the 1960s: this means that their respective ideological tenets hold only a marginal place in decision-making processes and outcomes (Carty, Cross, & Young, 2000; Turner, 1995). It is important, too, to appreciate that the parliamentary and economic (political, civil society, business, media, and others) mechanisms often cause non-incremental change to party policies, some of which are unpredictable, and some of which vary from issue to issue (Gormley, 2007). Further details of these mechanisms are noted in Chapter 9.

Liberal Party of Canada

The Liberals, or "Grits," were part of Canada's political structure at its founding in 1867. Christian and Campbell (1990) characterize the Liberals as comprising two ideological factions: business liberalism and welfare liberalism. These party factions are held together by the common traditional liberal values of liberty and individualism. Welfare liberalism places human rights above the economic rights of individuals. This type of liberalism expresses itself in the policies that impose taxation and other forms of economic regulation as well as those that facilitate the development of social welfare programs. Business liberalism, on the other hand, interprets taxes and regulation as economic restraints to individual freedom. The business faction of the Liberal Party prefers minimizing government law making and regulation, especially in economic matters.

Any interpretation of Liberal social policy must begin by assessing which side of the business–welfare liberalism tension is in the ascendancy position within the party. When business liberalism dominates, social policy focuses on costs and thus limits access to and reduces emphasis on universal programs. In contrast, when welfare liberals speak for the party, they emphasize universal access and standards in social policies. At these times, emphasis on the costs of *not* providing these services overrides concerns about the financial costs of providing them.

Conservative Party of Canada

The country's conservative tradition originated with the original Conservative Party (1867–1942) and the Progressive Conservative Party (1942–2003). The Progressive Conservative Party always had a wide spectrum of proponents. Those in the "Tory" tradition of eighteenth- and nineteenth-century England were conscious of the interdependence of socioeconomic classes and were more open to government involvement in the economy and society than many liberals. This group was once so powerful in the party that the Progressive Conservatives were known as "the Tories." Others in this party were stauncher advocates of the free market and individualism. In 1987, the Reform Party of Canada arose in Western Canada as a populist right-wing protest party, rejecting the "Toryism" of the Progressive Conservatives. Its presence split the right-wing vote, assuring a succession of Liberal Party governments in the late 1980s and 1990s. The Reform Party (renamed the Alliance Party in 2000) amalgamated with the federal Progressive Conservative Party in 2003, creating a new Conservative Party that came to federal power in 2005. At the provincial level, Progressive Conservative Parties remain in most Canadian provinces. The new Conservative Party of Canada, like its provincial counterparts, has strong ideological anchors in neo-liberalism and neo-conservatism. As a result, social policy proposed by the Conservative Party of Canada tends to promote reduced government involvement in social policy and increased reliance on self, families, and the economic marketplace. This approach has a lot in common with the market-state stage of social policy discussed in Chapter 2. A final point bears emphasis. Keep in mind that this entire definition emphasizes general principles only. For example, while it is true, on balance, that the Conservative Party of Canada prefers selective programs, some Conservative policies retain certain universal programs, as occurred with the creation of the Universal Child Care Benefit (2006).

New Democratic Party

The New Democratic Party is a social-democratic–oriented party that originated as the Co-operative Commonwealth Federation (CCF) party, established during the Great Depression of the 1930s among trade unions and farmer cooperatives. It was renamed the New Democratic Party (NDP) in 1961. The NDP has ideological roots in welfare liberalism and is a reaction to the Tory hierarchical view of society. A collectivist but egalitarian stance characterizes the Canadian socialism portrayed by the NDP. Legal equality and equality of opportunity are major features of their view of Canadian social democracy. NDP social policy tends to support universal programming, with broad access and a uniformity of distribution across Canada. To many party faithful, the costs of sustaining these social programs should be borne more prominently by corporate Canada.

Bloc Québécois Party

The Bloc Québécois, a federal political party that elected its first leader in 1991, has had as its principal mandate the promotion of Quebec sovereignty. In 1993, the Bloc gained the second largest number of seats in the general election and therefore became the Official Opposition (McMenemy, 1995). Although the Bloc has a very clear and precise political agenda, it has had support from diverse parts of Quebec society. For example, it is currently centrist but has also had trade union support and other social democratic influences. The Bloc is also closely associated with the Parti Québécois, a provincial political party founded in 1968 and also devoted to the sovereignty of Quebec.

A final point on these four political parties bears emphasis. Political parties are elected at the provincial and federal levels to govern for a maximum of five years. Governments can be elected with a majority of seats (half the seats plus one) or a minority of seats (less than half of the seats but with more seats than any other party). When acting as a majority, a governing party can pass legislation regardless of opposition if all members of that party vote. For minority governing parties, any legislation can be defeated if all members of the opposition vote against it. Thus, minority governments often need to negotiate with the other parties.

Theories of Social Welfare/The Welfare State

Ideology is the foundation of social welfare theory and the extent of programs and services delivered through the welfare state. Figure 4.2 illustrates the interconnection of ideology and the welfare state by demonstrating, in general terms, the relationship between ideology and social responsibility. For example, at the left end of the political spectrum, there is strong emphasis on societal responsibility, which results in an institutionalized approach to social welfare. Alternatively, at the other end of the spectrum, individuals are challenged to meet their own basic needs, with emphasis placed on the development of social or human capital. A current example is the use of welfare-to-work programs: these programs emphasize the development of individual skills to create greater social capital. *Social capital* is defined as the attitude, spirit, and willingness of people to

FIGURE 4.2   Model of Social Responsibility and Social Capital

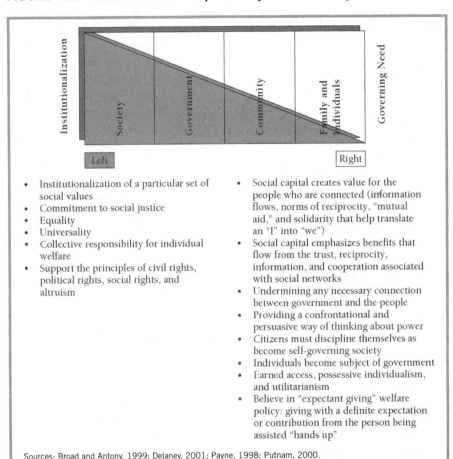

- Institutionalization of a particular set of social values
- Commitment to social justice
- Equality
- Universality
- Collective responsibility for individual welfare
- Support the principles of civil rights, political rights, social rights, and altruism

- Social capital creates value for the people who are connected (information flows, norms of reciprocity, "mutual aid," and solidarity that help translate an "I" into "we")
- Social capital emphasizes benefits that flow from the trust, reciprocity, information, and cooperation associated with social networks
- Undermining any necessary connection between government and the people
- Providing a confrontational and persuasive way of thinking about power
- Citizens must discipline themselves as become self-governing society
- Individuals become subject of government
- Earned access, possessive individualism, and utilitarianism
- Believe in "expectant giving" welfare policy: giving with a definite expectation or contribution from the person being assisted "hands up"

Sources: Broad and Antony, 1999; Delaney, 2001; Payne, 1998; Putnam, 2000.

engage in collective civic activities or networks of relationships with people in their community and family.

As with any continuum, the political spectrum contains a wide range of ideological beliefs, each with a distinct interpretation of social responsibility. This discussion is based on Mulvale's outline of six theoretical approaches to social welfare (2001, 15–29)—six practice frameworks used within the social work profession.

The first, a social democratic perspective, assumes that the welfare state emerged out of democratic political pressures, be it via trade unions, political parties, or other social institutions. Often these pressures come from the left end of the political spectrum (Struthers, 1994).

The second perspective, premised on Marxist thought, deems the welfare state an instrument of social control; for instance, it forestalls class insurrection. The welfare state serves the needs of capital accumulation—ensuring, for example, economic growth and relative peace with labour. It also serves the needs of the state: post-World War II economic growth financed a burgeoning welfare state, which in turn kept unemployment relatively low; political parties were elected in part on their ability to help facilitate these outcomes (Offe, 1984). Many Marxists believe social welfare has contradictory purposes in meeting the needs of the state and of capital. Some, in fact, accept right-wing arguments that some welfare programs create disincentives for work and diminish profit margins (Offe, 1984). Most see the post-World War II universal welfare state as decidedly a thing of the past. As elaborated in Chapter 2, economic growth in the 1970s faltered and governments abandoned the principles of intervening in the economy. Consequently, "two legs (high levels of employment and consumer demand, both premised on strong economic growth)" of the welfare state became wobbly; the third, the government's commitment to social welfare programs, was weakened as a result (Mulvale, 2001, 19).

A third perspective, based on feminist thought, sees the welfare state as having profoundly reinforced dependency of women and children on the breadwinner male. Women are fundamental actors in social welfare: as the clients, reformers, and state employees of the welfare state (Ursel, 1992). Yet the welfare state has been modest at best in meeting women's needs, and oppressive at worst in reproducing gender inequalities that arise within patriarchal structures. Income security programs, for instance, have been bifurcated into insurance-based entitlements for men, and needs-tested, stigmatizing programs for women. Feminist theorists call for greater support for women in the workplace, the expansion of affordable day care, and the transformation of income security programs to reflect women's needs, among many other measures. These concerns are elaborated in Chapter 6.

A fourth perspective is an anti-racist critique of the welfare state. One writer describes the double process of disadvantage experienced by members of ethno-racial communities. Their less-advantaged positions on economic and social grounds make them more reliant on the welfare state. Yet the welfare state treats them "on systematically less favourable terms than members of the majority community" (Pierson, 1991, cited in Mulvale, 2001, 23). This perspective is also discussed in Chapter 6.

Fifth, a green critique, sees the welfare state as "embedded in an industrial order"—meaning an economy based on growth that is no longer sustainable (Pierson, 1991, cited in Mulvale, 2001, 23). Green critics assert that the welfare state is premised on an expanded economy that overproduces, depletes resources, and creates pollution. These concerns are elaborated in Chapter 5.

The final perspective calls for a shift in social welfare from compensation to empowerment. Rather than emphasizing individual deficits and providing an agreed-upon community standard, such as a poverty line, empowerment social welfare assumes that all people require help in order to develop (Drover & Kerans, 1993, cited in Mulvale, 2001, 26–27). Central to this view is a critique of the way needs are interpreted and claims are made.

The market-state, discussed in Chapter 2, challenges several of these perspectives—particularly the social democratic perspective and any others that do not adhere to individualist or liberal assumptions.

Social Welfare as a Response to Need

Social welfare programs may be categorized as functioning in one of the following three ways (Macarov, 1995a):

1. Intervention is made before a problem arises. This is perhaps the least-addressed function of social welfare, given that scarce resources are most often used to address existing cases of economic hardship.
2. Maintenance is provided for at-risk individuals or groups, such as families with children, who receive various tax credits in the hope that they will not slip into the poverty ranks.
3. Social policy is directed at the amelioration of existing problems through such programs as social assistance. This is the most commonly used category. Governments and social agencies strive to develop clear indicators for identifying when personal economic troubles should fall within the realm of a social economic problem.

There is a great deal of debate about how to define need worthy of societal intervention, as well as how to respond to identified need. It is important to remember that there is a direct relationship between how a social problem is defined and its perceived solution. In this section, we will consider how poverty is defined and the solutions that are implied by these definitions. This will involve distinguishing needs from wants, categorizing types of economic need, and examining how benchmarks for measuring economic need to be addressed by societal intervention are created.

Need versus Want

A four-part typology helps social workers to determine the exact nature of a particular human need. The types include felt needs, expressed needs, normative needs, and comparative needs (Chappell, 1997):

➤ *Felt needs* are defined on a personal or subjective level.
➤ *Expressed needs* are felt needs that are communicated to others.
➤ *Normative needs* are determined by someone other than the individual, by applying a benchmark or standard to the individual case.
➤ *Comparative needs* are determined by comparing one individual or group to another.

Establishing the benchmarks for normative needs and the boundaries of specific social groups, such as those living in poverty, is of major concern for the creators and administrators of social policy.

Theoretical and/or ideological perspectives influence how social policy planners determine the nature of a human need. Psychologist Abraham Maslow's *hierarchy of needs* theory (see Figure 4.3) is an excellent means of considering these distinctions (Maslow, 1954; Macarov, 1995b). Maslow's theory categorizes needs according to a hierarchy ranging from *having* (physiological needs) to *loving* (social needs) and finally to *being* (self-actualizing needs) (Macarov, 1995b). Maslow defined the basic physiological needs (i.e., food, shelter, and clothing) as essential survival needs. Social policy is most often directed at this "having" aspect of need. Maslow's theory is based upon the principle of deficiency needs; that is, if a particular need is not being sufficiently met, then the person or group will seek to make up for this deficiency. This theory highlights a motivational element in meeting common human needs (adapted from Chappell, 1997).

FIGURE 4.3   Maslow's Hierarchy of Needs

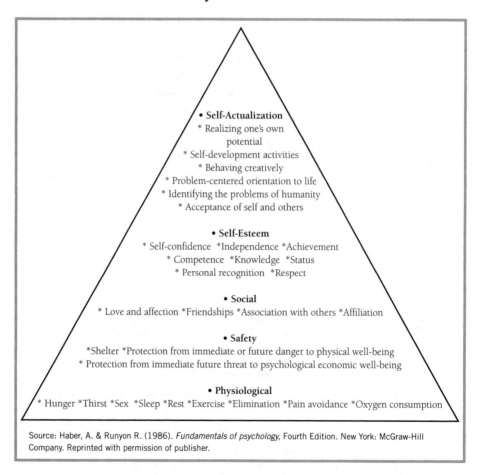

Source: Haber, A. & Runyon R. (1986). *Fundamentals of psychology*, Fourth Edition. New York: McGraw-Hill Company. Reprinted with permission of publisher.

Differential Human Needs

While Maslow's hierarchy distinguishes types of common needs, it does not address special conditions that create these specific needs. Macarov (1995) identified five categories of people with special needs:

1. the *incapable*, such as children;
2. the *unprepared*, such as recent immigrants to a new country and those who cannot read;
3. *disaster victims,* such as victims of war or environmental situations;
4. the *unconforming,* or those who do not abide by societal norms; and
5. the *unmotivated,* or people who lack the motivation to meet their own needs.

All five categories are essential to social policies.

Besides common human needs and special needs, some needs are created by society (Macarov, 1995). Institutionalized discrimination—along lines of race, gender, culture, or other areas of social diversity—may create obstacles to developing and implementing social policy. These include, but are not restricted to, lack of access to services, inadequate funding and representation in community-based programs, and ethnocentric values and practices in existing services and programs policy (Galabuzi, 2006). Discriminatory policies are examined in greater depth in Chapter 6.

Denying the impact of institutionalized discrimination affects the definition of the problems and, therefore, the anticipated solutions. This may lead to an interpretation of needs based upon membership in the unconforming and/or the unmotivated categories mentioned earlier. As a result, social needs—for housing, income security, or other things—may be restricted or even denied to a particular person or group, because they are evaluated as deserving or undeserving.

As society changes, the social attention to needs may also change. Policy-makers decide how and when societal resources are directed at certain needs and when social norms dictate that social institutions other than social welfare (e.g., the individual, family, or informal social networks) should be directed at finding a solution.

Measurements of Well-Being

There are several ways to measure well-being. Measuring the strength of a country's economy by means of the Gross Domestic Product (GDP) and Gross National Product (GNP) is one. GDP is "a measure of the total flow of goods and services produced by the economy over a specified time period" (Bannock, Baxter, & Davis, 1998a). GNP is a more comprehensive measure, which includes "gross domestic product plus the income accruing to domestic residents arising from investment abroad less income earned in the domestic market accruing to foreigners abroad" (Bannock, Baxter, & Davis, 1998b). Unemployment levels are another measure; a full employment economy means unemployment levels are 3 percent or less: anyone wanting a job could have one (albeit not necessarily a well-paying job). According to Vosko (2006), *precarious employment* refers to "forms of work involving limited social benefits and statutory entitlements, job insecurity, low wages, and high risks to health. It is shaped by employment status (i.e. self-employment or wage work), form of employment (i.e., temporary or permanent, part-time or full-time), and dimensions of labour market insecurity as well as social context (such as occupation, industry, and geography) and social location (the interaction between social relations, such as gender and race, and political and economic conditions" (3–4). New immigrants and racialized groups are over-represented among Canada's precariously employed (Galabuzi, 2006).

Several conditions related to precarious employment—such as job insecurity, excessive work hours, work–life conflict, effort–reward imbalance, and job strain—are also work-related determinants of health (Raphael, 2004, 97). The social determinants of health determine the conditions of a person's life. Table 4.1 lists other social determinants of health (Raphael, 2004, 13).

In 1990, the United Nations created a popular measure of human well-being called the Human Development Index (HDI). HDI is based on three indicators: longevity, education, and standard of living. These constructs are measured by analyzing the rates of life expectancy, adult literacy, enrollment in education facilities, purchasing power parity, and income. Canada often scores high; in 1992 and 1994 through to 2000, it had the world's highest HDI. In 2006, it ranked sixth out of 177 countries—following Norway, Iceland, Australia, Ireland, and Sweden (United Nations Development Programme, 2006).

Another recent measure of well-being results from people evaluating the well-being within their own lives—subjective well-being (SWB). SWB is measured by personal perceptions of life satisfaction as they relate to, for example,

TABLE 4.1   Social Determinants of Improved Health

1. Don't be poor. If you can, stop. If you can't, try not to be poor for long.
2. Don't have poor parents.
3. Own a car.
4. Don't work in a stressful, low-paid, manual job.
5. Don't live in damp, low-quality housing.
6. Be able to afford to go on a foreign holiday and sunbathe.
7. Practice not losing your job, and don't become unemployed.
8. Take up all benefits you are entitled to, if you are unemployed, retired, sick, or disabled.
9. Don't live next to a busy major road or near a polluting factory.
10. Learn how to fill in the complex housing benefit/asylum applications forms before you become homeless and destitute.

Source: Dennis Raphael (Ed.) (2004). *Social determinants of health: Canadian perspectives.* Toronto: Canadian Scholars' Press. Reprinted with permission from Canadian Scholars' Press Inc., 2007.

one's moods and emotions and one's living and work situations (Graham, Kline, Trew, & Schmidt, 2008). Understanding well-being in this manner is largely individualistic, but it provides a picture of a wide range of conditions that influence a person's happiness. According to SWB, happiness is more than simply monetary gains—in contrast to the corporate message promulgated through the popular media (Graham, 2008b).

Conceptualizing and Defining Poverty

Perhaps the most important concept of well-being in social policy is the notion of poverty. The concept of poverty dates back to ancient times. *Poverty* is a state of deficiency in money or in the means of subsistence. Welfare state governments want to know how many citizens live in a state of poverty, and these governments are not content to rely on subjective assessment. To this end, governments and organizations set *poverty lines* that measure the necessary amount of money for living at a determined *standard of living.* A standard of living refers to the "necessities, luxuries, and comforts" needed to sustain oneself or family at a determined level (Barker, 1991).

Defining poverty with a poverty line means measuring the difference between *what is* and *what should be.* As indicators of an income level below which living would be seriously difficult, poverty lines may be set at absolute or relative levels. Absolute and relative definitions of poverty are based upon destitution and disparity models, respectively. *Absolute need* definitions of poverty answer the question, "What is the bare minimum (destitution) level in order for an individual or family to survive?" Writing for the Canadian Council on Social Development, policy analysts Ross, Scott, and Smith (2000) set an absolute poverty line at about $2000 per person per annum in Canada (6). Adjusting this figure for inflation, in 2007 the absolute poverty line would be approximately $2400 per person per annum. This amount is a mere survival rate that includes using all local resources such as basic provincial health care, community shelters, food banks, and thrift shop clothing. In contrast, *relative need* definitions are based on social values, rather than absolute needs, and start with a prevailing standard of living and then deduce the level below this standard that is intolerable to society. Relative poverty lines are concerned with what should be—they establish the norm against which an individual or family can be compared.

Normative Basis of the Poverty Line

How do Canadians define poverty? Table 4.2 summarizes major indexes for defining Canadian poverty lines. Table 4.2 shows that Canadians cannot agree on a definition of poverty. Statistics Canada's low income cut-off (LICO) definition is the best known of these indicators. The LICO has been a standard since 1959 and is based on a 1959 survey of family spending patterns conducted by Statistics Canada. The survey showed that the average Canadian family spent 50 percent of

TABLE 4.2 Measuring Poverty

Poverty Lines in 2002	Cut-Off Income for Household of Four*
Statistics Canada: LICO	Before tax: $24 846 (rural) and $36 093 (large urban 500 000+ population)**
Statistics Canada: LIM	$30 514**
Statistics Canada: MBM	$29 343 (Toronto) to $22 167 (Quebec: community with population between 30 000 and 99 999)***
Toronto CSPC	$46 021****
Montreal Diet Dispensary	$25 962****
Sarlo Toronto (Fraser Institute)	$23 697****
CCSD	Before tax: $25 050 (rural) to $36 247 (large urban 500 000+ population)*****

Notes:
* A household of four refers to households with two adults and two children, or one adult and three children.
** Source: Income Statistics Division, Statistics Canada (2007). *Low-income cutoffs for 2006 and low income measures for 2005*. Income Research Paper Series, Catalogue No. 75 F0002MIE. Ottawa: Minister of Industry.
*** Source: Human Resources and Social Development Canada (2006). *Low-income in Canada: 2000–2002, using the market basket measure*. Catalogue No. 0-662-43389-0. Ottawa: Author.
**** CSPC = Community Social Planning Council. Source: National Council of Welfare (2006a). *Poverty profile 2002 and 2003*. Catalogue No. SDZ5-1/2003E. Ottawa: Minister of Public Works and Government Services Canada.
***** Source: Canadian Council on Social Development (2002). *2002 poverty lines*. Retrieved May 15, 2007, from: www.ccds.ca/factsheets/fs_lic02.htm.

its gross income on essentials: food, shelter, and clothing. It was estimated that any family spending more than 50 percent on these essentials was living in constrained circumstances, and any family spending more than 70 percent on essentials was designated as "low-income." In essence, these definitions created a poverty line. In subsequent years, the poverty cut-off has been adjusted using the same formula (i.e., spending on essentials for the average Canadian family, plus 20 percent). For example, in 1992, the poverty line was set at 54.7 percent of gross family income for essential expenditures, based on that year's survey. Since 1973, Statistics Canada has also distinguished among five different sizes of urban and rural communities—the larger the community, the higher the low income cut-off for any family (Statistics Canada Income Statistics Division, 2007).

In 1990, Statistics Canada calculated a second poverty line, based on median after-tax incomes rather than the average gross income. This measurement became known as the low income measure, or LIM. The LIM is based not on the proportion of income spent on food, clothing, and shelter, but rather on income itself. It is calculated on the basis of one-half of median gross (or after-tax) income, where median income is first adjusted for family size (that is, a one-person household earning $60 000 has significantly more disposable income than a four-person household earning $60 000). Be careful not to confuse *median* with *average*: the median income represents the income that half of all income earners earn more than and half earn less than, while an average income represents the sum of all incomes divided by the number of income earners. (Statistics Canada Income Statistics Division, 2006). An after-tax index may be a truer standard than the commonly used gross or before-tax measures. Statistics Canada nonetheless continues to use its LICO measurement as the standard for assessing poverty. As Table 4.2 makes clear, the LIM approach and the LICO provide different measurements. The LIM tends to reduce the number of people in poverty by two or three percentage points.

Another measure of poverty, and one that has been receiving recent attention, is the market basket measure (MBM). The MBM is distinct from the other two measures discussed here because it creates a measure of poverty that is based on the actual calculated market costs of shelter, food, clothing and footwear, transportation, and other goods and services—such as hygiene products and furniture (Human Resources and Social Development Canada, 2006). The MBM includes a greater spectrum of necessary goods and services for living a decent life, and is also calculated to a specific community, rather than being calculated as an average applicable to all Canadians.

Defining the Problem, Defining the Solution

In 1984, the Canadian Council on Social Development (CCSD) outlined the following four rationales for establishing poverty lines, all of which are still relevant today:

1. Poverty lines are needed to determine the number of people living in poverty. In Canada, the Statistics Canada LICO measurement is most frequently used to determine this figure.
2. Poverty indicators are used to inform and perhaps motivate those receiving and administering social service programs. This rationale explains why social assistance payments are set at a minimal level: to motivate people to view this financial program as temporary.
3. Poverty lines help set the parameters of an accepted "market basket" (the amount of goods and services consumed by a family or individual over the course of a typical month). This market basket approach contributes to the development of only a few of the major poverty indicators, such as the Metropolitan Toronto Social Planning Council's budget guides and the Montreal Diet Dispensary's budget guidelines of basic needs.
4. Poverty indices inform future social policy planners, especially with respect to setting income security levels.

The various poverty lines described above can be pegged across the political spectrum. The conservative right of the political spectrum is represented by the Fraser Institute (also referred to as the Sarlo measure, named after Dr. Christopher Sarlo of the Fraser Institute) and Montreal Diet Dispensary definitions of poverty. This position asserts that poverty levels using other standards are grossly exaggerated. The Toronto Community Social Planning Council figures represent the "left" or social democratic end of the political spectrum, or a more social-justice or equality focus. Statistics Canada maintains poverty measures that are closer to the political centre.

It should be stressed that the agreed-upon definition of poverty is the one that Canadian society accepts. In the face of rising numbers of persons living in poverty, society ultimately has three options, none of which are mutually exclusive. Society can

1. decide to leave more and more people behind;
2. find ways to distribute wealth more efficiently and equitably; or
3. hope to find ways for people to receive more income from their own efforts and work.

Economic inequality is a growing problem worldwide. A shocking 1 percent of the world's population holds 40 percent of its entire wealth, and 10 percent hold 85 percent of its wealth. At the other end of the continuum, 1 percent of the world's wealth is shared by 50 percent of its population—3 billion people (Davies, Sandstrom, Shorrocks, & Wolff, 2006). According to 2001 census data, in Canada, 10 percent of families held 53 percent of the country's wealth; and the wealthiest 50 percent of families controlled 94.4 percent of all wealth—leaving 5.6 percent to the bottom 50 percent (Kerstetter, 2002). In addition, economic inequality, measured by income or consumption, seems to be worsening in Canada and throughout much of the westernized world (Heisz, 2007). A recent Statistics Canada study reveals that inequality in after-tax family income increased between 1976 and 2004, driven by widening differences in family market income (the sum of earnings from employment and net self-employment income, investment income, and private retirement income, for all family members). Indeed, the report concludes: "This increase occurred at the same time as a reduction in the generosity of several income transfer programs, including the Employment Insurance and Social Assistance Programs (in some provinces), and decreases in income tax rates. This potentially reflects a weakening of the redistributive role of the Canadian state" (Heisz, 2007, 5). As discussed later in this chapter, income security programs and the income tax system still help moderate these income inequalities. A final point: the average family market income among the 10 percent of families with the highest incomes rose by 22 percent from 1989 to 2004. Meanwhile, among the 10 percent of families with the lowest incomes, it fell by 11 percent (Heisz, 2007).

Likewise, it is essential to note some of the changing parameters of poverty in Canada. A 2005 study by the Organization for Economic Cooperation and Development (OECD) compares Canada's record in combating poverty relative to those of 21 other OECD countries (Forster & d'Ercole, 2005). (See Figure 4.4.) As this figure shows, Canada has maintained a similar poverty rate across all three time periods and has not effectively lowered poverty levels. This is not to suggest that people are in a constant state of poverty. Some move in and out of poverty. In 2004, 11.2 percent of Canadians were in a low-income category (Statistics Canada, 2007a), compared to

FIGURE 4.4 **Poverty in Canada Compared with Other OECD Countries—
Poverty as a Percentage of Population, Mid-1980s,
Mid-1990s, and 2000**

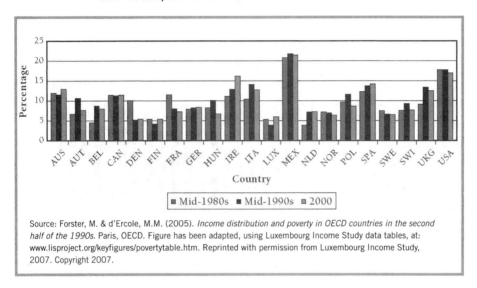

Source: Forster, M. & d'Ercole, M.M. (2005). *Income distribution and poverty in OECD countries in the second half of the 1990s.* Paris, OECD. Figure has been adapted, using Luxembourg Income Study data tables, at: www.lisproject.org/keyfigures/povertytable.htm. Reprinted with permission from Luxembourg Income Study, 2007. Copyright 2007.

15.7 percent in 1996 (Statistics Canada, 2006). Rates of low income for seniors have dropped over the last two decades. During the early 1980s, for example, approximately 17.5 percent of seniors had an after-tax income less than the Statistics Canada LICO measure, compared to 5.4 percent of seniors fitting into this category in 2004 (Hick, 2007). Many assert that the income security programs discussed in Chapter 3, such as Old Age Security and the CPP/QPP, have been especially important in reducing poverty among seniors. But within this cohort, there is a profound gender bias: 49 percent of unattached elderly females live in poverty versus 33.3 percent of elderly men—a reflection, in part, of the inequalities in workplace earnings that subsequently were translated into unequal pension rates upon retirement. Finally, it is important to emphasize that many elderly households have only barely been lifted above poverty levels, and, in fact, a significant proportion of the elderly fall into the category of *nearly poor*.

Young families are more likely to be poor than older families. What is more, poverty has increased dramatically among younger families. In 1981, approximately 20 percent of young families (in which the oldest/only adult is under 25) were poor; by 1991 this had increased to 41.5 percent; and by 2001, was approximately 57 percent—a rate that most readers will agree is deeply troubling (Campaign 2000, 2007). The next age cohort, those parents between 24 and 35 years of age, has also experienced increases in poverty rates (Morrissette & Zhangi, 2006). Within this age cohort there was a 31.1 percent increase in the incidence of poverty for these families between 1981 and 2001 (Campaign 2000, 2007).

Child poverty rates continue to be a great concern. In 2004, the most recent date for which there are data, 865 000 Canadian children under the age of 18 were living in poverty (National Council of Welfare, 2006a). This represents 12.8 percent of all

FIGURE 4.5   Child Poverty in Canada Compared with Other Countries, 2007

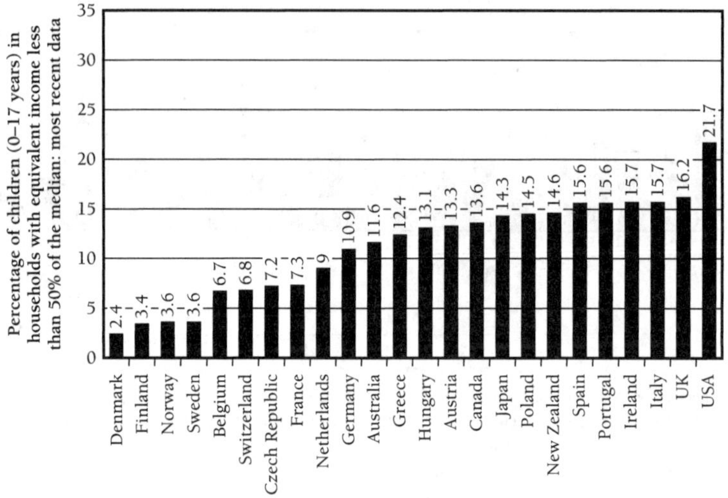

Percentage of children (0–17 years) in households with equivalent income less than 50% of the median: most recent data

Denmark	2.4
Finland	3.4
Norway	3.6
Sweden	3.6
Belgium	6.7
Switzerland	6.8
Czech Republic	7.2
France	7.3
Netherlands	9
Germany	10.9
Australia	11.6
Greece	12.4
Hungary	13.1
Austria	13.3
Canada	13.6
Japan	14.3
Poland	14.5
New Zealand	14.6
Spain	15.6
Portugal	15.6
Ireland	15.7
Italy	15.7
UK	16.2
USA	21.7

Source: Adapted from UNICEF, *Innocenti Report Card No. 7*, "Child Poverty in Perspective: An overview of child well-being in rich countries," United Nations Children's Fund, Florence, Italy, 2007.

Canadian children, a figure that still falls short of many advocates' demands for a total end to childhood poverty. Lone-parent families, particularly female-headed families, continue to be most vulnerable to poverty. In 2004, of the 550 000 lone-parent families headed by women, statistics showed a shocking 36 percent with low income. As noted in Figure 4.5, Canada's child poverty rates are higher than those of many other advanced industrialized countries.

The face of poverty has likewise changed in Canada's provinces and regions. The percentage of all poor families in Newfoundland dropped from 18.1 percent in 1981 to 12.8 percent in 2003. A similar trend has occurred in all Atlantic provinces and Quebec (National Council of Welfare, 2006a). But during this same period, in Alberta and British Columbia, the share of poor families increased from 11.3 percent to 15.7 percent in British Columbia, and from 11.8 percent to 14.6 percent in Alberta. Much of Western Canada's increase in poverty occurred in the 1980s (National Council of Welfare, 2006a). In the 1990s, Ontario's share of poor families rose by more than 7 percent above the late-1980s rates of poverty. But by 2003, it decreased somewhat to 11.3 percent of families, compared to 10.8 percent back in 1981. Poverty rates across family and unattached individual categories climbed during the 1990s but lessened during the early years of the twenty-first century.

Aboriginal peoples, minority peoples, and people with disabilities are particularly vulnerable to poverty, both historically and at present (Ross, Scott, & Smith, 2000; Statistics Canada, 2002). In 2002, based on the LICO measure, 38.0 percent of Aboriginal people and 38.0 percent of visible minorities were poor; and based on the MBM, 35.8 percent of persons with disabilities were poor (Human Resources and Social Development Canada, 2006; Statistics Canada, 2003). These rates are significantly higher than the 2002 national average of 11.6 percent, based on the Statistics Canada post-income tax LICO measure (Human Resources and Social Development Canada, 2006); and they are also higher than the 13.7 percent national rate determined by the 2002 market basket measure (MBM) (Human Resources and Social Development Canada, 2006).

Durations of poverty differ. For roughly 60 percent of the poor, poverty is a temporary state, unlikely to be repeated within a 10-year period. For 40 percent of the poor, poverty is "a more chronic problem, with longer spells of poverty and a greater likelihood of becoming poor again" (Ross, Scott, & Smith, 2000, 119). According to the National Council on Welfare (2006a), between 1996 and 2001, a total of 7.6 million Canadians experienced poverty for at least one year. There is considerable variability from one person to the next; taking aggregate statistics, the average poor person in Canada spends about five years poor—counting single and multiple experiences of poverty—while 5 percent remain poor for 10 years or more. Between 1996 and 2001, 2 million Canadians lived in poverty for only a single year, while 1.5 million people were in poverty across the entire span of those six years (National Council of Welfare, 2006a). Certain groups of people are more likely to experience longer spells of poverty: lone parents, people with disabilities, members of visible minority communities, recent immigrants, individuals with low levels of education, and single people. The longer that one is poor, the more difficult it is to escape poverty.

Education remains an important factor in distinguishing the poor from the non-poor, as shown in Figures 4.6 and 4.7. Social policies that encourage people to stay in school and that encourage post-degree continuous learning are potentially useful in reducing lifelong poverty.

Social Policy and Economic Policy

Chappell (1997) suggests that Canadian social and economic policies are related in three ways and that these reflect the Canadian experience of economic insecurity.

1. The state of the economy determines which social programs are needed. For example, in times of high unemployment, the demand for social services such as social assistance, mental and physical health, and child welfare increases.

2. Recent patterns of social spending have been dependent not upon need but upon the government's economic priority of fiscal restraint in order to reduce deficit spending.

FIGURE 4.6 **Rates of Unemployment Compared to Highest Education Attained**

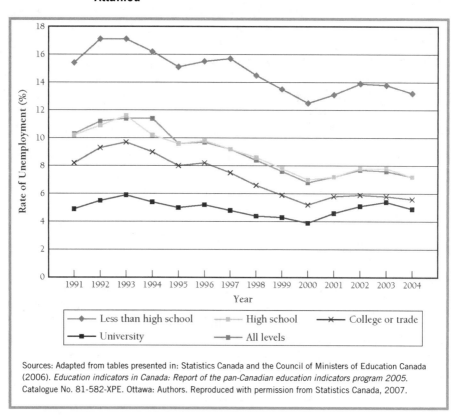

Sources: Adapted from tables presented in: Statistics Canada and the Council of Ministers of Education Canada (2006). *Education indicators in Canada: Report of the pan-Canadian education indicators program 2005.* Catalogue No. 81-582-XPE. Ottawa: Authors. Reproduced with permission from Statistics Canada, 2007.

3. Some people believe that social programs discourage economic growth because they decrease the spending power of working individuals and increase the debt/deficit situation. This, however, is a highly debatable point. Indeed, several observers argue that social programs promote economic growth by putting more money into more hands (Battle, 1993; Mendelson, 1993).

Income Redistribution

The *Gini coefficient* (see Figure 4.8) is a means of comparing three types of income levels with each other across time. In the Gini coefficient, 0 indicates perfect equality of income, where every Canadian receives the same amount of money. A score of 1 represents perfect inequality, where one person gets all the income and everyone else receives nothing. Both of these are ideal or theoretical scenarios that would probably never occur. The value of the Gini coefficient is that it provides the extreme parameters (0 and 1) between which we can make comparisons.

FIGURE 4.7   Education Makes a Difference

Note: For families, relates to the education level of the major income recipient.

Source: National Council of Welfare (2006a). *Poverty profile, 2002 and 2003*. Ottawa: Minister of Public Works and Government Services Canada. Reproduced with permission from Public Works and Government Services Canada, 2007.

FIGURE 4.8   Income Distribution in Canada: The Gini Coefficient

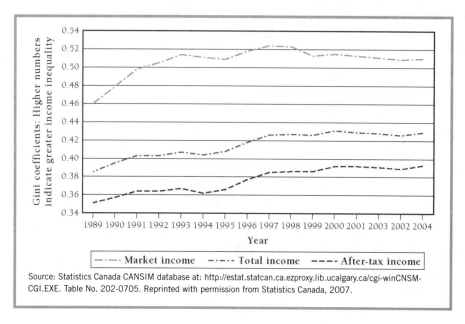

Source: Statistics Canada CANSIM database at: http://estat.statcan.ca.ezproxy.lib.ucalgary.ca/cgi-winCNSM-CGI.EXE. Table No. 202-0705. Reprinted with permission from Statistics Canada, 2007.

Figure 4.8 highlights the influence of income security programs and the tax system as tools of income redistribution. The highest line, which is also the one that shows the least equal income distribution, represents "earned income" prior to taxes. Individuals who do not have income from work are assigned an income of zero. The next highest line shows what happens when "earned income" is combined with income derived from income security programs such as social assistance, the Canada Pension Plan, and Employment Insurance. This line reveals the equalizing effect of income-security social policies. The third line, which tends to a greater state of income distribution, represents income *after taxes*, demonstrating the greater equalizing effects of the income tax system.

However, the income tax system does not benefit all Canadians equally. Scholars and policy analysts insist that many tax credits and tax deductions are used by the rich more than the poor, and benefit the rich more than the poor. Two write-offs that favour well-to-do individuals are Registered Retirement Savings Plan (RRSP) contributions and child-care expenses. Far more high-income earners claim RRSP contributions than do low-income earners (Statistics Canada Pensions and Wealth Surveys Section, 2005). In addition, as one policy document remarks, "high-income Canadians are much more able than low- and middle-income Canadians to put money towards RRSPs, and, because tax assistance is provided in the form of a deduction, RRSP owners in the top bracket enjoy larger tax savings" (Torjman & Battle, 1995a, 5). Moreover and more generally, tax breaks to individuals and corporations drain billions of dollars from government budgets and thereby contribute to the retrenchment of social programs (Torjman & Battle, 1995a, 5; Guest, 1997, 188–189; Muszynski, 1987). For example, tax break measures implemented in the 2007–08 federal government budget will result in just over $3 billion of forgone revenue to Ottawa in that fiscal year alone (Department of Finance Canada, 2007b). This has serious implications if a government is going to erode funding for social programs— which in turn hurts all Canadians, particularly those who are poorer and hence particularly vulnerable.

Paying Taxes

Death and taxes are claimed to be the two things in life that are unavoidable. Typically, Canadians are most aware of two types of taxes: personal income tax and consumption taxes, especially the goods and services tax (GST) and provincial sales tax (PST). Personal income tax is the largest source of government revenue in Canada (Martineau, 2005). Although the GST and PST are the most noticeable forms of consumption taxes, "sin taxes" on consumer items such as tobacco and alcohol have received increased public attention. Payroll taxes, business taxes, import taxes, property taxes, and resource taxes are other levies made upon the citizens of Canada. The proportion of Canadian income going toward income taxes has increased over the past several decades, as shown in Figure 4.9. One of the most recent studies reveals that in 2003 the average family earned $57 782 and paid $27 640 (47 percent) of that income in personal income tax (Beauchesne, 2004).

FIGURE 4.9   Income Tax Payment in Canada

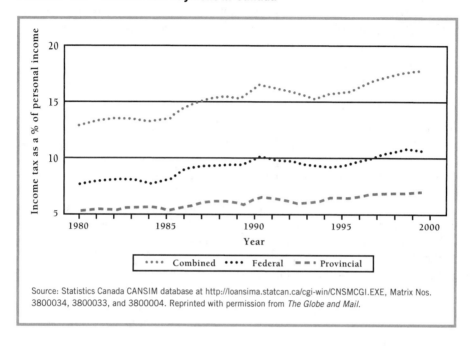

Source: Statistics Canada CANSIM database at http://loansima.statcan.ca/cgi-win/CNSMCGI.EXE, Matrix Nos. 3800034, 3800033, and 3800004. Reprinted with permission from *The Globe and Mail*.

Tax systems generally operate on either regressive or progressive principles (or on a combination of both). *Regressive tax systems* impose the same tax level on all citizens, which, in effect, imposes the greatest burden on those least able to pay (Muszynski, 1987). A provincial sales tax (PST) is a Canadian example of a regressive tax. It is levied on a particular good at the same percentage regardless of a person's income. Because they have less disposable income, persons with low incomes pay a greater portion of their incomes in PST payments than do those in higher income brackets.

A *progressive tax system* bases the level of taxation upon a person's ability to pay, such that those with higher incomes pay proportionately higher taxes. Canada's current income tax system contains both progressive and regressive elements. It is progressive insofar as it has multiple tax brackets, with a progressive increase in the percentage of taxable income paid as one's income rises. In this sense, the income tax system differentiates between those with less money (and in lower tax brackets) and those with more (and in higher brackets). But critics point out that it could be still *more* progressive, with richer people and corporations paying more. Because poor people pay a greater proportion of their income to taxes than do rich people, the system has definite regressive elements. If well-to-do individuals and corporations paid more, it would be more progressive and less regressive.

A recent income tax option that is not based on this progressive principle is the "flat tax." Alberta's provincial income tax is no longer calculated as a percentage of federal tax payable. Rather, as of 2007, it is 10 percent of taxable income (hence a flat tax) above the personal exemption of $14 899 per year (hence a small progressive aspect in that people under the threshold are not responsible for the 10 percent payable). A flat tax brings a simplicity and efficiency to the current complex tax system with less emphasis on tax loopholes than the present system. But it tends to make the income tax system less progressive, and hence a less powerful instrument of income redistribution.

Changing Demographics

An international trend reflects what is described as a "vast gulf in birth and death rates amongst the world's countries." The wealthier, more urban nations—particularly in Europe—have shrinking and aging populations, while poorer, rural countries—particularly in Asia and Africa—have demographic growth and younger populations (Kent & Haub, 2005, 5). Largely because of Latin immigration, the United States does not face as strong a demographic pressure as Europe. But Canada is close, experiencing the twin themes of decline in birth rates and aging of its population. In partial response to both, immigration has become increasingly important to the growth of the Canadian population over the last 30 years (Figure 4.10). In 2005, immigration accounted for 66 percent of all population growth in Canada (Lapointe, Dunn, Tremblay-Cote, Bergeron, & Ignakzac, 2006). As Figure 4.10 illustrates, immigration will become increasingly more important to the sustainability of population growth in Canada into the future. This is not to downplay the problems of population growth, particularly as outlined in the next chapter in its comments about sustainable economic growth.

FIGURE 4.10 Change in Total Population in Canada, 1976–2051

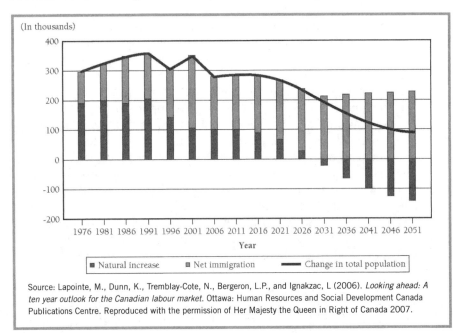

Source: Lapointe, M., Dunn, K., Tremblay-Cote, N., Bergeron, L.P., and Ignakzac, L (2006). *Looking ahead: A ten year outlook for the Canadian labour market.* Ottawa: Human Resources and Social Development Canada Publications Centre. Reproduced with the permission of Her Majesty the Queen in Right of Canada 2007.

Age and retirement have become a topic of focus in national and international contexts over the last decade. Some critics describe the situation as a "demographic crisis," in which people throughout the developed world are not bearing enough children to sustain themselves economically (Cohen, 2006). Today, nearly half of the world's population lives in countries with fertility at or below replacement levels. Further, by the mid–twenty-first century, three of four countries now described as developing are projected to reach or slip below replacement fertility (Morgan & Taylor, 2006).

Another major demographic factor is that people in advanced industrialized countries are living longer and retiring earlier (Townson, 2006; United Nations, 2002). During the Paleolithic era, life expectancy at birth was 20 years. Ten thousand years later, for those in the Roman Empire, it had risen to 27 years. Fifteenth-century England and Wales had a life expectancy of 33 years; by the mid-nineteenth century, life expectancy had risen to 40 years, and by 1900 to 50 years (Usher, 2003, 5). Major changes in life expectancy occurred during the twentieth century. In 1920, Canada had life expectancies of 59 for men and 61 for women: the average person was not expected to make it to 65, the age of retirement that emerged as an OECD gold standard several decades after Bismarck's Germany introduced an old age social insurance program in 1889 (Germany originally set the age at 70). By 1950, average Canadian life expectancies were 66 for men and 71 for women. In 2004, they were over 82 years for women and 78 for men—and rising yearly (Statistics Canada, Health Statistics Division, 2006). In the early 1970s, working age people (18–64) accounted for 57 percent of the population, climbing to 64 percent in 1995 (Chiu, 1996). As recently as 2002, though, this figure had fallen to 61.3 percent and is projected to fall even further to 51.3 percent of the population by 2041 (Guillemette, 2003). The culmination of these two factors (low fertility and longer life expectancy) has created a situation known as demographic aging (Cheal, 2002). In response to this challenge, in 1998, the OECD published a report suggesting that national governments throughout the developed world need to reform legislation to remove incentives for early retirement to reduce the economic implications of an aging population (Townson, 2006).

Many Canadians, particularly when the issue came to the media's attention in the 1990s, wondered how social programs and retirement funds (private and public) could be sustained. A recent study projecting current fertility rates, immigration levels, and moderately rising life expectancy shows that the ratio of the population aged 65 and over to the population of traditional working age (18–64) will rise from 20 percent in 2006 to 46 percent in 2050 (Guillemette & Robson, 2006, 1). A further possibility looms on the horizon. Future projections in labour market characteristics suggest that between 2006 and 2015, 70 percent of all newly available jobs will be a result of people retiring (Lapointe et al., 2006). A combination of factors—the shrinking proportion of available workers to retired people and the increase in available jobs as a result of retirement—could essentially lead to higher numbers of jobs than there will be available or qualified workers to fill them (Lapointe et al., 2006). What is the future of the notion of "unemployment," as well as social programs such as health care and retirement, both of which are heavily used by retired people but are funded particularly by those who work (through the income tax system and payroll deductions)?

Some Consequences of Social Policy

Paradoxes of intervening in the economic life of some Canadians have long been recognized. For example, financial assistance programs may sometimes decrease the incentive to paid work for some recipients; that is, some programs contain inherent labour force participation disincentives. The authors of this textbook, like other progressive observers, insist on the need for plentiful jobs offering meaningful employment and decent wages. More than any other factor, decent jobs would alleviate much of the problem of such labour force participation disincentives (Clarke, 1997). In addition, some observers blame social policies themselves for the absence of a full-employment economy. The following components of social welfare programs tend to act as disincentives to paid work:

➤ the decreased purchasing power of current "minimum wages";

➤ health care benefits that exceed those of many jobs;

➤ insufficient coverage for back-to-work expenses;

➤ high tax-back rates for earning exemptions; and

➤ lack of affordable, accessible childcare (National Council on Welfare, 1993).

Canada's transition from an institutional approach to a market-state approach has reduced the scope and impact of such programs as Employment Insurance. As a result, "social assistance has moved from its original intent. It has grown into a major front-line program—larger than Employment Insurance in some provinces. An unpopular and stigmatizing program, it nonetheless has proved stubbornly resistant to reform" (Torjman, 2007, 1). Some proposed changes would particularly assist the unemployed who can seek work, as well as the precariously employed. These include making social assistance a genuine program of last resort; providing earnings supplementation measurements separate from social assistance; making work more remunerative than welfare; improving minimum wage levels; introducing working income tax benefits for the working poor; and improving childcare benefits for the working poor. (Torjman, 2007; National Council of Welfare, 2007).

Other critics stress that the demoralization of Canadians receiving welfare should be addressed by mandatory workfare programs as a condition for receiving social assistance and EI services (Handler & Hasenfeld, 1991). Proponents of workfare suggest that it promotes the "moral merit of work" in a "failed system of subsidized poverty" (Sirico, July 27, 1997, E15). Self-respect, taking responsibility, the development of a "worker" identity, and the acquisition of work skills and work experience are among the moral benefits suggested by advocates of workfare programs. Such programs are based upon separating out the able-bodied recipients from those who are unable to work. To some, this division seems a

"Thick" needs, in contrast, represent needs within their particular cultural context. Diversity is central to this concept of need. Thick need is not objectified and measurable but rather is viewed as subjective. Its meaning is constructed by individuals or groups through their particular experiences. As Kerans notes, neither category of need is as clear as definitions presume, and neither can stand on its own as the basis for social policy. However, application of thick and thin ideas of need can help us explore the relationship between diversity and social policy. Challenges to the welfare state by diverse groups can be understood as insistence upon recognition of "thick" conceptions of need. That is, diverse groups are insisting upon their particular history and experience as factors in defining need and in satisfying it through social policy initiatives.

Conclusion

Fraser (1995) poses two important understandings of injustice. One is socioeconomic, which is rooted in the "political-economic structure" of society (70). This is the primary kind of injustice addressed by redistributive social safety net policies discussed in other chapters of this book. The other kind of injustice, referred to as insufficient "recognition," is cultural and symbolic rather than material. Members of subordinate populations (Kallen, 2004) are subject to both kinds of injustice, which frequently interact to reinforce each other.

Fraser argues that in the current era, class has become decentred; group identity and calls for recognition have to some extent supplanted class interests as the "chief medium of political mobilization." The goals of recognition politics stand in some contradiction to the goals of the first form of injustice. Whereas redistributive forms of redress call for dissolving differences in the quest for equality, groups seeking recognition of identity seek acknowledgment of their differences from others. Fraser's challenge is to acknowledge both forms of injustice and to better understand the kinds of redress needed for each of them. She concludes that a transformative social and political agenda is the only way to address the goals of both kinds of injustice.

Chapter ⑦

Social Policy and Social Work Practice

Social work is about helping people. But the assistance a social worker provides—be it to an individual, a family, a group, or a community—occurs in a social policy context. This chapter elaborates why and how social workers need to understand social policy and policy processes. Without this understanding, social workers can never be fully effective, and the help that they provide their clients will never be fully satisfactory. This chapter also explains how the relationship between social policy and social work processes has evolved in the literature. Understanding this relationship is crucial to a final objective of the chapter: appreciating the relationships between the practice skills of direct intervention and the skills of social policy comprehension and analysis.

Why Study Social Policy?

Social policy students and practitioners in Canada may be more aware of relationships between policy and practice now than in past decades. An overall shift in general policy from support for the welfare state to the dismantling of programs and restricting of access to social services has made social workers aware of the ways policy effects direct practice. In the 1990s, social workers saw the effects of job loss and long-term unemployment. Many found themselves in the position of refusing clients services previously offered; many have observed substantial withdrawal of funding and cutbacks to the programs they run. Yet social work training programs and literature maintain a sharp division between the ideas and skills of direct practice and those of social policy development and analysis. This chapter focuses on exploring those relationships, as well as examining policy-based knowledge and skills useful in practising social work.

In spite of the recognized importance of social policy to direct practice, few students enter social work hoping to focus on social policy itself. Many social work students in Canada express the goal of "helping others." Familiarity with social policy may appear a remote and dubious route to this goal. The social policy field has been dominated by white males, who have tended to write and talk about this field in a somewhat abstract and impersonal manner. Perhaps one reason social work students so often avoid social policy is that it has indeed been too far removed from the messy "real life" experience of practice and does not seem to assist them in obtaining the resources their clients need. Universalizing tendencies aggravate this problem, for students cannot easily recognize, in abstract descriptions, the individuals and problems they work with in direct practice settings. Finally, as Wharf and McKenzie (2004) point out, practitioners and their clients are generally not included in the policy making process.

One of the unique features of social work is its focus on the individual in a wider context (within a family system, an organizational system, a community, or a society), as well as the complex relationships between the individual and these broader structures. This emphasis on appreciating the individual in broad contexts is sometimes called understanding "the person in environment"—a key skill that social workers must cultivate.

In the early years of social work, this "environment" clearly included social policies and the requirement to use, develop, and change them for the benefit of clients. Pioneers of social work, such as Mary Richmond, Bertha Reynolds, and Jane Addams, focused on both the personal and the social context when framing ideas about the new profession. As Wharf (1990) notes, agencies such as settlement houses, located in inner cities, provided appropriate settings for social workers to observe the effects of social policies on individuals and to apply their efforts to individuals and to social causes simultaneously. In fact, these early social workers became leaders because of their commitment to social causes. "They cared desperately about people, they had a vision of the good life, and they were morally indignant about social evil" (Burns, quoted in Wharf, 1990, 16). These leaders considered social action, along with the promotion of legislation that would alter the conditions of life for individuals they cared about, to be a natural part of their work. But in 1915, Abraham Flexner, addressing a social work conference, issued a stinging indictment of this approach to social work. He urged social workers to enhance their own status as a profession by emulating the medical profession. Flexner said that if social work wanted to become a "real" profession, its members would have to develop a recognizable technology as doctors have done, and would have to demonstrate this technology in their everyday practice with individuals where it could easily be seen.

As Popple and Leighninger (2001) argue, after Flexner, the social work profession focused on individuals and families as the route to professional success and largely abandoned social action. Flexner's work was important for highlighting the individualism that pervaded social work through the rest of the century. Certainly, by the 1920s, casework had established itself as the "nuclear skill" of social work (Lubove, 1965). Supported by the curriculum of most schools of social work, the majority of social workers have since been directed toward and trained in interventions with individuals and families. This trend reached a peak in the psychoanalytic training of the 1950s. During the 1960s and early 1970s, intense focus on social issues shifted emphasis back toward social action for many members of the profession.

However, social workers have continued to find pressing reasons to maintain their focus on individuals. One reason is that individuals and families present themselves directly to us; they are immediately available as the focus of possible changes, whereas policy changes are slow. In the political climate of the new millennium, many social workers may even believe that larger social change is beyond possibility. In *The Cult of Impotence*, McQuaig (1998) explores the widespread belief that social forces affecting individuals are now too powerful and overwhelming to be changed. Such disempowering myths reinforce for social workers the idea that the only useful point of intervention is the individual. McQuaig argues that the Canadian public has been fooled into believing that access to social programs and good jobs are now out of reach because of "globalization" and that social change is impossible. Finkel (2006) provides an example showing that rapid, significant, and positive social change is still possible. In the 1980s, the Cree people of Northern Quebec were considered among the most impoverished in the developed world. A decade later, following active protests and social development efforts, the same community was named by the United Nations as one of 50 "exemplary communities in the world" (325).

Changes in the Canadian political and economic context may make social workers aware of the importance of understanding and changing social policies. Downsizing, for instance, has eroded job security for social workers themselves. Cutbacks mean that some of the traditional casework jobs on which social work relied are disappearing. Cutbacks in related sectors, such as nursing, mean other professions may claim traditional areas of social work as their own. The substantial reduction in the size and number of institutions, such as hospitals, has meant clients previously counselled in institutional settings are now living "in the community" and requiring assistance to find resources. Social workers must be intimately familiar with the relevant social policies and their related service provisions in order to be useful. Neo-liberal social agendas mean that a profession geared toward seeking social justice must become knowledgeable about and insistent upon policy development and change in order to work toward justice goals.

Theory: Understanding the Person in their Social Context

Over the century of its existence, social work has struggled to theorize connections between individuals and their environment. Mary Richmond is generally recognized as the first to theorize and extensively explore this relationship. In *The Long View* (1930), she expanded on the idea of casework:

[O]ne perfectly good definition of social casework is the development of the character and welfare of the individual through adjustments effected between him (or her) and his social surroundings. Sometimes the surroundings need to be radically changed, sometimes the person needs to be, but more often a change, to be permanent, must be effected in both (577).

She recommended that caseworkers "consciously and deliberately" examine their work at the points of intersection with social movements, and strive to improve their work at these points. The casework movement, she thought, would inform the caseworker and in turn direct the workers toward the movement.

Sociologist C. Wright Mills' notions of private troubles and public issues, explored in Chapter 3, have also been crucial to the exploration of the personal and the social. A "trouble," he said, is a problem that has to do with the self and the limited areas of social life with which a person is involved. "Issues," on the other hand, have to do with matters that transcend local involvement. An issue is a public matter, incapable of private resolution. In the conclusion to his important work *The Sociological Imagination* (1959), Mills offered this advice: "Do not study merely one small milieu after another; study the social structure in which milieux are organized . . . Know that many personal troubles cannot be solved merely as troubles, but must be understood in terms of public issues . . . and know the human meaning of public issues must be revealed by relating them to private troubles" (224–6).

Feminists later explored this general terrain, elaborating on it and changing the emphasis to create the slogan "the personal is political." This notion, expanded in models of feminist practice (Dominelli & McLeod, 1989), suggests that private troubles are intricately connected to the public and political worlds. Through feminist analysis, problems previously viewed as private and personal came to be seen as common and widespread (Callahan, 2004). For example, a man's violent behaviour toward his female partner is now widely understood as part of a larger social problem of violence against women, not as an interpersonal problem between one man and one woman. The arrangements of society, including social policy, are implicated in creating and maintaining problems experienced by individuals. These insights reveal the reluctance of the Canadian state to establish policies to promote equality for various minorities, including women. Recently, the concept of "caring" has been employed to reveal this reluctance (Neysmith, 2000). Analysis by feminists of the concept of caring shows how private issues of performing caring labour reflect the gendered expectations and hierarchies of the social world, including the organization of social work itself. Several feminists (e.g., Little, 2005) have focused on the welfare state, examining the ways social programs reinforce unpaid, undervalued caring expected of women in both the public and private realms. This approach shows the necessity of changing the fundamental structures through which social policy is shaped as a method of changing the daily realities of individual women.

Some social work theorists and writers have employed ideas from Marx and the Critical School to explore the relationship between the person and the social environment. Marx and Engels (1846, trans. 1947) observed that the state is itself based upon the contradiction between public and private, and between general and particular interests. Social work's original purpose was to mediate this contradiction, helping to soften the worst effects of public life on individuals and proposing remedial public policies. A Marxist perspective also theorizes that society and individuals have mutually constructing relations; in other words, people both create and are created by their social world. Writing about this idea from a social work perspective, Leonard (1975, 1984) examined how individuals internalize ideological constructs that help to shape their personality. In the aggregate, the characteristics of these individuals then appear to justify public policy. Internalized constructs tend to be those that support and recreate the status quo. Girls, for instance, have traditionally been socialized to be caring and passive, qualities that, if internalized, ensure the continuation of unpaid caring labour upon which the economy depends. Social work has at least two possible responses to this public/private dilemma. According to Pearson (1975), it might come to rest on a "false split" between society and individuals; or it can enhance the potential of people in both the private and social realms (Leonard, 1975).

A related view of the policy–practice relationship is the idea that social policy creates the world in which it practises. Rein (1983) points out that "the things we think about and the ways we think about them, as well as the ways we act, are shaped by the institutional arrangements of the society we live in" (223). Of course, practice also contributes to policy. The activities of front-line workers are not merely neutral instruments of broad objectives. The activities themselves act to alter intentions (Rein, 1983, 40). "The lowest field officer," as Handler (1979) notes, interprets rules and guidelines for specific cases. This idea was taken up in considerable detail in Lipsky's book, *Street Level Bureaucracy* (1980). According to Lipsky, each encounter with a client represents an instance of "policy delivery." These encounters help entrench policy on the personal level. For instance, they help to socialize citizens about social expectations and rules. Through the creation of precedents, these encounters determine eligibility for the services created through policy. Lipsky focuses on the collective behaviour of staff in public service organizations, arguing that their practical behaviour actually *becomes* the policy they carry out. "Street-level" workers actually make policy in two ways. First, they exercise discretion on an individual basis, which is an expression of policy. Second, in its aggregate form, this discretion then becomes agency policy.

Swift (1995) used the terrain of child welfare to explore the way social workers help to create social policy development through their casework practices, including agency records. She examined how the individual decisions of "anonymous" social workers become the raw material through which the concepts of child abuse and neglect are developed and legitimized. Simultaneously, their records have been used as evidence of the individual failings of the clientele. This idea had previously been explored by Rein (1983), who observed that service intervention can actually magnify problems, especially for vulnerable populations. The rich, he noted, are able to sort out problems, using their own private resources to do so. The poor, on the other hand, become subject to a "problem formulation process," which then legitimizes the organization of services and creates identifiable "targets" for social policy.

Lipsky also identified the mediating influence of the organization in the dialectic (or interaction) between individual workers and the policy level. Perhaps one reason social workers often fail to recognize the relationship between social policy and their own everyday work is that policy is filtered through organizational processes and practices. Agencies themselves also set policy, which is much more visible to front-line workers than macro-level policy is likely to be, but this may be viewed by social workers not as policy but merely as agency "rules." Lipsky shows the importance of the "mezzo" or organizational level in the processes of both enacting and making policy.

What most of these theoretical perspectives have in common is the idea that policy is not simply a top-down process carried out by the social worker in everyday practice. Rather, there is a dialectic relationship between policy and practice through which policy is not only carried out but created, maintained, and changed by social workers in their everyday practice.

Practice Models

An impressive literature has developed exploring the ways social work can integrate direct practice skills and policy skills to forge a more effective practice. These models are discussed separately below. Most share certain core values and ideas, such as the dialectic between practice and policy, the "social justice imperative" (Figuera-McDonough, 1993), and the belief that the intersection of direct practice and social policy is the natural terrain and most powerful field of endeavour for social work.

Systems and Ecological Approaches

Beginning in the 1960s, social workers began to use and promote systems theory and its heir, ecological theory (focusing on the relationship between individuals and their social contexts), as a method of integrating direct practice with social (or, as social work uses the term, "environmental") issues. Building on the sociological writings of Talcott Parsons and other sociologists, systems theory explored the interactions between people and the systems they are enmeshed in. Applied to social work (Schwartz, 1974), systems theory regarded the social worker as a bridge between the individual and the environment. A systems approach called for a "generalist" social worker, comfortable working and intervening in the social environment as well as directly with the individual. Johnson (1986), for instance, describes the generalist approach as requiring social workers to determine which "system" is the appropriate unit of attention for the change effort. She lists 26 social work approaches that might be employed, from those focused on the individual to models of social action and social planning. Since the 1980s, ecological theory, as espoused in the writings of Germain and Gitterman (1980, 1996), has found favour among social work students and educators. Ecological theory seems to capture the relationships between people and their immediate surroundings in a concrete way that social workers can visualize and work with. Both systems and ecological theories focus on helping people cope with and develop within a social context. Although both approaches are intended to create a balance in social work activity between the two spheres, in practice, they usually emphasize direct work with individuals and families and recommend knowledge and skill development in that area.

Certainly, both models have been criticized. A serious criticism has been the assumption that once a need for social change is identified, it is easy to achieve it. Canadian society has continued to reproduce and legitimize major social inequities—including child poverty, racism, and violence against women—in spite of many advocacy efforts to create change. A related criticism is that these approaches fail to conceptualize power and power relations adequately. The knowledge and skill base evolving from systems and ecological theories does not include analysis of power elites, power bases, or power processes common in Canadian society. This critique suggests that social workers hoping to challenge and change oppressive social policies using systems or ecological approaches are left without appropriate tools to carry out this work.

Radical Practice

Developing alongside systems and ecological models of practice have been a number of social work practice models specifically aimed at challenging social policies and structures. Significant contributions to this literature were made by Galper (1975) and Bailey and Brake (1975). Their approach to social work focuses on the position and problems of oppressed people within the social and economic structures of their lives. Leonard's (1975) contribution describes the aims of radical practice:

1. improving education, referring primarily to consciousness raising;
2. linking people with systems to serve their interests; and
3. building counter-systems.

Referring to Marxist thought and analysis, Leonard proposed exploring the "contradiction" as a primary method of radical practice. Through this exploration, social workers can identify and supply both misinformation and missing information to help explain relations between public and private experience. For instance, social workers could look for relevant information about clients' living conditions that is not asked for in agency forms. A problem labelled as child neglect might then be viewed as a problem of poverty. Recognition of contradictions experienced in everyday practice can reveal to social workers the discrepancies between expressed aims of social policy and the actual experiences of their clients.

According to Thompson (1993), only toward the end of the 1980s did social work education begin to take seriously the impact of racial oppression and discrimination on clients and communities. Earlier "radical" texts focused primarily on class analysis and referred infrequently to issues of race (and even to gender, notwithstanding the substantial contribution of feminists). Most of the major published theorists of radical practice were themselves white males. Furthermore, much of this work was premised on classical Marxist analysis, which did not include race, gender, or other forms of "difference" in its scope.

Dominelli's work, *Anti-Racist Practice* (1988), and Thompson's work, *Anti-Discriminatory Practice* (1993), both published in Great Britain, and Mullaly's publications on challenging oppression (2002, 2007) offer well-developed analyses of the relationships between oppression and social work practice. They also explore practice methods and propose the kinds of policy challenges social workers must deal with at the policy–practice intersection. They propose using anti-discriminatory practice to move away from the individualistic approach to an approach that emphasizes "difference." Social workers need to focus on the impacts of policies that assume, entrench, or subtly allow racism and other forms of discrimination, and on the impacts and experiences of discrimination on the individual and the group. Thompson (1993) argues that any model of social work practice that does not take account of oppression cannot be seen as good practice, regardless of whether standards are high in other respects. Social workers play the role of mediators between clients and the state and its apparatus. If policy is misused or used for inappropriate control purposes, lives of clients can be made worse, as when social workers moved many Aboriginal children from their homes to residential schools and foster homes during the "sixties scoop" (Johnston, 1983). The practitioner, Thompson notes, may be encouraged through policy to provide either care or control, and to enhance either the empowerment or the oppression of individual clients. Similarly, Leonard (1975) noted that social systems and policies can be both oppressive and supportive: it is a crucial function of social work to enhance the possibilities of the latter and reduce the potential for the former.

Thompson (1993) identified the three essential building blocks of radical practice:

1. the understanding of the social and political contexts within which their clients' experiences occur;
2. the acknowledgment of the danger that their own practice could contribute to and reinforce oppression; and
3. the recognition and use of opportunities for the emancipation of clients from oppressive circumstances.

These three precepts also inform related models of practice that attempt to explore the relationships between policy and practice, including feminist practice, the structural approach, and anti-discriminatory practice.

Closely related to both radical and anti-discriminatory models is the structural model, developed by Moreau (1989) and elaborated by Mullaly (1993, 2007). The structural approach pays systematic attention to race, class, and gender in the assessment of individual problems presented to social workers. The practitioner's tasks include helping clients recognize the structural antecedents of their problems and the social changes that need to occur in these social structures. The client–practitioner relationship is less focused on therapeutic processes than on consciousness raising and mutual social critique. Roles of the practitioner emphasize advocacy, mediation, and brokerage.

Community Development Models

For several decades beginning in the 1960s, schools of social work recognized community organization and development as comparable in importance to casework and group work. Community work could involve helping communities become more self-sufficient, participating in social planning tasks, and, most prominently, taking social action. For some years, however, the community development approach has been in decline, perhaps largely because policy makers who grant funds do not value social action and the possibility of public policy challenges, as many in the social work profession do. Caragata (1997) argues that the skills of community development and organization should not only be preserved and used but also be incorporated into all facets of social work. The principles of community development, she argues, can help build bridges between the macro and micro areas of practice. They also help raise clients' consciousness concerning social change by involving them explicitly in efforts to change social structures. Furthermore, community organization is helpful in strengthening communities that are under stress as the result of neo-conservative political agendas.

Wharf and McKenzie (2004) distinguish between the organization of geographic communities and the organization of interest or policy communities. Geographic communities share common interest and common space. Policy communities are "loosely knit groups of individuals interested in and knowledgeable about a particular aspect of public policy" (99). An example of a policy community is Campaign 2000, an effort to pressure the federal government to make good on its United Nations commitment to end child poverty by 2000 (**www.campaign2000.ca**). Through this campaign, organized largely by social work practitioners and academics, a national coalition of individuals, schools of social work, and community groups has obtained funding, carried out research, and participated in widespread lobbying efforts. The campaign has given the issue of child poverty a high profile and has produced media and public support for the goal of changing social policy to provide more generously for poor children and their parents. The goal of ending child poverty is far from realized, but this campaign has successfully pressured the federal government to re-examine policy options and to create a different approach, one result of which was the Canada Child Tax Benefit (CCTB). While the CCTB proposal is far from perfect (Swift & Birmingham, 1999), its development does demonstrate that social workers committed to improving the lives of vulnerable children can collectively reshape the policy agenda.

Closely related to community organization approaches to social work are "alliance" models that connect practice and policy. This approach is captured in Bishop's (2002) work, *Becoming an Ally*. Alliance models encourage social workers to ally themselves with social movements, such as labour unions, the women's movement, poor people's organizations, First Nations groups, and various coalitions, and to provide supporting activity and expertise in targeting social change goals. Texts advocating this approach often speak not to professionals at all but to large groups of like-minded people, such as "activists" (Bishop, 2002) or "women" (Ricciutelli, et al., 1998). Alliance-building approaches ask social workers to move beyond the "elitist" professional sphere to work with a wide variety of people toward common goals. This approach is often, but not only, taken "after hours" by committed social workers who have strong community ties and interests in addition to their "day jobs." It asks social workers to contribute to a cause that uses both their professional knowledge regarding the effects of policy on individuals, and their professional practice skills in organizing and in policy development. This approach specifically works toward coalition building, combining skills and experiences to develop a stronger challenge for change.

Everyday Relationships Between Policy and Practice

In the everyday world of work, social workers specializing in direct practice may find themselves feeling cut off from social policy and analysis, whereas those in social policy development and analysis may feel cut off from issues of direct practice. Even—or perhaps especially—in social work education, these two fields of endeavour have been conceptualized and organized separately, and they often appear as distinct "silos" (Caragata, 1997) or even bunkers to both students and practitioners. Typically, social work courses are cast as either direct practice or social policy. In the world of work, the skills and tasks of policy and direct practice also tend to be organized in different spheres, so that practitioners do not see themselves as involved in policy development, and policy analysts do not come into frequent contact with the people who are most affected by their policy efforts. In addition, the policy-making process rarely includes those most affected by policy—that is, practitioners and service users (Wharf & McKenzie, 2004). Schorr (1985) pointed out some time ago that social workers in fact "practise policy" when they choose instruments to employ in their interventions, make decisions influencing organizations, and attempt to change policy. However, many social workers and students remain unclear about how policy is practised and how practice reflects policy.

In the dogma of the field, social policy analysts have generally been characterized as "progressive," while direct practitioners frequently labour under the stigma of being the conservatizing agents of the profession. However, as Lecomte (1990) observes, "all methods of social work have the potential to be conservative or progressive" (45). Adams (2002) stresses the relationships between social work and social policy, noting they are both "inseparable from politics" (29): they draw on common theory and concepts, use similar language, and are linked through legislation. Much theory, as we have seen, directs us to see and act on the ongoing connections between these two apparently separate endeavours. This section of the chapter identifies the tasks and skills needed for work in each arena and emphasizes the potential complementarity between them.

Policy Practice

Popple and Leighninger (2001) refer to social work as a "policy-based profession." They argue that over the past century, professions, including social work, have become firmly embedded in organizations and bureaucracies. They also suggest that social work and some other professions, such as the law, base their authority on mastery of complex cultural traditions, rather than on precise and specific techniques. These two characteristics of social work legitimize and, in fact, require social policy as a central feature of the profession. Following theoretical formulations outlined earlier in the chapter, Popple and Leighninger list several ways that social policy, including policy at the organizational level, shapes the tasks and attention of direct service to individuals and families. First, policy determines the major goals of service. For example, public policy is shifting away from universal and accessible social welfare services to a "leaner, meaner" model of reduced budgets and privatization of service delivery. Second, policy determines the characteristics of the clientele. For example, policies may grant services on the basis of marital status, physical or mental abilities, age, immigration status, and so on. At the agency level, eligibility may be further limited geographically, or in terms of religion or other characteristics. Third, policy may specify and restrict service options. For instance, abortion counselling services may be restricted on the basis of the age of the mother. Finally, policy can determine the theoretical or ideological focus of services. In Canada, for instance, multicultural policy underlies ideas of "inclusive" service provision, while human rights policies direct attention to such issues as who is hired to deliver services.

Popple and Leighninger identify policy at three levels—*macro, mezzo,* and *micro.* Macro-level policy includes legislation and regulations formulated at the federal, provincial, and municipal levels. These policies, many of which are outlined and described in previous chapters of this book, set the basic framework for the provision of services and benefits. Mezzo policy involves organizational guidelines, rules, protocols, and precedents that "direct and regularize" operations of the agencies where social workers are employed (Popple & Leighninger, 2001). In turn, these operations mediate between macro policy and service delivery, translating policies into response systems. It is often at the mezzo level that social workers attempt to translate and reshape policy. McKenzie (1997) has developed a Canadian model examining the importance of the mezzo level. He points out that it is at the agency level that the connections between policy and practice take on real meaning. Micro policy describes the transactions that occur as social workers deliver services to particular individuals and groups. This is the level of potential discretion described by Lipsky (1980).

Taking a somewhat different tack, Jansson (1990) examines the practice component of social welfare policy. He suggests that contemporary realities require social work practitioners to become conscious and active participants in the shaping of social policy. In the current neo-liberal era, wealth is accumulating at the top, and public resources are shrinking. Jansson suggests that serving the needs of clients in this climate of increasing inequality requires social workers to become more proactive in policy development. His "policy practice" approach is defined as "the use of conceptual work, interventions, and value clarification to develop, enact, implement, and assess policies" (25). Skills required for "policy practice" include:

➤ conceptual skills, including data gathering, identification of policy options, comparisons of merits of various options, and drafting of proposals;

➤ political skills, including exploring feasibility, locating power resources, and developing political strategies;

➤ interactional skills, involving developing contacts, building networks, developing and using group processes, and creating individual relationships; and

➤ value clarification skills, including identifying moral and ethical considerations in both proposals and strategies and determining how these considerations will shape strategy.

Of course, these same skills may be and frequently are used in direct practice. For example, in working with a client who has been cut off from assistance, a social worker will analyze the relevant policy to determine if the client meets eligibility requirements, employ political skills to locate allies with the power to support access, use interactional skills to tap into potential helping networks, and evaluate and act on the moral considerations of potential courses of action. Jansson states that conscious application of these skills extends a social worker's options because it uses knowledge of policy to help solve client problems.

Practice to Policy

A different yet ultimately similar approach has been taken by McInnis-Dittrich (1994). This approach begins with the traditional problem-solving skills of direct practice and shows how they can be used in policy development. Steps in this model include:

➤ assessment of the problem, including information gathering, problem identification, identification of resources and obstacles, and goal setting. Needs assessment may also be included in this process, involving the development of procedures to locate community services required to meet needs. In this phase, specific facts and figures are accumulated to answer specific questions about needs;

➤ exploration of alternatives, considering a wide range of possibilities and their potential consequences;

➤ development of an action plan and selection of alternatives;

➤ implementation—translating plans into specific tasks and allocating them to particular people; and

➤ evaluation of results.

The recommendations of Jansson and McInnis-Dittrich regarding both direct practice and policy work overlap considerably. Both require conceptual and planning tasks, political and relational skills, and ethical considerations, although the language used is somewhat different.

Use of Power

Central—although often implicit—to all discussions concerning the interaction between policy and practice is the issue of power. Traditionally, social workers have been taught less about power than about authority. Lukes (2005) defines authority as a form of power exerted and complied with because both parties agree on its legitimacy. Certainly, social workers accept the authority of supervisors (most of the time), of executive directors, and so on. However, this traditional definition suggests that the existing relations that vest authority in some people are reasonable and normal and should not be challenged.

Typically, the social work functions of authority and helping are not necessarily mutually exclusive (Kadushin & Martin, 1988). However, social workers often have considerable difficulty negotiating these apparently opposing functions in their everyday work (Swift, 1995). Furthermore, the business of challenging existing policies and practices very likely involves questions about appropriate authority, including the authority vested in organizational bureaucracies through which most agency policy is made. Authority and the way it has been addressed in social work literature have not offered sufficient or clear guidance to social workers in working to relieve oppressive conditions. A direct focus on power may be more helpful. Recent attention to the work of Foucault (1972) has made many social workers and students aware of the complexity of the concept of power. However, as a profession, social workers have been reluctant to acknowledge its importance in our work.

The concept of power, as Lukes (2005) points out, has deep historical roots and has been written about by many of the most authoritative scholars of the last two centuries. Lukes has developed a conceptual map of power that considers power in four dimensions. First is the scope or range of issues over which power is being exerted. Second is the contextual range or circumstances in which power is operative. The third dimension is the relationship between power and intention. The fourth distinguishes between active and inactive power, demonstrating that power can be effective even if not actively pursued.

Power—perhaps several kinds of power—is present in all relationships, and power held by each person continually shifts in the course of action. Jansson identifies several kinds of power that may appear in "policy practice."

One kind is *person-to person power*. Expertise, coercion, reward, charisma, and authority characterize this kind of power. It is perhaps most familiar to direct practitioners, since they engage in much person-to-person interaction and are made aware in education and training of the potential for misuse and abuse of personal power. In a client–worker relationship, the worker may be presumed to be more powerful most of the time, because he or she brings the mandates, policies, and resources of the organization and of macro-level policy to the encounter. However, clients find ways to exert power as well. Resistance, withholding, avoidance, withdrawal, aggression, deception, and dishonesty are all strategies employed by clients to assert themselves in relations they consider to be to their disadvantage. Clients, individually and in groups, may also try to influence a social worker to become interested in an issue or to take up a cause. Both kinds of power can provide social workers with information about social policies that have an impact on the people with whom we work.

Substantive power refers to the content of policy proposals. Those who attempt to shape policy spend considerable time compiling arguments and evidence supporting one position or another and discrediting alternatives. Constantly at play in this work is the question of how particular content will be received by different parties and with what consequences. Attempts to make policy changes appear non-threatening, and the inclusion of provisos such as time limitations demonstrates how this type of power is deployed.

Jansson calls the third kind of power *procedural power*, which is often overlooked in discussions of power exerted by social workers. The skills of controlling the agenda, chairing, and participating in meetings are used by all social workers at some time or other. Procedural skills can help ensure that a topic reaches the floor for discussion, that challengers are satisfied or avoided, that barriers are bypassed, and that rules of order are used to advantage.

A related type of power in Jansson's taxonomy is *process power*, through which the tenor or scope of an issue is set. Social workers generally become familiar with and use complex and sophisticated means to develop and encourage processes favourable to their cause. Team-building skills, tact, emphasis on opportunities for key players, timing, and broadening or restricting participation are all strategies used to influence processes, and therefore the outcome of a cause.

Finally, Jansson identifies the *power of autonomy*, the ability to develop policies of one's own, at times in defiance of existing policies. Social workers have considerable latitude in some circumstances to use this kind of power. In some situations, a group of social workers might discover and share a common issue and prepare a proposal for dealing with the problem. A proposal might request a grant to fund a programmatic response, suggest a change in organizational policy, or move to challenge macro policy. Social workers are also at times inventive in resisting unwanted policies, for instance, by circumventing rules they consider damaging to clients and by ignoring meaningless recording requirements. Of course, there are also more overt forms of power. Physical threat or actual violence is one. Usually this kind of power is more familiar in the police and military but may be an important factor in the lives of some clients. Economic power is also relevant for social work practitioners. Capital, as Finkel (2006) points out, is sometimes invisible but always an important player in social policy. The power to grant or withhold money or resources can be exercised not only by the state but also by corporations, employers, agencies, and intimate partners.

In direct social work practice, uneven power relations between worker and client are somewhat hidden by the concept of the "helping relationship." As radical social workers have warned, unacknowledged power can increase oppression for the client. Social workers who want to decrease oppressive experiences need to be aware of how power operates in various facets of social work. They also need to be aware of the risks to themselves in challenging established authority.

Moreau (1989) identified five kinds of power that can be learned, practised, and brought to bear in direct practice with clients. One kind is *expert power*, including access to information, resources, and networks of help. Another is *referent power*, meaning the ability to attract others to a cause. The third is the *power of numbers*: direct social work provides many opportunities to gather data about individuals and their experiences. In the aggregate, these data can provide powerful support for a cause. Fourth is *legitimate power*, the power that parole officers, welfare workers, and child protection workers have. Finally, Moreau speaks of *coercive power*, the power to reward or punish. This kind of power may be overused in mandated forms of social work and underused when challenging oppressive policies. Social workers need to be aware of their own power and put it to use in service of the client. Because many social workers are women, and because women are not generally socialized or encouraged to take and use power, this remains an arena for further exploration and skill development.

Empowerment has become almost a cliché in social work, to the point that some people no longer use this word. However, there can be no doubt that significant contributions to professional work have been developed under the label of "empowerment." Quoting Rappaport, Wharf (1990, 158) defines empowerment as "the process by which people, organizations, and communities gain mastery over their lives." For Chamberlin (1997), a psychiatric survivor, empowerment is a process rather than an event. Popple and Leighninger (2001) also define empowerment as a process, one that increases personal, interpersonal, or political power in an "active, self-creating process" (123).

In an unpublished study written by a master's degree student (Marno, 1997), empowerment was related to various political ideologies. Marno found that neo-conservative policies have eroded the concept of empowerment as employed in social work. She concluded, however, that social democratic and Marxist ideologies can produce a practice of empowerment that explores one of the major contradictions facing social work—that social work draws its funding and legitimization from the very sources that activists seek to challenge. It is perhaps this contradiction that prevents many social workers and students from fully developing and using their considerable skills in both practice and policy arenas. The next chapter helps social workers link the practice and policy arenas.

Conclusion

Social workers are developing new visions for resolving contradictions between the policy and practice world. These proposals grow out of concerns about the market-state characteristics of the welfare state, described in Chapter 2. A generally shared proposition is that social work has the potential to redirect social welfare from control to caring. Writing from a sociological perspective, Dominelli (1997) suggests that social work can be profoundly revolutionary, challenging governments' current focus on economic priorities, and arguing that human needs must be the organizing force in the development of new forms of welfare. Leonard (1997) also speaks of human need as a crucial focus for social work in the future. He describes welfare as an emancipatory project, requiring not only cool analysis, but also courage and the strength of moral outrage. Wharf and McKenzie (1998) say the task of building a more humane social environment requires social workers to "surrender the desire to control." They recommend focusing instead on an "inclusionary practice" as the most important reform in human services.

How would social workers begin to address such a goal? Wharf and McKenzie (2004) recommend developing genuine alliances between practitioners and service users. In the long term, such alliances can be practical and effective for influencing the policy development process. Without the serious input of those who need and use services, social policies are doomed to be incomplete and inappropriate, at best. Wharf and McKenzie also propose the development of "vertical-slice policy groups" as a mechanism for creating a more inclusive practice. These are groups that involve people at all levels of a policy process, including social workers and service users. To increase the potential for creating and changing social policy, Dominelli (1997) suggests that local issues be brought to national and international attention. An example is the appearance of Canadian social workers at the United Nations, protesting that the country's rating as the "best place to live" ignores our escalating rates of child poverty. Dominelli further suggests that social workers focus on making connections among different forms of oppression and help develop new paradigms that account for these connections. Leonard's (1997) proposal is "welfare building"—the construction of new policies and practices promoting human welfare. This project, of course, would require the power and resources of the state. His suggested strategy is the development of a "confederation of diversities"—a movement or even a political party with sufficient power to wrest needed resources from the state. Such a movement, he suggests, might involve feminists, trade unions, anti-racist groups, and the ecology movement, as these are some of the more active and solidified social movements in contemporary times.

These and other emerging proposals require work, knowledge, and skills at the micro, mezzo, and macro levels. Among the threads that tie these visions together is the insistence that social work move beyond the "silo" approach so that the potential power of the practice–policy relationship can be fully realized.

Chapter 8

The Policy-Making Process

This chapter discusses how social policy moves from ideas into action. The first part explains how world views shape unique perceptions about society, people, and people in society and how these perceptions simplify reality to conform to each world view. Not only does each world view correspond to a social policy, but each also prescribes how to convert that social policy into public policies, programs, and services. For example, a neo-conservative world view would accept inequality as a mechanism for promoting competition and stimulating individual initiative and would be relatively unconcerned about equality issues in policies and programs. In contrast, a social democrat world view would highly value equality and insist that public policies and programs promote greater equality. Moreover, each of these world views would also prescribe who is to be involved in the policy-making process and how power and decision-making authority would be distributed.

This chapter examines different approaches to the policy-making process, including comprehensive, incremental, and other approaches. As noted in Chapter 1, each model for policy-making has advocates who believe that their model best serves the people of Canada. Much like world views, models for policy making are based on notions that assign value to citizen participation, political and economic power, evaluation and feedback, and other related areas, which are discussed in Chapter 9.

The following four short stories convey in narrative form the notion of world views or social constructions of reality and show how these affect how we see the world.

Story 1: You and a friend are walking down a country road on a beautiful autumn day. As you turn a corner, you spot a cluster of maple, oak, and elm trees sporting a magnificent array of fall colours. For a moment, you are enthralled by the beauty of these colours reflecting against the brilliant blue of the sky. You experience a sense of wonder at nature's glory and feel content. Then your friend says: "Look at those poor leaves. All spring and summer they work to provide nourishment for the tree. Then in the fall, the trees remove the chlorophyll, the leaves return to their natural colour, and they are condemned to die. What a shame! Can you imagine anyone admiring a dying leaf?" You feel deflated and say nothing.

Story 2: It is the month of June, and you are driving along the Trans-Canada Highway in Northwestern Ontario. You see a beautiful lake surrounded by trees and wild grass, so you stop to take a picture at the roadside. As you exit your car, you are immediately attacked by hordes of blackflies. Fighting off the flies, you quickly take a picture and get back into your car. At home, you proudly display an enlargement of the picture that always attracts comments of how beautiful and peaceful it looks and how people wish they were there right now. You remember the blackflies.

Story 3: It is 1944, and the International Red Cross is sending a delegation to visit Theresienstadt, a ghetto the Germans claim to be a paradise for Jews. Prior to the visit, the ghetto sees a flurry of activity, as fresh paint is applied, rooms are refurbished, activity centres are created, and the Jewish people are clothed and cleaned. When the delegation arrives, children are playing, music from live bands fills the air, food is available, arts and crafts are on display, and the Jewish people themselves are friendly and open. The delegation members, even with some reservations, speak highly of this ghetto and the Germans' treatment of these Jewish people. When the delegation leaves, all food, furnishings, and clothes are removed, and the Jewish people begin an exodus from this camp by cattle trains to the death camps and eventual "final solution."

Story 4: It is 1998, and Canada is experiencing positive economic growth. New jobs are being created, and the federal government and many of the provinces are moving toward balanced and surplus budgets. Employment Insurance is experiencing a billion-dollar surplus, and workfare is being introduced in some provinces to give the poor an opportunity to get back into the workforce. Companies and governments are becoming more efficient, and private interests are being encouraged to become involved in public-sector activities. Canada is a viable member of the North American Free Trade Agreement (NAFTA) and has been invited to join an international consortium through the Multilateral Agreement on Investment (MAI). The economic health of Canada is vastly improving as governments free the private sector to conduct business.

World Views and the Policy-Making Process

What do these stories have in common? Each illustrates how a world view or social construction can frame our notions of "reality" and why it is sometimes easier to believe stories than to try to confront "reality" as critical thinkers. The first story, about the dying leaves, shows how difficult it can be when our assumptions about reality are challenged. One such reality today is the issue of poverty. Neo-conservative domination of Canada's media has resulted in a constant negative image of the poor: women having children so they do not have to work; people cheating on welfare; unemployed people taking advantage of Employment Insurance premiums; young people going on welfare so they do not have to live with their parents; lack of common sense among the poor; and so forth (Saul, 1995). This creates the impression that everyone is relatively well-off in our society, and if they are not, then it is probably due to a character flaw or bad life choices. Yet as the Senate Committee on Poverty (1971) stated a generation ago, "the time has come for a little common honesty. The poor, after all, are not, as some still pretend, poor of their own accord . . . . They are casualties of the way we manage our economy and our society" (xxvii).

The second story, about the photo and the blackflies, relates to what it is like to view society from a distance. When one is removed from the helplessness and hopelessness, the poor-quality housing and food, the violence, the tensions, the frustrations, and the pain and the emotional injury, it seems as if people choose to remain poor and refuse to be responsible citizens. When one is far away enough not to see poverty, soup kitchens, hostels, street kids, low-paying, no-benefit part-time and casual jobs, pay inequity, and minority discrimination, Canada seems to be doing very well in the global economy.

The story about the Jewish ghetto alludes to the social cosmetics and "spin" that can be placed on reality. In Ontario, the recent decision to introduce private sector "boot camps" for young offenders was carefully orchestrated—only the best candidates were chosen, the process was carefully followed, and the results were well publicized and even mentioned in the Throne Speech. Young offenders are presented as really bad people needing to be shamed and disciplined with a firm hand—often the very reality that has shaped these young people in the first instance. Positive publicity for boot camps is given prominence by newspapers essentially owned by those supporting conservative government reforms.

The final story, about Canada's current economic growth, shows why social policy analysts must constantly listen past the stories created by those in positions of public and economic power. Through the clever use of rhetoric and propaganda, power groups perpetuate social myths in order to minimize criticism and maximize conformity (Saul, 1995). For example, instead of acknowledging that companies are firing large numbers of employees, they say these companies are "downsizing." Furthermore, these companies are not downsizing to increase profits, but to demonstrate "fiscal responsibility." Today, governments are not in the business of promoting equality and protecting the welfare of their citizens, but in the business of making profits (called surpluses). Just as the Gulf War created new media euphemisms, such as "sanitizing" to mean "killing people," corporations are inventing euphemisms that make government programs and public workers seem uncaring and uneconomical and other euphemisms to suggest that corporate models and corporate leaders are necessary for proper management of human resources, especially where there is "a rush to use machinery—inanimate or human—while these are still at full value, before they suffer a depreciation" (Saul, 1995, 162). Moreover, Clarke (1997) asserts that the Business Council on National Issues and its allied corporations have heavily funded the Fraser Institute, the C.D. Howe Institute, and the Reform Party in order to manufacture opposition to government interventionism. Not only have these think tanks been successful in creating a negative image of government, but they have also been able to hide the fact that they play a powerful, behind-the-scenes role in determining public policy-making in Canada.

The policy-making process is manifold. On the one hand, the prevailing world view implicitly creates the social policy-making process of the time by ascribing privilege and power to those it favours and ascribing a reduced or nominal role for those it does not favour. It answers such questions as: To whom do politicians listen? How are people appointed on commissions and other bodies studying public and social policy? Is there a process for making social policies? Do some people have a greater say on which social policies will drive society? The answers determine how social policy will be made.

Many people are involved directly and indirectly in the policy-making process. Some of these people, such as members of the governing party, have the power to legislate policies into law. Others, such as business leaders, wealthy individuals and families, labour leaders, and entertainment notables, may become involved as advocates for policies that best reflect their own interests or values. Still others, such as consumers, average citizens, or interested people, may become involved in the policy process as advocates for policy options that are relevant to the communities in which they live.

As noted at the beginning of the chapter, everyone who becomes involved in the policy-making process brings their own world views and life experiences into the policy debate. From a social work perspective, Wharf and McKenzie (2004) suggest that policy-makers have a professional responsibility to ensure that issues of social development and social justice are included in the policy-making process. Citing Flynn (1992), they recommend that policy-makers keep the acronym *SCRAPs* (sexism, classism, racism, ageism, and poverty) in mind as a reminder that many of society's victims of discrimination only receive "scraps" from most policy initiatives. To evaluate the impact of policies on people, Reamer (1993) recommends exploring how the concept of equality is being applied. Reamer suggests that equality has a range of definitions:

➤ *Absolute equality* exists where resources, such as wealth, property, and access to services, are divided equally among all people (also known as *equality of result*).

➤ *Equality of opportunity* is concerned with the opportunity individuals have to gain access to desired resources. This might also include remedial services to enhance opportunities to compete for scarce or limited resources.

Reamer recommends that in order to enhance equality and minimize inequality, policy-makers should use the following mechanisms:

➤ *Maximum policy*, which simply seeks to maximize the minimum—that is, to raise minimum standards for items such as income, housing, health care, and education;

➤ The *ratio of inequality* approach, which seeks to increase the resources of those worse off in relation to those who are better off;

➤ The *least difference policy*, which seeks to reduce the range of inequality;

➤ The *mini-max principle*, which seeks to reduce the advantage of those who are most privileged—that is, minimize the maximum (27).

Review the exercise "Are You a Number One?" at the end of Chapter 1. Advocates of social justice seek a social order where the societal distribution of resources and rewards is as just as possible and where exploitive inequalities are removed. Again, examine your own reality within the existing social order. What policy solutions would benefit you in relation to the distribution of resources and rewards and exploitive inequalities? You might wish to identify existing policies that continue to promote inequalities in your own life. You might wish to break into groups and share your discoveries. Are there common themes? Are there common solutions? Do you or members of your group feel disempowered to remedy inequality in your lives?

Gil (1998) suggests that social work's Code of Ethics requires all social workers to integrate a social justice approach to their practice setting, regardless of the resistance they receive. Similarly, Titmuss (1974) warns that because social policies are simply choices that direct government action toward given social ends, they may very well promote or create social injustice, discrimination, and oppression. For example, apartheid in South Africa was a social policy, as was racial segregation in several American states. It is important to question all policy initiatives. Are current neo-conservative and liberal initiatives toward the poor, women, children, and the unemployed further promoting social injustices, discrimination, poverty, and oppression? Keep in mind that these same initiatives have resulted in workfare, limited insurance for unemployment, reduced benefits for welfare recipients, reduced support for women's and minorities' programs, reduced support for all levels of education, and reduced health-care benefits

Powerful groups justify the policies they create by appealing to the public about needs and responsibilities. For example, recent leaders have justified cutbacks to social programming because of the "need" to reduce government debts and deficits. But evidence suggests that a large portion of Canada's national debt is due more to tax breaks and loopholes for wealthy individuals and corporations and to high interest rates than to government spending on social programs (Turk & Wilson, 1996; McQuaig, 1993; Minoto & Cross, 1991). Yet government spending is where the majority of cuts have been directed.

The world views of the rich and powerful shape Canada's social policies and help determine who influences policy decisions and the policy-making process. Of major concern to social workers is the constant decrease in government funding to support organizations that promote the interests of those who are not rich and powerful. This, of course, means that not everyone is in the same position to influence the policy-making process, and indeed, some people may be deliberately ignored. Being ignored as partners in the constitutional debates leading to the Charlottetown Accord was one of the complaints of Native groups. Many people on social assistance have been upset by the failure of some provincial governments to invite or to include their opinions, experience, and knowledge in the policy-making process. This is especially true of neo-conservative governments, whose view of the poor is often hostile and dehumanizing. In 1996 in Ontario, advocates of the poor attempted to use both public protest and the court system to stop the severe cuts to social assistance implemented by Mike Harris's Conservative government, on the basis that these cuts infringed upon their human rights. These efforts failed, and the cuts remained and even deepened. Yet when the medical profession and the legal profession were angered over anticipated cuts to their domain, the same government backed down and granted concessions.

Given that many people representing many interests and world views are involved in the policy-making process at many different levels of power and influence, understanding the process is not easy. It can best be understood within a framework that incorporates models of policy-making, the role of political ideology and power, institutional structures supporting the policy-making process, and participation in the policy-making process. The policy-making process is constantly influenced by such factors as globalization; dominant political ideologies; institutional structures; public values; social and economic power holders; economic prosperity; degrees of social and economic equality and equity; quality of social, political, and civil rights; and the degree of public participation. These, therefore, are some of the important variables that must be considered when examining the various approaches to the social policy-making process.

Models of Social Policy-Making

The Comprehensive Approach

When comparing the social policies of different countries, researchers often use social indicators representing quality-of-life measures. These social indicators reflect how public policies, social institutions, social programs, and social services work in each country and how they influence the various elements that make up a society of people. For example, countries may be compared to each other based on child poverty; the social equality of women; the quality and availability of educational institutions and health (physical and mental) resources; social welfare spending as a percentage of gross national product; criminality and correctional resources; child welfare services; and income security levels, among others. As such, social indicators provide a comprehensive overview of each nation's social policies in practice, and in turn, allow nations to be ranked based on the various social indicators.

This approach is called the *comprehensive approach* to policy-making because it begins with global objectives based on social values and then translates these policies into public policies, social institutions, social programs, and social services. The advantage of this highly centralized approach is that policy is equally applied to all parts of a country.

The following provides a summary of representative models of social policy. These summaries are helpful to review and revisit as you proceed through the chapter.

The Rational Model (Simon, 1957)

The rational decision-making model uses the following sequence of tasks:

a. identify and clarify a social problem;

b. identify and rank goals with respect to that problem;

c. develop strategies that can remedy the problems (or achieve the goals);

d. carefully examine all possible consequences; and

e. decide on which policy best achieves government/organizational goals.

The Incremental Model (Braybrooke & Lindblom, 1963)

The incremental model suggests that the rational model fails because it cannot account for everything and therefore must be incomplete at design level. This model instead views policy-making as "muddling through" by making incremental adjustments to existing policies.

The Mixed-Scanning Model (Etzioni, 1968)

The mixed-scanning model suggests that the substantive (political or social) issues need to be addressed by rational decision-making; then adjustments need to be made to the policy in order to reflect unforeseen social realities and unintended consequences.

Rights Model of Social Policy (Marshall, 1965)

The rights model argues that the best way to ensure the welfare of citizens is to institute universal entitlement to the following three rights: (1) civil rights that guarantee individual liberty and equality before the law; (2) political rights that ensure the right to vote and seek political office; and (3) social rights that ensure equal access and opportunities to all social institutions. Social policy advocates rely on the legal system to monitor and correct any abuses of these rights.

Titmuss's Three Historical Models (1974)

1. *The Residual Welfare Model of Social Policy*

The residual welfare model argues that the private market and the family are responsible for meeting an individual's needs. Only when these break down should social welfare institutions come into play. This model is favoured by the neo-conservatives and economists such as Friedman and Hayek.

2. *The Industrial Achievement-Performance Model of Social Policy*

The industrial achievement-performance model argues that social needs should be met on the basis of merit, work performance, and productivity. Known as the "handmaiden model," it is favoured by positivists and other economic and psychological theorists who advocate incentives, effort, and reward.

3. *The Institutional Redistributive Model of Social Policy*

The institutional redistributive model argues that social welfare is a major integrated institution in society, providing universal services outside the market based on the principle of need. It is based on a model incorporating systems of redistribution in command over resources through time. In other words, society must ensure that major income redistribution systems, such as income tax and regional distribution transfers, are moving constantly toward achieving equality.

Titmuss also coined the phrase "The Iceberg Phenomenon of Welfare" to compare perceived and real welfare spending. *Occupational welfare* (benefits such as pensions and health insurance, which are derived by workers through employment) and *fiscal welfare* (tax benefits to individuals and corporations, including all deductions) formed the majority of the iceberg that is hidden under the water, whereas social assistance welfare is a smaller portion visible above the water. In other words, many people other than the poor benefit from welfare, but this other welfare is concealed. Titmuss found that the majority of welfare spending actually is distributed upward to the rich through "hidden welfare benefits" (pensions, work-related benefits, tax deductions).

Values Competition Model (Rein, 1974)

The values competition model suggests that social policy is, above all, concerned with choice among competing values. Society consists of people holding diverse values (world views) who are in competition with each other and, consequently, with each other's values, in an effort to achieve maximum power. Values are so ingrained in every aspect of social, economic, and public policies that a major role of policy-makers is to learn how to control their own values and prejudices.

Social Justice and the Comprehensive Model of Social Policy (Gil, 1992, 1970)

The comprehensive model suggests that social policies are guidelines for behaviour that have evolved through societal processes. They specify, maintain, or transform the structures, relations, values, and dynamics of a society's particular way of life. As such, comprehensive and rational social policies govern societal life and are therefore of great concern to social workers and other human-service personnel. Good social policies should be concerned not only with life-sustaining activities that ensure minimum basic needs, but also with life-enhancing activities that stimulate human potential.

The Value Criteria Model (Haskins & Gallagher, 1981; Wharf & Mackenzie, 2004)

The value criteria model suggests that after determining what the problem is and what policy alternatives are available to address the problem, policy makers must use value criteria, informed by universal and selective values, and cost–benefit analysis to evaluate each policy alternative. In short, the best policy is the one that maximally reflects these value criteria.

The Garbage Can Model (Kingdom, 1995)

The garbage can model suggests that the three types of policy processes—problems, solutions, and politics—operate individually and independently until a crisis occurs that requires all three to come together. Resolving the crisis is dependent on (1) how the public perceive the problem, (2) what the current political agenda is, and (3) who the participants are. Getting an issue on the policy agenda becomes a function of whether or not there is a crisis or situation that creates a need for the three processes to come together.

Drawbacks of Comprehensive Approaches

Some advocates believe that social policy should work along the lines of the garbage can model. Politicians and policy analysts should determine what each country's social policies should be and then put these policies into practice. Social policy is thus the aggregate of all social indicators and a statement about society's values. But applying programs universally doesn't guarantee equality. For example, when the Canada Assistance Plan was enacted in the late 1960s, the federal government was able to ensure that all Canadians received equal treatment under the act, regardless of what province they lived in. The same is true for the health care system, which also ensures that all Canadians have equal access to health care. In contrast, the recent creation of Employment Insurance (EI) signalled a limiting of benefits to the unemployed. The disadvantage of the comprehensive approach for EI is its universality and equality: it ends up being less sensitive to Canada's social and regional diversities, especially regarding seasonal employment.

Comprehensive policy approaches can also backfire if they are not solid. Consider the Canada Assistance Plan (1966), which the federal Liberal government replaced in 1995. In order to balance the budget and reduce the public debt, the government determined that it was more advantageous to negotiate lump-sum transfers of money to provinces than to make transfers based on actual cost. The Canada Assistance Plan originally paid dollar for dollar what the provinces paid for programs that qualified under the act, including social assistance. It also allowed for assistance to be granted to people in need or likely to become in need, thus allowing for prevention services. In 1996, the Canada Assistance Plan was replaced by Canada Health and Social Transfer Regulations, with enabling legislation in the Federal–Provincial Fiscal Arrangements Act (1985, 1995). The federal government no longer cost-shares the actual program costs of each province, nor does it enforce uniform standards. Canada's poor are no longer protected; soup kitchens and flophouses have reappeared; and Canada has lost an act that provided public policy protection.

At the same time, even though health costs have been greatly increasing, the government did not substantively change the Health Act (1984) to compensate for these increases. The Health Act simply restricted the provinces from instituting direct patient charges. Moreover, even though the core principles of universality, comprehensiveness, accessibility, portability, and public administration remained, the means to provide for them did not.

Yet the political right remains committed to dismantling comprehensive programs and reinstating needs- and means-based programs that require meeting eligibility criteria. The argument is that this approach ensures that those most in need receive the benefits, while those who are better off do not. Given this logic, what is next for the health care system, one of the last remaining universal programs in Canada? The provinces of Alberta, Quebec, and Ontario have begun to challenge the Health Act and have committed to privatizing some parts of health care. Moreover, most provinces have reduced medical and prescription services covered by the health care system. What do you believe it will take to turn this process around? How empowered do you feel in being a part of the effort to redirect these policies? Comprehensive policies often have a "power-over" feel to them, and solutions are often limited to "power-over" strategies. You may wish to examine these issues by exploring the concerns raised by Jackson and Sanger (1998); Blake, Bryden, and Strain (1997); Finlayson (1996); McQuaig (1995); Wein (1991); and Carniol (1987).

The comprehensive view of social policy maintains that a scientific, rational approach to social policy-making is feasible and desirable. But social policy is about accomplishing what is termed *net value achievement*, rather than about pleasing everyone on every issue. Net value achievement means that the rewards gained from society's common values, as chosen by the policy-makers, more than compensate for any values that may have been sacrificed. For example, a country may value stable economic growth to the point where it chooses to control inflation by increasing interest rates. These increased interest rates will result in higher borrowing costs, making it more expensive for companies to borrow money and to have large inventories. This process usually concludes with companies laying off staff and creating more unemployment. Although the country may value employment and regret the layoffs, it may value stable economic growth more and be prepared to sacrifice employment for stability. The choice about which values to sacrifice is often a function of the value preferences of those who have the power to determine social and public policies. Analyzing social and public policy-making from a net value achievement perspective often focuses on issues of economic, social, and political power and how this power influences value-based policy choices that serve the interests of the powerful. In the above example, had the workers themselves been consulted, they might very well have preferred to sacrifice some economic stability in favour of maintaining or increasing employment levels.

Rein's Model

Social and public policies are often about struggles between value preferences and how some values become dominant and why. Rein (1974) suggests that social policy is about choice between competing values. From his perspective (see Figure 8.1), the social policy process stresses the interaction between values (input), operating principles (conversion process), and outcomes (output). Because Rein's model provides a comprehensive view of the policy-making process, it will be examined in some detail.

People who hold positions of political and/or social power disproportionately influence which values (input) win. When the debate about values is limited to ideology and world views, rather than the real world and the needs of real people, then social policy process suffers from what Rein calls *detached ideology*—that is, choices are made strictly in accordance with values, regardless of the outcome and consequences to others. Statements such as "It is important to reduce employment in order to control inflation"; "Adjustments to the safety net are required if Canada is to overcome its national debt"; or "Social services must be limited to what a country can afford" are simply the values of the people in power (in this case, economic well-being) being used to justify reduced opportunities and services (i.e., reductions in another value) for the average Canadian (social well-being).

Consider the following holes that detached ideology creates in social policy. The political right believes in deregulation, decentralization, and free enterprise. A pro-globalization orientation gives corporations freedom from government intervention and advocates for minimal government programs and a balanced or surplus (profit) government budget. What options are available to advocates of this ideology when confronted with rising costs, such as those associated with health care? The Canadian Institute for Health Information reports that the cost of drugs is the fastest-growing segment of health care and is now second only to hospital costs. Obviously, controlling drug costs would seem to be a logical policy direction; but how likely is the current ideology to introduce new health care coverage? Would a corporate world view not prefer to reduce health costs associated with hospital and doctor care, while allowing drug costs to spiral upward?

Discuss the following questions in small groups: How important is balancing the federal/provincial/municipal budgets, and what priority should this goal have relative to other problems? What factors have contributed to Canada's determination to balance budgets and to allow globalization to direct Canadian social and economic policies? Who do these policies benefit the most? Are poor and marginal income groups being asked to carry the major burden in reducing the public debt? Is it possible for any government to escape its own detached ideology? How much of the discussion you are having is being influenced by each participant's detached ideology?

FIGURE 8.1   Rein's Overview of the Policy-Making Process

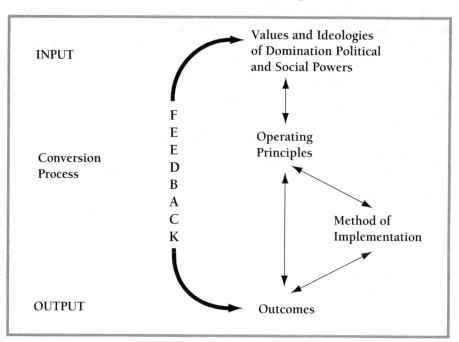

Input for social policy design and analysis consists of the values and ideologies of dominant political and social powers. In Canada and all democratic societies, governments are elected by the people to lead the nation. Part of that leadership is the implementation of the "political platform," which states the vision the party has for the country or the province. This vision reflects the world views and ideologies that constitute the value base for that political party. In other words, different political parties—such as the Liberal Party, the Bloc Québécois, the New Democratic Party, and the Conservative Party—inform the public of what they will do if elected.

Once in power, a majority government can pass legislation that creates new social policies and alters existing policies. These policies, called public policies, are a purposive course of government action designed to deal with issues of public concern (Anderson, 1990). Berkowitz (1980) notes that social choices made in the policy process only rarely benefit the interests of all without being adversely consequential to some. Thus, the political influence held by various alliances and interest groups in Canada can limit universality. These influential groups can include the economic/business sector; special interest groups such as the elderly, women, or people with disabilities; and international monetary institutions.

As noted in Chapter 1, when social policy becomes public policy, it also becomes legitimate and universal and controls the forces of coercion. For example, in the early 1990s, Canada underwent a debate about gun registration, with many people disagreeing with or wanting amendments to the proposed registration policy. In 1995, Bill C-68 was introduced; it contained stricter gun control legislation and a requirement for all guns to be registered. However, once the policy became law in late 1998, gun registration became mandatory regardless of different opinions (legitimacy); it applied to everyone in Canada (universal); and the police were sanctioned to enforce the law (monopoly of coercion). On the other hand, physician-assisted suicide has not become legal in Canada, and it is therefore illegal (illegitimate) for anyone to assist in suicide, regardless of personal beliefs, with prison or a criminal record awaiting any who choose to do so (use of coercion). In Holland, physician-assisted suicide is legal, provided all criteria are met, and there are no social sanctions. Further discussion of the law-making process can be found in Chapter 9.

If a political party comes to power with a pro-business and anti-welfare agenda, social workers can anticipate negative public policies regarding the poor and the disadvantaged. Wharf and Cossom (1987) warn of potential efforts to restrict the role of citizens in policy-making and policy decisions through *consociational democracy*—that is, "government of elite control designed to turn a democracy with a fragmented political culture into a stable democracy" (267). Marchak (1988) goes so far as to speculate that should the demands for the redistribution of power and wealth become public policy, the elites of Canada would break away from democracy and take power by force.

While these may seem like dire warnings, Saul (1995) identifies the modern corporate advocate as promoting economic objectives that are similar to those that were advocated by the early fascists in the early 1930s:

1. to shift power directly to economic and social interest groups;
2. to push entrepreneurial initiatives in areas normally reserved for public bodies; and
3. to obliterate the boundaries between public and private interest—that is, to challenge the idea of the public interest (91).

A recent example of the use of power by Canada's economic elite is the 1989 Canada–United States free trade agreement (FTA), which eventually became the 1994 North American Free Trade Agreement (NAFTA). As Trudeau (1990) noted:

[T]he commendable goal of promoting freer trade has led to a monstrous swindle under which the Canadian government has ceded to the United States of America a large slice of the country's sovereignty over its economy and natural resources in exchange for advantages we already had, or were going to obtain in a few years anyway through the normal operation of the GATT. (385)

GATT is the General Agreement on Tariffs and Trade, which was adopted in January 1948. Not only did Canada give up a large measure of sovereignty, but thousands of Canadians lost their jobs as well.

Another major problem for social workers working with communities and with the poor is "social dumping," which occurs when corporations invest in countries with fewer labour rights and lower wages, thus driving down the wages and job security in Canada. The recent push to join the Multilateral Agreement on Investment (MAI) would have enhanced the rights of investing corporations and further weakened Canada's sovereignty (Clarke, 1997).

Social policies are based on operating principles, which combine with implementation methods and create a *throughput* or *conversion process*. *Operating principles* are "attempt[s] to integrate various social ideals with a practicable rule of application" (Rein, 1974, 297–298). These include universality, citizen participation, housing and in-kind benefit subsidies, earned access, equity, and other such principles that are held to be of value by society. Not all of these principles support a social work value system, and it is incumbent on social workers to carefully analyze and articulate the operating principles associated with social policy decisions and positions.

The *methods of implementation* consist of organizations, including social agencies, specifically designed or altered to provide the services prescribed by implemented social policies. For example, social policies and public policies regarding children have resulted in a myriad of social agencies, such as schools, Children's Aid Societies, Children's Mental Health Clinics, and Young Offender facilities. However, many of these agencies and the professionals within them can prefer a particular value (children/youth should or should not be involved in agency policy-making; family is or is not the primary institution in a child's life; or children have or do not have the same human rights as adults) or a particular practice methodology (psychotherapy, brief therapy, task-centred therapy, or community-based practice). This prescribed value or practice methodology can in fact compromise the policy and operating principles to the extent that they become congruent with the prevailing value or practice methodologies. In effect, the agency or staff members could be doing the same thing but under a different name and could be acting in a manner that is counterproductive to the values and objectives of the new policy. This debate about the principles of implementation is known as *doctrinaire insulation* (Rein, 1974, 298). In Canada, other examples of doctrinaire insulation include situations where southern-based practice methodologies and specializations are applied directly to northern environments without adaptation or citizen consensus; and situations where public policies do not account for the values and views of groups other than the policy-makers, such as women's groups, ethnic groups, religious groups, and gay groups (Delaney & Brownlee, 1995).

The output of social policy is its outcome. The importance of outcome centres on whether the outcome and the purpose of the social policy are congruent and *in whose estimation*. Often social policy success is measured by social impact studies or by feedback from those whom the social policy was intended to benefit. However, the degree to which citizens are allowed to give feedback and influence social policy is in itself a fundamental issue for social policy analysis.

Rein views values, operating principles, and outcomes as inseparable and in fact completely interrelated. Rein explains this interrelationship in the following manner:

Policies are in fact interdependent systems of: (1) the abstract values we cherish; (2) the operating principles which give these values form in specific programs and institutional arrangements judged acceptable for public support; (3) the outcomes of these programs which enable us to contrast ideals and reality; and (4) the often weak linkages among aims, means, and outcomes, and the feasible strategies of change this pattern suggests. (298)

Gil's Model

Another social policy theorist who supports Rein's notions of value-driven social policy is David Gil (1998; 1992). Gil maintains that human beings and human development should form the basis of social policy. Gil believes that throughout history, systemic inequalities have resulted in social arrangements that benefit selected members of society and disadvantage the remaining members of society. He calls this process *patterned inequalities* and suggests that, over time, people do not even recognize the injustice or the inequalities. The result is the creation of social institutions that serve to benefit the interests of the few, while dehumanizing, marginalizing, discriminating against, and/or oppressing the many. Gil believes that most societal violence stems from the damage these social institutions do to people.

Gil argues that social policy must promote and enhance human development and potential and in doing so, serve as "guidelines for behaviour, evolved through societal processes, which specify and maintain or transform the structures, relations, values, and dynamics of a society's particular way of life" (Gil, 1992, 21–22). Gil defines social policy as a set of guiding principles that govern societal life and that therefore must be of great concern to social workers and other human service personnel. In effect, social policies should control all other public policies, excluding religion and foreign trade, but including economic policies.

From this perspective, social policy should reflect long-range visions of what a just and non-oppressive society would look like (Gil, 1998). Gil's vision also stresses values and ideologies affirming equality, individuality, liberty, cooperation, community, and global solidarity, rather than the currently prevailing values and ideologies that support inequality, individualism, selfishness, domination, competition, and disregard for community. For example, if Canada and other nations used the *Universal Declaration of Human Rights*, as adopted by the United Nations in 1948, as the centrepiece for all social policy, then all social policies would have to conform to this declaration in order to be established as public policies. By signing the UN document, Canada committed itself to eradicating poverty and ensuring basic human rights—and then did not do it.

Gil's comprehensive view of the social policy-making process suggests that social policies should govern natural and human-created resources; all aspects of employment, including human issues; the production of life-sustaining and life-enhancing resources; social, political and civil rights; mechanisms for the distribution of rights and privileges; and mechanisms for the assignment of social status (Gil, 1992, 24–25). Therefore, all social problems are the result of a flawed social policy; thus, the policy, not the problem, needs to be redressed. As such, social policies are "potentially powerful instruments for planned, comprehensive, and systematic social change rather than reactive measures designed to ameliorate (in a fragmented fashion) undesirable circumstances" (Gil, 1970, 413). The primary domain of social policy is "all possible sets of human relationships and the quality of life or level of well-being in a given society" (415).

An important feature of Gil's approach to social policy is his insistence that social policies must address not only life-sustaining activities that ensure minimum basic needs but also life-enhancing activities that promote and support human growth and potential. Social change theorist Paolo Freire (1968) argued that every person has an "ontological vocation"—that is, each person is born with the desire to search for meaning in his or her life. Oppressive societies thwart this drive to maximize one's humanity. In this sense, Gil agrees with Freire that the ontological vocation for humans is to become more fully human and that social policy should be a mechanism to ensure that all humans have equal opportunity and equal access to society's resources to this end.

Swift (1995) suggests that existing social policies do in fact discriminate against the poor and, in particular, poor women. In order to gain resources, mothers "must appear incompetent in order to qualify for the resources" (125) and, in effect, present themselves as failed mothers. And yet the alternative is to live in poverty with inadequate resources, with the result of many mothers being labelled "bad mothers," rather than people who have been failed by society. Similar criticisms of social policies, as they relate to other areas of social diversity, are outlined in Chapter 4.

For social workers, Gil's notion of social policy conforms to the profession's value and ethical base. Having social policy address the challenges and realities of the human condition is certainly an ideal worth seeking. Making the interests of all people, their families, and their communities the first principle for societal governance emphasizes *the common good* rather than the *public* or *private interest*. As social welfare philosopher Frederic Reamer (1993) puts it, there is a substantive difference between the common good and the public interest, with commensurate implications to social policies. The common good refers to "that which constitutes the well-being of the community—its safety, the integrity of its basic institutions and practices, the preservation of its core values," and human end-states such as human flourishing and moral development. While originally referring to national security and prosperity goals, due to the neo-liberal world view, the public interest has now come to mean "a rational alliance of primarily self-interested individuals whose collective good is constituted by the collection or aggregation of private interests" (Reamer, 1993, 35). Thus, powerful groups can argue that they are promoting public interest by enhancing the individual pursuit of self-interest. Thus, social workers, who have a particular commitment to social justice for society's most marginalized, must hold notions of the common good as sacrosanct, despite changing notions about the public interest.

Implementing Gil's approach would require society to agree on what set of values should govern social policies. But in societies where political, ideological, and economic power is in the hands of fewer and fewer people (Bishop, 2002), this degree of social transformation is unlikely to occur. In the neo-conservative world view, life enhancement is something to earn, and society is responsible only to provide minimally life-sustaining needs.

An Incremental Approach

Other social policy theorists do not take as comprehensive a view of social policy as Rein and Gil do. Wharf (1992) distinguishes between the *ordinary* and *grand* issues of social policy. *Grand* issues are "those pertaining to the fundamental structure of political–economic life" (14), including distribution of income and wealth, political power, and corporate prerogatives. *Ordinary* issues of social policy include "the governance of child welfare services, deinstitutionalization and the development of community support programs, the struggle to raise social welfare rates in Ontario, and the debate about abortion politics in Nanaimo" (15). Wharf argues that *ordinary* issues should be of concern to social workers because these issues directly affect the lives of people, can be managed and redressed by community-based organizations, and are sometimes the unintended consequence of earlier reforms.

When dealing directly with the *ordinary* issues of social policy, social workers often employ the rational decision-making model used by incrementalists. The incremental model views the social policy-maker as having to:

➤ define and rank governing values;

➤ specify objectives compatible with these values;

➤ identify all relevant options or means of achieving these objectives;

➤ calculate all the consequences of these options and compare them; and

➤ choose the option or combination of options that would maximize the values earlier defined as being important (Hogwood & Gunn, 1984, 46–47).

Wharf (1992) makes note of the "goal-directed-muddling-through" approach to the policy process (where goals emerge in a way that might not be clear at the outset of the intervention) that is used by community workers. This inductive approach allows the community worker to ensure that the people's interest is known and that the policy process is "anchored in a philosophical position and a vision for change" (233). Because it permits a high degree of flexibility, practice wisdom, and discretion in pursuing objectives, Wharf believes it is an adaptive approach to policy-making. For most social workers, who will only rarely be exposed to global social policy issues, the values and ethics of social work are often the only firm base they have in policy.

A criticism of the incremental approach is that social workers and other human service workers become too preoccupied with resolving local or immediate issues stemming from social policy and do not pay sufficient attention to the social issues that may be creating the problem in the first place. For example, when the new EI program limited the time people were able to collect benefits, many regions with high seasonal unemployment organized against this policy. But the Liberal government did not alter it, which suggests that it was committed to globalization and to a right-wing policy agenda (Clarke, 1997). How then should regional groups have attacked the Liberal government's policy position? Would they have obtained better results from local (incremental) efforts that challenged this policy within the region, or from national (comprehensive) initiatives that challenged the national policy direction?

The Mixed-Scanning Model

Etzioni (1968) argues that there may be a method of reconciling the differences between a comprehensive policy-making process and an incremental policy-making process. The "mixed-scanning model" can bridge the gap between these two approaches. After making a rational, comprehensive policy decision, policy-makers adjust the policy incrementally, based on information gained from its implementation. Thus, policy-makers can focus on the greater issues without becoming bogged down in details (Hess, 1993).

Table 8.1 compares the sequences of tasks for each approach. The *policy agenda* refers to the need to identify problems in a priority manner and to make policy makers aware of this priority. *Policy formulation* refers to the development of clear and acceptable ways of solving problems or at least addressing them in a policy. *Policy adaptation* refers to the development of support and acceptance for the policy by such means as advocacy and accommodation. *Policy implementation* refers to the actual application of policy to the problem. *Policy evaluation* seeks to answer whether or not the policy worked.

Table 8.1 shows that each theory has its strengths and weaknesses. Anderson's sequence is rational and easy to understand, but it fails to address who is benefiting from these policies and why policies are directed to their benefit

TABLE 8.1   Sequencing the Policy-Making Process

Anderson (1990)	Wharf (1992)	Wharf & McKenzie (1998)	Rein (1974)
Policy agenda	Initiation	Problem identification	Values
Policy formulation	Formation	Identification of value criteria	Operating principles
Policy adaptation	Execution	Assessing alternatives	Method of implementation
Policy implementation	Implementation	Feasibility assessment	
Policy evaluation	Evaluation	Recommendations	Outcomes

(Mason, Talbott, & Leavitt, 1993). While Wharf's sequencing appears similar to Anderson's, his approach is much more analytical and substantive, with a very clear community-organization perspective. Wharf's sequence addresses concern about which people are involved in the policy-initiation process; whether the problem the policy is addressing is correctly defined or whether it can be redefined; and whether sufficient resources, including people and funding, are available. Like Wharf, Rein recognizes that the policy-making process is not linear and that each stage is subject to problems and to political manipulation.

In the mixed-scanning model, policy makers choose different paths through the sequence. They can start with Wharf and McKenzie's value criteria model (1998), which requires them to evaluate costs, benefits, and alternatives after defining the problem and the policy alternatives. Or they can use the garbage can model's three types of policy processes (problems, solutions, and politics), allowing them to operate independently until a situation or crisis arises. If a particular issue does not get on the policy agenda, then it may have to wait until a new opportunity arises or may have to be removed if it appears to be resolved. In other words, whenever there is a public concern, such as those being expressed over water quality in Ontario or farm subsidies in the Western provinces, then all components come together. When the crisis is over, they separate again, only to be re-engaged when another crisis strikes. While these processes are separated, there is little opportunity for social change.

The mixed-scanning approach is important because it allows social workers to understand both the anticipated and unanticipated impacts of social policy, as well as potential or actual shifts in social policy in Canada. Pierce (1984) notes that "social workers also need to be able to identify policies that actually constitute a part of their practice world. If policy is to be used in generalist practice, its definition must come from the practice parameters and perspectives of line social workers" (4). However, the policy analyst should keep Wharf's (1990) cautions regarding four limitations associated with generalist practice models based on the ecological systems perspective:

➤ The mixed-scanning approach assumes that problems, once identified, will generate a demand for change—that is, change will occur and the problem will be solved.

➤ This approach ignores power and its distribution in Canada—that is, goodness-of-fit for the rich is good to excellent, while the goodness-of-fit for the poor is bad to terrible. Who has the power and the will to change this—the rich who are benefiting?

➤ This approach does not assign social workers responsibility to bring about change.

➤ This approach does not address the issue of auspices—that is, the fact that social workers work in agencies that are given their mandates by those holding political power. The social worker's efforts to change the system are limited by each agency's political and social agenda.

Controlling the Policy-Making Process

If anything is apparent from the preceding discussion on policy-making approaches, it's the number of factors that can derail the policy-making process. In Canada, there are four major types of pressure groups involving social policy:

➤ business groups, including the Canadian Manufacturers' Association (CMA) and the Business Council on National Issues (BCNI);

➤ labour groups, including the National Labour Congress;

➤ professional groups, including the Canadian Association of Social Workers and the Canadian Association of Schools of Social Work; and

➤ advocacy groups including the Canadian Council of Social Development, the National Anti-Poverty Association, and the Canadian Welfare Council.

The most successful groups over the past few decades have been the business pressure groups. Corporate models essentially reflect a "power-over" (Bishop, 1994) approach, promoting the value of competition, hierarchy, and separation. Separation here refers to groups of citizens uniting to promote their best interests against the best interests of others. Bishop suggests that the end product of this type of "power-over" approach is a society infused with "sexism, racism, ageism, adultism, heterosexism, and ableism" (21). The question is simply this: what is needed to motivate people who are benefiting from the existing system (and who have the political, economic, and ideological power to maintain their advantage) to share their benefits with those less fortunate?

Consider the following example. Cancer patients in Southern Ontario who have to travel to Northern Ontario for radiation treatment have their travel, hotel, and food expenses covered; Northern Ontario residents who travel to Southern Ontario are not reimbursed equally. In one example reported in *The Globe and Mail* (June 11, 2000, A3), a cancer patient from Iroquois Falls travelling to Sudbury (about 360 km) a half dozen times received $109.89 in support payments. Cancer patients travelling from Southern Ontario cities to Northern Ontario hospitals received approximately $5000. The reason: Northern Ontario patients are covered by Northern Health Travel Grants, whereas Southern Ontario residents are covered by the more generous Cancer Care Ontario. The same problem in opposite directions makes a difference of $4900.

By limiting resources to those less well-off (such as the geographically isolated, the unemployed, the poor, the marginal income earners, and many post-secondary students) or those in need of protection (such as abused children, battered women, and dependent elderly), power groups create an environment of competition for funds. For example, the simple tightening of EI criteria has prevented thousands of seasonal workers from receiving benefits. Reducing social assistance and introducing tighter eligibility criteria has forced thousands of people off welfare. Reducing public housing projects ensures that thousands of people live in inadequate housing, which many cannot even afford. Reducing subsidies for women's shelters ensures that many women are left with horrific options should they need to flee a dangerous home situation. These are all current examples of human deprivation and suffering in one of the world's richest countries. How can a nation such as Canada justify there being more food banks than McDonald's restaurants?

Social policy advocates such as Bishop (2005), Banks and Mangan (1999), and Wharf (1992) have increasingly focused on the need to engage the community in the policy-making process. By engaging the community, policy advocates can also link with existing community resources, such as local social and economic planning councils and citizen advocacy groups. These linkages ensure not only that the policy issues being discussed are relevant to the community, but also that obstacles to policy development are identified. Policy advocates can also translate new policy initiatives and existing public policies into terms that communities can understand.

Controlling the policy-making process is one of the major challenges facing policy advocates. Not only do political interest groups control the government public policy-making mechanisms, but they also play a large role in the economic life of Canada and its communities. Advocates for progressive social policies must put away their individual differences (avoiding separation) and unite as allies seeking the same end despite different self-interests. As Bishop (1994) notes, "Commitment to social justice means beginning a completely unknown journey—a journey that can unfold only one step at a time, with confusion and danger along the way" (124).

Figure 8.2 presents an overview of the policy-making process as discussed in this chapter.

FIGURE 8.2 An Overview of the Policy-Making Process

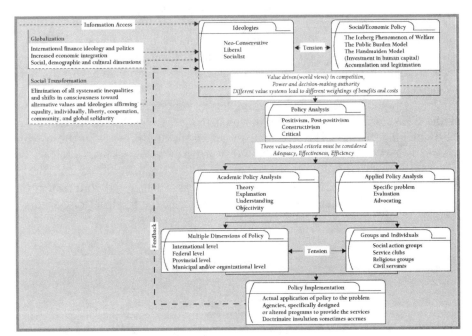

Figure 8.2 shows that the tensions created by the conflicts in globalization and social transformation challenge the ideologies that influence Canada's economic and social policies. Currently, the forces supporting globalization have been moving policies away from social transformation and citizenship and more toward a social responsibility and accountability model. At the policy analysis level, the dominant neo-conservative world views shape the policy debate by infusing its ideological interpretations of social and economic benefits and corresponding social and economic costs into public policy. At the next level, the theoretical and critical analysis of academic policy analysis comes into conflict with the applied policy analysis process—the process of actually transforming policy into structure. The next level represents tensions between the political dimensions of a policy and the positions of interest and advocacy groups. Policy committee representatives (selected individuals to represent affected constituencies) tend simply to represent their constituencies, rather than providing direct feedback. Neysmith, Bezanson, and O'Connell (2005) advocate using a direct feedback mechanism, one that lets people understand "how policies play out in the lives of citizens from the perspective of those who experience them—those for whom . . . they are designed" (14). At the bottom level, policy becomes implemented in practice. A final feedback loop assesses whether the policy in structure is congruent with the original objectives. But whose voice actually is heard in the feedback process? And if concerns are raised, is anybody listening?

Conclusion

This chapter explored how different world views shape unique perceptions about society, people, and people in society. It also examined the power of world views to convert social policy into public policies, programs, and services; to prescribe who is to be involved in the policy-making process; and to distribute power and decision-making authority. Finally, it discussed different approaches to the policy-making process.

Every model of social policy-making has its supporters and detractors. Academic debate still flourishes around which model is most effective. However, the tightening of control over Canadian policy-making process by those with the most economic and political power signals a challenge to advocates for social justice to unite in a common cause—to let Canadians know "the other side of the story." Chapter 9 discusses issues associated with implementing social policies and strategies to bring social justice to the forefront of Canadian public policy.

Chapter 9

Implementing Social Policies

The goal for all advocates of a specific social policy is to shape the public landscape in a manner that reflects the values and objective of their policy position. This chapter discusses how these goals are accomplished. Having political power, especially in the form of a majority government, allows a group to introduce its social and economic policies into public policy with little opposition. This process is evident in provinces like British Columbia and Ontario, where reform governments over the past 10 to 20 years created tremendous public policy changes. Dare (1997) details major public policy changes made by Ontario's Harris government in its first five months in office:

➤ dismantling the Workplace Health and Safety Agency (incorporated by Workers' Compensation) and eliminating worker input; and limiting the Wage Protection Fund, which had included wages, benefits, severance, and termination pay, to simply wages and benefits;

➤ reinstating the "spouse-in-the-house" rule, where single women who are alleged to be living with a man are cut off from welfare;

➤ imposing a three-month wait for welfare if applicants quit their jobs;

➤ cancelling 390 co-op and non-profit housing projects and Jobs Ontario, and closing 25 halfway houses for offenders;

➤ cutting welfare rates by 21.6 percent, the Ministry of Health budget by $1.5 billion, school board budgets by $1 billion, and grants to municipalities by 48 percent over two years.

Recently, the federal Conservative government has been seeking similar measures. Even with a minority government, the Harper government seeks to create changes in areas that tend to support multinational businesses and negate unions and the environment. For example, the decision to support the SPP (Security and Prosperity Partnership) provided an opportunity for business leaders to participate in semi-secret policy debates. Unions and advocates for the environment and for various groups (such as women and immigrants) were not invited to these meetings.

This chapter will explore how laws are made in Canada (both federally and provincially); what laws look like and why they are important; the role of courts in the policy-making process; how power and influence play a major role in policy selection; and the role of citizen participation in this process.

The Canadian Political System

Like the United States, Switzerland, and Australia, Canada is a federal state. A federal state has two levels of government: national and state/provincial. The role of the national government is to promote the best interests of the whole country, to offset the diversity and chaos that could be created if each province or state sought its own best interests. Canada has two major forms of government—federal and provincial—built on a parliamentary model with a constitutional monarchy. The British North America Act, 1867 (now known as the Constitution Act, 1867), and the Constitution Act, 1982, established the governance domains for both the federal and provincial governments. While the territories—Nunavut, Northwest Territories, and the Yukon—are based on similar parliamentary models as the provinces, they are headed by a commissioner, rather than a lieutenant governor.

The federal parliament governs issues associated with Canada as a nation and makes laws to support the peace, order, and good government of Canada, such as international agreements and the right to levy taxes across the country. The provincial parliaments govern issues associated with the province, including hospitals (except marine hospitals), natural resources, municipal and provincial institutions, property rights, marriages, and social services; they have the right to levy taxes for provincial purposes.

To learn more about the history of the Canadian parliamentary system of government, visit www.parl.gc.ca/information/library/idb on the Web, or check out Landes, R. (1998), *The Canadian Polity: A Comparative Introduction* (5th ed.). Scarborough: Pearson.

At the federal level, Canada has a governor general (representing the Queen of England), a senate, and a House of Commons. The governor general appoints members of the senate on the recommendation of the prime minister. The 105 members of the Canadian senate, called senators, are appointed on the basis of 24 seats for the Western provinces, 24 seats for Ontario, 24 seats for Quebec, and 24 seats for the Maritime provinces. The remaining 9 seats represent Newfoundland and Labrador, the Northwest Territories, the Yukon Territory, and Nunavut. Senators maintain their seats until 75 years of age.

The 308 members of the House of Commons, known as members of Parliament (MPs), are elected from across Canada and its territories. The executive authority for Canada is vested in the Queen, who is represented by the governor general (the lieutenant governor in provinces). By tradition, the governor general conforms to the will of the cabinet, which is headed by the prime minister, who is the leader of the political party with a majority of seats (or the largest minority party if no majority is elected, as determined by the governor general). The cabinet, which is the executive branch of government, consists of a small group of MPs, known as ministers, who have been selected by the prime minister and assigned specific ministries. These ministers are responsible for all policy development within their ministerial portfolio and the promotion of these policies in cabinet. Obviously, a strong minister will achieve greater success in moving policy to law or programs.

The legislative branch of government essentially consists of the House of Commons, including all parliamentary committees. Should the governor general become incapacitated, the chief justice of the Canadian Supreme Court becomes administrator of Canada and serves on behalf of the governor general.

At the provincial level, a lieutenant governor represents the Queen of England for a provincial parliament. Provincial parliaments follow the same process as the federal government, except that the head of the provincial cabinet is called a premier, and there is no provincial senate. The Quebec provincial parliament is called the National Assembly, and members are called Members of the National Assembly (MNA). The Newfoundland and Labrador provincial parliament is called the House of Assembly, and members are called Members of the House of Assembly (MHA). The Ontario provincial parliament is called the Provincial Parliament and members are called Members of Provincial Parliament (MPP). All other provinces and territories call their provincial parliament the Legislative Assembly, and members are called Members of the Legislative Assembly (MLA).

Making Laws

The initiative to create a new law or reform an existing one can come from various sources. For example, strong public opinion, such as the current fear of terrorism, can influence ministers, as can people lobbying for industry or other interest groups. As noted in the beginning of this chapter, the political platform of newly elected governments can also shape political opinion. In addition, the bureaucracy for each ministry can promote public policy initiatives based on their own operations, including program evaluations and need surveys.

Essential policy debate on a proposed legislation (called a bill) occurs in cabinet, often in secret, before it ever reaches Parliament. Committees of cabinet, including the Treasury Board, examine the bill. Other constituents, such as the party's caucus (elected members of the ruling party), may be involved in discussions, particularly for controversial or marginally supported bills.

Laws can originate in many ways, but some routes are more effective than others. Explore this further by reading newspapers, magazines, and public opinion surveys and search for the answers to the following questions: Who is sponsoring the proposed new or reformed legislation? Who is likely to benefit from this legislative initiative? Who is likely to be negatively affected?

When a draft of the bill is ready, the minister introduces it to the House of Commons or Legislative Assembly. It must then pass three separate readings and votes. By use of a "party whip," the governing party ensures that party members who are not in cabinet (known as backbenchers) vote in support of the proposed legislation. Sometimes, when a piece of legislation has deep moral or social meaning, party members are allowed to vote according to their own conscience and not necessarily with the party's position. If passed, Parliament sends the bill to committees composed of representatives from all parties for fine-tuning and minor amendments.

There are two common types of bills. Public bills are proposals that will impact the public as a whole, and they are usually introduced by the appropriate minister. Private bills usually concern individuals or local matters. However, there are also private members' public bills, private senators' public bills (federal only), private senators' private bills (federal only), and senate government bills.

Once a federal bill passes three readings in the House of Commons, it then goes to the senate, where the process is repeated. If it passes all three readings in senate, it goes to the governor general for royal assent. Once the governor general signs it, it becomes law. Provincially, the bill becomes law once it passes its three readings in the provincial Legislative Assembly and receives royal assent by the lieutenant governor.

Each department or ministry in the federal and provincial government has statutes (acts) that empower these ministries and departments to do their business. For example, the minister assigned to the Department of Family and Community Services in New Brunswick works under the following statutes: Charitable Donation of Food, Family Income Security, Health Services, Intercountry Adoption, Nursing Homes, Family Services (except Part 7), and Vocational Rehabilitation of Disabled Persons. As well, it operates under some sections of Change of Name, Education, Employment Standards, Hospital, and reciprocal Enforcement of Maintenance Orders statutes. It is important for social policy advocates to know which acts govern which ministries or departments and to become familiar with those acts that affect their work.

Municipal governments, which govern cities, towns, villages, counties, districts, and metropolitan regions, are established by the provincial legislatures. Provincial and territorial legislatures grant municipalities all their powers. Officials such as mayors, reeves, and councillors are elected on a basis determined by the provincial legislature.

The Internet provides ready access to provincial and federal ministries and departments. Most sites allow downloading or printing of acts and regulations associated with the different ministries. Try looking up ministries or departments that interest you and examine the statutes that govern their activities. Provincial government sites can be found at www.gov.nf.ca (Newfoundland and Labrador); www.gov.pe.ca (Prince Edward Island); www.gov.ns.ca (Nova Scotia); www.gov. nb.ca (New Brunswick); www.gouv.qc.ca (Quebec); www.gov.on.ca (Ontario); www. gov.mb.ca (Manitoba); www.gov.sk.ca (Saskatchewan); www.gov.ab.ca (Alberta); www.gov.bc.ca (British Columbia); www.gov.nt.ca (Northwest Territories); www.gov. yk.ca (Yukon); and www.gov.nu.ca (Nunavut).

Municipal governments provide an array of local services, including water supply, sewage and garbage disposal, roads, sidewalks, street lighting, building codes, parks, playgrounds, and libraries. Some provinces, such as Ontario, have granted municipalities a greater role in social welfare programs. For example, Ontario Works (1997) downloaded workfare and social assistance to municipalities. Schools are generally looked after by school boards or commissions elected under provincial education acts but are often funded at the municipal level.

As noted in Chapter 1, laws are powerful instruments that impact all Canadians. Despite controversy and opposition, once a bill becomes law, all citizens must obey it or suffer sanctions, such as fines or even imprisonment. Certainly, issues such as capital punishment, abortion, and marriage definitions are still being debated in the general public, but existing laws frame what options are legal. Nevertheless, people who believe their rights are being infringed have options.

The Court Option

People who believe they have a legitimate case against an existing law can take their case to court. Canada has two levels of courts: federal and provincial. While the Constitution provides that most courts are created by provincial legislatures, judges from county courts up are appointed by the federal government (with the exception of probate courts in Nova Scotia and New Brunswick). Under the Judges Act (1952), the federal government in Canada appoints and pays all federally appointed judges. However, removing judges is a different issue. Judges of the provincial supreme courts (called the Superior Court in Quebec), the Federal Court, and the Supreme Court of Canada may be removed only by the governor general. This provides these courts with a great deal of independence from governing parties. Nevertheless, judges are appointed by a governing party, and there is a tendency for parties to select judges who reflect their political ideology or orientation. A judge with a neo-conservative orientation may adjudicate differently on the same issue than a judge with a social democratic orientation.

People who believe their rights are being violated or who wish to contend with how a particular act is being interpreted may address their grievances through the court system. What is important is that the ruling of the Supreme Court of Canada is final. This process is very expensive and time consuming, but is still an option for advocates of human and social rights to redress social injustices. For example, the Supreme Court has been asked to rule on such issues as the right of gay partners to receive the same employee benefits as the partners of heterosexual employees; the right of an individual to have physician-assisted suicide; and the right of citizens to practise active euthanasia.

Power and Ideology

Power has been defined by Etzioni (1975) as the ability to enforce compliance to authority, and by Brager, Specht, and Torczyner (1987) as the potential for and the exercise of influence. Other theorists (Gil, 1992) have viewed power in terms of its ability both to create compliance and to resist being made compliant. This ability to resist being made compliant is a critical issue for social work and all the helping professions. In terms of social policy, Wharf (1992) suggests that power is, in effect, the capacity to alter policies and decisions.

This capacity may be exercised through persuasion, rewards, or other means of securing compliance; but where these strategies fail, policy-makers can bring about change on a unilateral basis. Influence refers to any attempt to convince policy-makers of the need for change. Policy-makers have power, even though their ability to secure compliance may at times be slight because of the pitfalls of implementation. On the other hand, social reform organizations possess influence, but not power (Wharf, 1992, 25–26).

In terms of political advocacy, Gil (1990) reminds social workers that they cannot be politically neutral if they value the social well-being of those they serve, because their practice "either confronts or challenges established societal institutions or it conforms to them openly or tacitly" (20).

According to Woodsworth (1986), while power operates on many levels, it takes many forms:

➤ big business and big government;

➤ management and bureaucracy;

➤ professional and interpersonal relationships;

➤ religious organizations; and

➤ professional, scientific, and technical leaders.

While acknowledging *pluralism* as a central concept in Canadian political life, Woodsworth notes that there is also an elite group in Canada that wields considerable power. *Pluralism* means that "there are many competing influences on the way people behave toward each other" (71). *Elitism* refers to the chosen or most carefully selected part of a group or society. Elitism in social policy terms implies that social and public policy do not reflect the demands of the people so much as they do the interests and values of the powerful few. Elitism views the masses as largely passive, apathetic, and poorly informed—a situation that allows the elite to manipulate mass sentiments by the use of power gained from monopolistic control of the boards of major corporations and financial institutions and by their overwhelming presence in government. This leads to a situation where the elite "develop policies to favour big business, and when in business they find ways of influencing public policy" (71):

Perhaps the central question for social workers is the extent to which the methods and goals of government and business (aimed at standardization and control) are accepted and continued by professionals in their ways of working with clients (70).

Galbraith (1983) suggests that power is derived from three sources: (1) personality (with leadership a major asset); (2) wealth or property (including disposable income); and (3) organization (viewed as most important). Wharf (1986) views politicians, bureaucrats, and pressure groups as having the most influence on policies, with provincial and federal cabinets being the most important units in the Canadian political system. In terms of pressure groups, Wharf notes that having well-organized groups with influential people who are known to those in power is essential for successful influencing. The Canadian Manufacturing Association, the International Bank, the Chamber of Commerce, the Canadian Medical Association, and the Canadian Bar Association are examples of business and professional groups. The National Council of Welfare, the National Anti-Poverty Organization, the Canadian National Institute for the Blind, and the Canadian Council on Social Development are all examples of pressure groups from the social welfare arena.

The influence of an ideology supported by powerful political and economic forces is enormous. Ideology is essentially a confirmed belief that a political and social order is correct. In effect, an ideology with political, economic, and sometimes religious clout becomes so dominant that other perspectives are viewed as dangerous or irrelevant. In effect, oppression and power-over thinking comes to pervade the policy-making process. For example, Schragge (1997) suggests that the new political agenda of the 1990s promoted an ideology that not only "bashed the poor" but also created a whole new ideology about the "underclasses." Not only have social programs been cut after being blamed for creating the public debt, but a meaner and dehumanized ideology has also ascended into policy prominence, legitimating workfare as progressive policy development despite research that suggests it is repressive and counterproductive. The following quote from a conservative writer exemplifies how neo-conservative ideology blames the poor for their social conditions:

Social Work's reluctance to see that personal failings play a role in poverty is worse than unrealistic: it positively hurts the poor. Modern social workers have taken the position that environmental factors—the economy, racism, sexism, and so on—account for neediness, and sadly, many have preached this doctrine to their clients. By telling them that someone else is to blame for their fate, they encourage scapegoating and whining, and undermine the motivation to succeed (Payne, 1998, 109–110).

An oppressor's goal is to maintain absolute control by planting fear and doubt in the minds of the oppressed, who are only rewarded for public docility and compliance. As Fromm (1967) notes, human freedom has historically been restricted by "the use of force on the part of the rulers . . . and, more importantly, the threat of starvation against all who are unwilling to accept the conditions of work and social existence that were imposed on them" (183).

Institutional Structures Supporting the Policy-Making Process

The primary policy-making bodies in Canada are the federal, provincial, and territorial parliaments. All public policies stem from these bodies, and the power granted to municipalities stems from the provincial and territorial governments. As discussed in Chapters 2 and 3, under the Canadian Constitution, provincial governments have historic jurisdiction over health, welfare, and education. Any federal government intrusion into these jurisdictions—such as occurred with Unemployment Insurance (1940, Section 91, 2A), Old Age Pensions (1951, Section 94A) and pensions extended to cover survivors, disability, and supplementary benefits (1964)—requires constitutional amendments. The provinces did contest Family Allowances (1944) (*Angers v. Minister of National Revenue*), but it was eventually allowed under the constitutional provision of "peace, order, and good government" (Report for the Interprovincial Conference of Ministers Responsible for Social Services, 1980).

The two most important components of the policy-making process are the prime minister/premiers and the cabinet (Yelaja, 1987). The prime minister and premiers have the power to appoint cabinet members and to remove them as well. Each cabinet minister is given a specific area of government responsibility called a portfolio. This portfolio may be just one ministry or department or it may include more than one. For example, Alberta has the Ministry of Family and Social Services; Ontario has the Ministry of Community and Social Services; New Brunswick has the Department of Health and a Department of Family and Community Services; Prince Edward Island has a Department of Community and Cultural Affairs and a Department of Social Services and Seniors; the Northwest Territories have a Department of Health and Social Services; British Columbia has a Ministry of Children and Family Development and a Ministry of Community Services; and Manitoba has both a Department of Family Services and Housing and a Department of Health. The titles of these ministerial portfolios change often with the election of new governments.

The Charter of Rights and Freedoms (1982) is a major piece of social policy legislation that has the potential to ensure that citizens have the opportunity to challenge any legislation or amendments that might restrict, interfere, or impinge on those rights and freedoms claimed in the Charter. However, as Hess notes:

When interpreting complex and sometimes ambiguous sections of the Charter, the courts will inevitably play an increasing role in social policy, despite the fact that many people in Canada's judicial system have limited experience and understanding of social policy issues and the implication of their decisions on policies and programs (Hess, 1993, 45).

Citizen Participation

Citizens can participate in the social policy-making process in many ways. Before exploring the options, we need to explore the issue of citizen participation. The role of citizens in the policy-making process is a major concern for social workers, in terms of both social work's value base and its code of ethics. People in a democratic country have a right to participate in issues affecting the public interest and the common good. However, there are problems in motivating people to participate.

Wharf and Cossom (1987) suggest that the *principle of affected interest* is a major issue in promoting citizen participation. This principle states that everyone "who is affected by the decisions of a government should have a right to participate in that government" (271), especially in terms of the following three criteria:

➤ *Personal choice* reflects the degree to which a person wants to be involved, especially in terms of how much people believe the policy will affect them. For example, university students may become involved in decisions to raise tuition but not feel affected or interested in decisions to raise the price of admission to local swimming pools.

➤ *Competence* suggests that some decisions are accepted because experts made them. As well, for issues of complexity, such as pollution and nuclear waste, citizens need a degree of knowledge in order to participate. Complexities, such as the overuse of rules of order or presentations by technocrats, can intimidate people into not participating.

➤ *Economy* suggests issues of efficiency, rationality, and preservation of scarce resources. It also refers to the time, energy, and money people have to participate. For example, single mothers may not be able to attend meetings because they do not have money for bus fare or babysitters.

Another problem stems from Canada's political process. Canada's political system is based on the principle of representative democracy. Each political party in Canada is permitted to choose a candidate to represent that party in each federal/provincial electoral riding. In each riding, members of the party select from among a number of eligible candidates the person they wish to represent the party at the next election. Once an election is called, this member then runs against candidates selected by other parties in the same way. The winner is supposed to represent all those in the riding, including all members of other parties. Yet the member becomes a member of the party caucus and is expected (and even coerced) to vote along party lines. It is easy to see why people can feel alienated and powerless in getting their voices heard when the very system that is there to represent them is so removed from them as individuals. Moreover, it is difficult for an elected member not to feel a sense of obligation to those who helped to win the election and to feel fewer obligations to those who were trying to defeat her or him.

Governments can involve citizens in the policy-making process in several ways. At the input or formative stage, governments can establish commissions with the mandate to explore a public issue in depth and to bring back a community-informed recommendation on actions the government should take. The Senate Committee on Poverty in the late 1960s is an example of such a commission. This committee visited several cities in Canada and listened to thousands of delegations representing multiple interests. It prepared a final report including these recommendations, which was made public.

Also at the input level, the government may appoint policy committees. The recent popularity of policy committees reflects the disparity of influence between "the haves" and "the have-nots." The core of policy committees consists of representatives from government, agencies, and institutionalized interest groups, who have the real power in the policy-making process (Hess, 1993). Other groups that lack status or resources, such as academics and advocacy groups, are given the status of "attentive public," and their contribution is limited to what they contribute to the public debate and the policy discussion.

This unequal power and influence means that the power of specific pressure groups can increase the probability of a policy outcome (Hage & Hollingsworth, 1977). Mishra (1995) notes that pressure or lobby groups "are associations of people with common interests which seek to influence public policy" (67–68). Pressure groups can either be interest groups that seek to enhance members' interests (such as chambers of commerce, rifle associations, trade and business associations) or promotional groups that "espouse a cause . . . or advocate on behalf of a particular group (such as the poor, the homeless, the disabled)" (68). Wharf (1986) recommends that any group wishing to influence public policy must be well organized and made up of influential people who are known by senior civil servants and politicians.

In other words, influencing public policy at the input stage is both strategic and expensive. Large corporations hire lobbyists who are often ex-politicians or ex-senior civil servants to advance their causes and to ensure that public policies reflect their best interests. The poor, the injured, the unemployed, the sick, people with disabilities, and dependent groups cannot compete and are often dependent on the policy advocacy of others, such as The National Council on Welfare, National Anti-Poverty Association, the Canadian Council on Social Development, Canadian Association of Social Workers, and other promotional groups.

At the policy evaluation stage, governments once again seek citizen input. However, many of the problems that reduce citizen involvement at the input level also affect it at the evaluation level. Some people assume that policy-makers reflect on their policy decisions because of the feedback. However, Grob (1992) and Galster (1996) suggest that this is not the case. Essentially, policy-makers are receptive to research findings that support their ideology, especially when the research is easy to understand and to use. Timing is another important factor, because research becomes attractive when there is a current, controversial public issue, and less attractive when there is no public controversy.

Unfortunately, very few built-in structures in Canada ensure that citizens—both those directly affected by policy or those with an interest in policy—have the opportunity to be heard. Certainly, not voting for a party in the next election is one means of protest; but if one is a member of a minority group, it is of little consequence unless the majority understands the issues as seen by the minority.

Getting information to the public is another means of consciousness raising that can influence policy. However, in a country where the vast majority of media—such as television, newspapers, radio, and magazines—are owned by the privileged few, it is unlikely that the minority and politically left views will be deemed newsworthy. Meanwhile, the media are more likely to accept reports from a neo-conservative ally source, such as the Fraser Institute, without question or analysis. Those in power are able to maintain a "power-over" posture that maintains hierarchy (who rules, who follows), separation (we are not responsible for each other), and competition (the proving ground for competence and character), because decision-makers favour their own group and give themselves increasing power.

These powers serve to sever those with limited power or no power from any substantive role in the policy-making process. It is essential that social workers and other human service professionals strive to open the channels for citizen involvement.

The Role of the Social Worker in the Policy-Making Process

The call to use community as a basis for policy-making development is not new (Wharf, 1992), nor is the *strengths perspective,* which views the strengths and resources of people and their environment as the central focus of social work (Chapin, 1995). Together, they provide an excellent framework for conceptualizing societal needs in new ways, to allow a more inclusive approach to policy formulation and a wider opportunity to develop more meaningful and realistic policy options. Communities have personal, firsthand knowledge of *respect, collaboration, caring, trust, sacredness, vision,* and *neighbourliness,* and they are familiar with ways these ideas translate into community needs.

Obviously, the trust and value the community places in the social worker plays an important part in how well these resources work together. Earning this trust without violating or compromising one's social work values and ethical base requires great skill and time. The knowledge social workers gain through their position of trust gives them a unique ability to relate the policy-making process to social impacts by doing the following:

➤ objectively analyzing the anticipated and unanticipated impacts of social and public policies on the communities they serve;

➤ examining the congruence between social policies and agency policies (their own and other agencies) and advocating for adjustments to align these policies;

➤ increasing community consciousness regarding existing social and economic policies and any potential consequences for these communities;

➤ organizing community responses to social policies with negative consequences;

➤ developing coalitions between communities to enhance the response to negative social policies;

➤ ensuring that those social policies that benefit communities are acknowledged;

➤ developing a research capacity of sufficient sophistication to allow information pertaining to the community to be collected; and

➤ developing mechanisms to ensure this research information is made available and acknowledged by policy-makers, even if lobby or pressure groups must be employed.

For many social workers, social policies often seem abstract concepts with little or no connection to social work practice. However, policy advocacy and policy practice are both instrumental components of social work practice.

Conclusion

At a time when social programs and agencies are being downsized and even eliminated, social workers need to become involved in the policy-making process. As political and economic interest groups dominate Canada's policy-making process, the helping professions, especially those in the public sector, are being called upon to engage in collaborative partnerships with their client groups and their communities (Barter, 1996; Delaney & Brownlee, 1995; Graham & Barter, 1999) to fight for their inclusion as citizens who can take part in policy-making, and not just as citizens who are passively affected by social and public policies.

While there are and probably will continue to be many different approaches to the policy-making process, social workers should advocate for citizen participation in all policy-making activities. Within the framework of social justice and equality, social workers can go a long way toward ensuring that all voices are heard by policy-makers and that no voice is given preference over others. The objective is not to make social policy a matter of easy choices but of informed choices that benefit all the people of Canada.

Social work is being called upon to resist neo-conservative interpretations of social realities and to maintain its own vision and critical analysis to promote social and human justice. Social workers and human service professionals must maintain their ideals in a storm of cynicism about people and human value. As Homan (1994) states: "Idealism is not to be confused with naiveté. Idealism is a purposeful, powerful belief . . . . An idealist simply refuses to capitulate to a prodding dullness of spirit . . . . Someone may say to you, 'You are an idealist.' Take it as a compliment." (32).

Appendix

Social Welfare History Chronology, Canada

Prior to European colonization, Aboriginal peoples are in North America and have long-established traditions of social care.

1520s–1763: European settlement along the St. Lawrence River; establishment and growth of French colony in North America—New France. Formal European contact had preceded this date along the eastern coast of North America. European colonization in North America transforms Aboriginal communities across the continent. Colonization brings with it European social welfare institutions such as education, hospitals, and charity.

1759: The fall of New France leads to the 1763 Treaty of Paris and the creation of a British colony. British social welfare institutions, like their French counterparts, assume limited, local government (parish) responsibility for the poor and indigent. A residual approach to social welfare.

1867: The British North America Act establishes constitutional jurisdiction over provinces for health, social services, and education. Residual approach persists. There is an increase in the scope and number of voluntary charitable services during the latter half of the nineteenth century.

1872: The Nine-Hour Movement, in defiance of the existing law stipulating that labour unions were illegal, results in labour rights rallies throughout Ontario and Quebec. Later that year the Trade Unions Act is passed, making trade unions legal. But it would require several decades of strikes, and the subsequent deaths of several strikers, to gain union recognition in many employment sectors.

1873–1878: The Canadian Labour Union (the first national organization for unions in Canada) was created and abolished. Local unions, though, would continue to flourish—by 1890 there were approximately 240 local unions across the country.

1876: The Indian Act establishes the Crown as a separate authority for services to Aboriginal peoples based on treaty obligations. The act places Aboriginal peoples in a distinct legal category, as wards of the federal government, without the privileges of full citizenship. To gain citizenship rights, Aboriginal people would have to apply for enfranchisement (a culturally insensitive and completely discriminatory process of total assimilation within Canadian society), a condition of which included relinquishing their status rights and cultural identity.

1883: The Labour Congress of Canada was created out of meetings with the Toronto Trades and Labour Council and the Knights of Labour, later being renamed the Trade and Labour Congress of Canada (1886–1956).

1886: Early forms of Workers' Compensation legislation are introduced. Voluntary welfare organizations emerge over the early to mid-nineteenth century, with greater intensity at century's end. Highlights include the Toronto Children's Aid Society (1891), Red Cross (1896), and Victorian Order of Nurses (1897).

1900: Dominion Elections Act is passed, permitting only those people considered eligible to vote in provincial elections the right to vote in federal elections. As a result, Aboriginal people, visible minorities, and women do not gain voting rights.

1914: The country's oldest social work school is established at the University of Toronto. Others follow at McGill University (1918) and the University of British Columbia (1928).

1914: Workers' Compensation is established in Ontario; other provinces follow.

1914–1918: World War I. Returning veterans provided retirement annuity insurance assistance (1920), settlement assistance (1927), and allowances (1930) to veterans, widows, or orphans with insufficient means.

1914: Voluntary welfare organizations proliferate after World War I. They include the Toronto Family Service Agency (1914), Canadian Mental Health Association (1918), Canadian National Institute for the Blind (1918), Canadian Council on Social Development (1920), and Canadian Association of Social Workers (1926).

1916: Mothers' Allowances, a selective program, is established in Manitoba; other provinces follow.

1916–1920: During this period approximately 1600 worker strikes were undertaken. Workers were requesting standards to be implemented that legally only allow for an eight-hour work day, that unions become recognized, and that wages be improved.

1919: The Winnipeg General Strike, consisting of 25 000 to 30 000 strikers, began May 15 and ended on June 26. During these few weeks two Canadian workers were killed and a few dozen others were injured.

1920: Amendments are made to Dominion Elections Act. Voting rights are extended to all except Aboriginal people and visible minorities. The vote is accorded to women federally; between 1916 and 1920, seven provinces also accord women the vote. PEI gave women the vote in 1922, followed by Quebec in 1939.

1927: Old Age Pension Act is introduced. It is federal, selective, and cost-shared with provinces.

1928: The Sexual Sterilization Act is passed in Alberta, forcing the sterilization of all those in mental institutions. The act was not repealed until 1972.

1929: Five Canadian women successfully sought legal recognition as persons under the British North America Act.

1930s: The Great Depression. In 1933, the national unemployment rate is 25 percent. Municipal governments face difficulties paying for Unemployment Relief; many go bankrupt. An uploading of responsibilities to higher levels of government occurs.

1937: The Rowell-Sirois Commission on dominion–provincial relations is established, releasing its report in 1940. The report examines the economic and financial basis of Confederation. It advocates greater taxing provisions for the federal government; a national system of Unemployment Insurance and pensions; and revenue transfers to provinces.

1939–1945: World War II—domestic conditions set the stage for the onset of a universal welfare state.

1940: Unemployment Insurance (1941–1996), a federal program resulting from constitutional amendment, is introduced.

1943: The Marsh Report, a wartime blueprint for a federal welfare state, is released.

1944: The Privy Council Act 1003, an emergency order by the federal government, in response to the growing number of strikers across the country, was passed in Parliament. The order further solidified in law the right for workers to organize, and ordered that businesses recognize the unions chosen by the majority of workers.

1944: Family Allowances (1944–1992), a universal program, is introduced.

1945: United Nations is created.

1946: Supreme Court Justice Ivan Rand rules that workers are obligated to pay union dues (known as the Rand Formula) regardless of status within the union. This, coupled with legislation similar to the Privy Council Act 1003 being passed in all provinces during 1946 and 1948, solidified the role of unions in negotiating labour standards and worker rights.

1948: Discriminatory sections that only provide voting rights based on race are repealed from the Dominion Elections Act.

1948: United Nations General Assembly passes the Universal Declaration of Human Rights.

1951:   The Old Age Security program becomes universal.

1954:   Ontario becomes the first government in Canada to establish that it is illegal to deny to any person service or accommodation by passing the Fair Accommodations Act. The other provinces would follow suit shortly thereafter.

1956:   The Hospital Insurance and Diagnostic Services Act sees the federal government agree to set up a plan in cooperation with the provinces, to provide hospital care for everyone.

1956:   The federal government passes the Female Employee Equal Pay Act, entitling women to equal pay as men for the same work.

1956:   The Canadian Labour Congress (1956–present) is formed by merging the Trade and Labour Congress of Canada and the Canadian Congress of Labour (1940–1956).

1960:   Aboriginal people are granted the right to vote in federal elections without giving up their treaty rights and entitlements first.

1960:   The federal government passes the Canadian Bill of Rights, which guaranteed such rights as freedom of the press, freedom of association and assembly, freedoms of speech and religion, equality rights before the law, and the right of the individual to life, liberty, security of the person, and enjoyment of property.

1962:   The Saskatchewan government of T.C. Douglas proposes the first medicare plan in North America (it had been announced in 1959 and was preceded by other initiatives from his government in 1947 covering hospital insurance). Medicare allows doctors to collect their fees only from the government.

1962:   The federal system of immigration selection begins to become more objective, yet individuals from European countries continue to be favoured in selection processes.

1966:   The Medical Care Act of the federal government extends health insurance to cover doctors' services. It is finally implemented in 1968 and it will take six years for all of the provinces to join. The Medical Care Insurance Act implements cost shared programs between the federal and provincial governments to finance provincially run health care programs.

1966:   The Canada Assistance Plan (CAP, 1966–1996), a cost-sharing agreement between the federal government and the provinces to split fifty–fifty the costs of provincially delivered education and social services, is introduced.

1966:   The Canada Pension Plan (CPP) and Quebec Pension Plan (QPP) are established. Intended to cover all working Canadians, the plans transfer income from workers to retired persons.

1966:   The Guaranteed Income Supplement (GIS), a supplement to Old Age Security for low-income earners, is introduced.

1967:   A points system is introduced to Canadian immigration in an effort to reduce the selection process's racial biases. Subsequent legislation further revises the immigration selection process.

1968:   The Employment Standards Act is introduced by the federal government. This act established a national labour code that set minimum wage standards ($1.25 per hour at this time), established the eight-hour work day and the 40-hour work week, and the entitlement to vacation time by employees.

1969:   The federal government's White Paper on Indian Affairs proposes the repeal of the Indian Act, the end of separate legal status for Aboriginal peoples, and conversion of reserve lands to private tenure. It is widely rejected by Aboriginal leaders, who begin a sustained campaign for separate constitutional and policy recognition.

1969:   Following the Royal Commission on Bilingualism and Biculturalism, the Official Languages Act is passed. This federal legislation recognizes English and French as official languages in the operations of all federal departments and agencies.

1971:   The federal government announces an official policy of multiculturalism. These principles are further elaborated in the 1988 Multiculturalism Act, among other policy documents.

1971:   The Unemployment Insurance program is considerably expanded in scope.

1971:   The Senate Committee on Poverty coincides with the creation of the National Council of Welfare and with more comprehensive publication of poverty data by Statistics Canada.

1973:   The Canadian Council on the Status of Women is established following the recommendations of a royal commission on the status of women.

1976:   The Coalition of Provincial Organizations of the Handicapped (COPOH) was formed (presently known as the Council of Canadians with Disabilities), acting as a national lobbying group to further the rights of people with disabilities in Canada.

1977:   The Established Programs Financing (EPF) Act, signalling changes to funding arrangements of the CAP and the Medical Care Act, is passed.

1977:   The Canada Human Rights Act is passed. An important inclusion of this legislation, which was missing from other human rights documents, was the disallowance of discrimination on the basis of a person's ability. Sexual orientation would not be amended into the act, as a ground to disallow discrimination, until 1996.

1981:   The Special Committee on the Disabled and the Handicapped pub-
         lished a report consisting of narratives about the barriers and obsta-
         cles that people with disabilities were facing in Canadian society.
         Policy outcomes developed from the recommendations in this report
         around improving the ways in which people with disabilities are
         integrated into Canadian society.

1982:   The Charter of Rights and Freedoms, expanding previous legisla-
         tion, provides individual rights and group rights to various com-
         munities in Canadian society. Marital status and sexual orientation
         have been recognized as categories for protection from discrimina-
         tion by the Supreme Court of Canada (*Miron v. Trudel* and *Egan v.
         Canada*, both in 1995), but presently have not been added to the
         Charter.

1982:   Mandatory retirement is abolished in Quebec, followed by Manitoba
         in 1983. This practice would not be recognized elsewhere in the
         country until the twenty-first century: Ontario, 2006; Saskatchewan,
         2007.

1984:   The federal government's Canada Health Act, outlining the conditions
         of universality—portability, public administration, comprehensive-
         ness, and accessibility—is passed.

1985:   The Indian Act is amended to eliminate discriminatory practices
         that were present in prior amended versions. For example, women
         no longer gained or lost their entitlement to register as a result of
         becoming married, and marriage of parents would no longer deter-
         mine the entitlement of a child. The concept of enfranchisement
         was removed from the Indian Act and all entitlements that had been
         a result of this policy were reinstated after application.

1989:   Changes to the income tax system make Old Age Security effec-
         tively a selective program. Over the 1980s and 1990s, other pro-
         grams are systematically eroded.

1992:   Family Allowances are abolished and replaced with selective child tax
         benefits.

1996:   Unemployment Insurance is replaced with Employment Insurance.
         Retrenchment of the terms/conditions of this program and others
         continues.

1996:   CAP and the funding arrangements for health care under EPF are
         replaced with the Canada Health and Social Transfer.

1998:   The National Child Benefit Supplement (NCB), which provides sup-
         plemental income to low-income families over and above the amount
         received through the Canada Child Tax Benefit, is introduced.

1999:   The federal government and the provinces join in a Social Union
         initiative to coordinate delivery of social and related programs.

2000:   In response to a 1999 Supreme Court of Canada decision regarding same-sex couples, legislation defining spouses to be opposite or same sex for Canada Pension Plan, Old Age Security, and other income security programs is introduced.

2002:   Superior Court of Ontario determines that disallowing same-sex marriages is discriminatory and unconstitutional in the *Halpern v. Canada* case (similar rulings are passed down from the courts in Quebec and British Columbia), but allots two years for the federal government to amend applicable legislation. The federal government later in the year appeals this decision in the Ontario Court of Appeal.

2003:   The Ontario Court of Appeal passes a ruling upholding the decision of the Superior Court of Ontario in *Halpern v. Canada*. Within this new decision, the Ontario Court of Appeal removes the interim period and states that the ruling will be effective immediately. An opposition motion to uphold the historic definition of marriage was defeated in the House of Commons.

2004:   The Canada Health and Social Transfer is divided into two separate transfer arrangements—the Canada Health Transfer (for health-related programs) and the Canada Social Transfer (for programs related to education, social services and support, and child development).

2005:   The equal marriage law (Bill C-38) was passed in the House of Commons, extending equal marriage rights for same-sex couples across all of Canada.

2006:   A motion is introduced and defeated in the House of Commons that would allow the government to vote again on Bill C-38, with the government's intention to repeal the law.

2006:   The Universal Child Care Benefit (UCCB) is introduced, and provides a monthly payment to the primary caregiver of a child under the age of six at a rate of $100 per month. The program is universal and is provided to all families with children meeting the age requirements regardless of financial need.

2007:   The Supreme Court of Canada issues a ruling on the case, *Health Services and Support – Facilities Subsector Bargaining Assn. v. British Columbia, 2007 SCC 27*, stipulating that collective bargaining is protected by the Canadian Charter of Rights and Freedoms.

Glossary

Aboriginal peoples: Native persons indigenous to Canada. Aboriginal communities consist of First Nations peoples (those Aboriginal peoples with treaty status), Métis (Aboriginal people who, following eighteenth- and nineteenth-century intermarriage of First Nations peoples with traders/settlers, founded distinct societies in Western Canada), and Inuit (Aboriginal peoples who live north of the tree line).

Alms: A historical term describing charity in cash or kind provided to the needy.

Block grant: A cash transfer provided by one level of government to another, the amount of the transfer being fixed independently of the purpose to which the funds are put. Also known as a general-purpose grant. Its opposite is a *specific-purpose grant*.

Breadwinner male: A term coined by scholars to describe the social construction of men as the principal income earners. Notions of the breadwinner male have had mutually reinforcing relationships with some social programs, but have been challenged by feminist thinking and some contemporary social programs. See also *women's domesticity*.

Canada Assistance Plan (CAP): Introduced in 1966, this program allowed provinces and the federal government to cost-share on a fifty–fifty basis education, health care, and social welfare services. Provinces administered these services and received federal money, subject to federal standards. The CAP gradually eroded during the latter part of the 1970s, 1980s, and 1990s, and was ultimately replaced in 1996 by the Canada Health and Social Transfer (CHST), with looser federal standards.

Canada Health Act: Federal legislation enacted in 1984 that reaffirms five principles of our universal health care system: its universality, comprehensiveness, accessibility, portability, and public administration.

Canada Pension Plan/Quebec Pension Plan (CPP/QPP): Both pension plans were introduced in 1966. The Canada Pension Plan applies to all working Canadians except for those in Quebec, which has its own contributory pension plan, the QPP. Both are publicly administered and are based on employees' workplace contributions.

Canadian Charter of Rights and Freedoms: The only Charter of Rights entrenched in the Canadian Constitution. It came into force in 1982.

Canadian Constitution: A body of fundamental principles and established precedents on which the Canadian state operates, and which determine legislative and administrative responsibilities among the three levels of government: federal, provincial, and municipal. Named the British North America Act in 1867, it was renamed the Constitution Act in 1982. Every law that is inconsistent with the Constitution is, to the extent of the inconsistency, of no force and effect.

Capitalism: An economic system in which the production and distribution of goods and services are controlled through private ownership and open competition.

Collectivism: A world view wherein the rights and welfare of the group or society are placed above those of the individual.

Comparative needs: Needs that are determined by comparing one individual or group to another.

Conditional grant: A transfer of money from one level of government to another, and tied directly to an expected type of service delivery. The Canada Assistance Plan (1966–96) is an example of a conditional grant. CAP provided federal transfers to provincial governments to cover the latter's delivery of health, education, and social services.

Consumer Price Index (CPI): An economic measurement consisting of a typical and predetermined "basket" of consumer items, from which analysts may measure and compare changes in inflation over time.

Debt: A cumulative, multi-year calculation based on the total amount of money that is owed.

Deficit: A yearly calculation based on annual operating costs. It occurs when spending exceeds revenue.

Detached ideology: Those political values that create policy choices that are made strictly in accordance with one's values, regardless of the outcome and consequences to others.

Dictatorship of the proletariat: According to Marxist theory, the control of communist parties that begins immediately following a revolution. Marxist theory projects the dictatorship as ending with the development of a classless society.

Diversity: A concept that conveys differences between people on the basis of age, culture, ethnicity, gender, nationality, race, range of ability, religion, and sexual orientation, among other social factors.

Egalitarianism: A world view that values human equality politically, socially, and economically.

Elitism: A world view that sees society organized around groups that are unequal in power and resources.

Employment Insurance (EI): Formerly Unemployment Insurance (introduced 1940), this publicly administered, universal, employment-based contributory insurance program was initially intended to provide for the hazards of temporary unemployment, but has been expanded to include other reasons for temporary cessation of work, including maternity and parental benefits. Renamed Employment Insurance in 1996.

Equalization payment: Also known as an unconditional grant, an equalization payment is a transfer of money from one level of government to another; no particular commitment by the recipient government to tie the grant to an expected type of expenditure is required. Its opposite is a *conditional grant*.

Expressed needs: Needs that are communicated to others.

Family Allowance (FA): A universal program, introduced in 1944 and withdrawn in 1992, that provided mothers a monthly payment for each child under their care. In 1992, the universal FA program was replaced by a refundable, income-tested (i.e., selective) tax credit.

Federal system of government: In this type of system, political power is divided between the national and provincial governments. Canada is a federal system. Most countries are unitary, meaning political power is centralized in one national level of government.

Felt needs: Needs that are defined on a personal or subjective level.

Fiscal capacity: A particular level of government's ability to change the total or composition of its revenues (e.g., taxes) or expenditures (e.g., a social program).

Globalization: A current, pervasive trend of international finance, ideology, and political arrangements. As a result of globalization, money is invested quickly and easily across national borders. Principles of transnational competition for lucrative markets and inexpensive labour are actively pursued. In the absence of powerfully constraining national legislation or intra-national structures, multinational corporations have growing sovereignty to pursue their objectives.

Grand issues of social policy: Those issues relating to the fundamental structures of political–economic life. Examples include distribution of income and wealth, political power, and corporate prerogatives. Grand issues are contrasted with ordinary issues of social policy.

Gross domestic product (GDP): A measurement of a country's economic productivity over time.

Horizontal imbalance: An unequal relationship in fiscal capacity between richer and poorer provinces.

Human rights: Those legal, social, and political entitlements that are justly claimed to belong to any individual in society. These include, but are not restricted to, the right to justice, equality of opportunity, and religious freedom.

Ideology: A pattern of ideas based on experiences, values, and beliefs, and profoundly influencing one's political views. Ideologies shape, organize, and justify a course of action, and are used to legitimize the power held by the active political party.

Individualism: A world view wherein freedom, worth, and self-determination are foremost attributed to the individual rather than a group.

Intergovernmental finance: The web of financial movement that links governments in a federal system.

Low income cut-off (LICO): A relative measure of *poverty* and the standard *poverty line* (see below) used by the federal government since 1959. It is calculated based on information from a survey of family spending patterns conducted by Statistics Canada.

Means of production: According to Marxist theory, the land, labour, and capital that are used by a society to produce material goods.

Normative needs: Needs that are determined by someone other than the individual by applying some benchmark or standard to the individual case.

Old Age Security (OAS): Introduced as a selective, means-tested program in 1927, Old Age Security was transformed into a universal program in 1952, providing all Canadian senior citizens a monthly income. The introduction in the late 1980s of income tax "claw-backs" for individuals and couples having or surpassing a particular net income has called into question whether OAS may truly be considered a universal program today.

Operating principles: The policy results that occur when various social ideals are integrated with a practicable rule of application.

Ordinary issues of social policy: Those policy issues that directly affect the lives of people in a community and the technical operating principles of direct social work intervention. These are often managed and redressed by community-based organizations, and are sometimes the unintended consequence of earlier reforms. Examples include how child welfare service organizations are structurally administered, or the deinstitutionalization and development of community support programs. Ordinary issues of social policy are contrasted with grand issues.

Poverty: A state of deficiency in money or in the means of subsistence.

Poverty gap: How far below a particular *poverty line* (such as the *low income cut-off*, or *LICO*, above) one's income falls. If the poverty line is $15 020/year, and one's income is $13 020, then the poverty gap would be $2000.

Poverty line: A measure representing a minimal level of human need. An absolute poverty line presumes that there is some fairly objective means for determining the absolute minimum an individual or household requires for food, shelter, clothing, and any other physical necessities. A relative poverty line assumes that poverty is to be defined relative to prevailing community standards, as opposed to absolute criteria.

Power: In social policy, power refers to the capacity to alter policies and decisions.

Principle of affected interest: A principle of social policy relating to community or citizen participation, and affirming that anyone who is affected by the decisions of a government should have a right to participate in that government.

Proletariat: According to Marxist theory, the proletariat consists of individuals and families who are members of the working class, particularly manual and industrial labourers.

Public policies: Legislated acts, regulations, and by-laws (including all associated policies in the ministerial, agency, and public arenas) at the federal, provincial, and municipal levels of government.

Selective programs: Social welfare programs implemented on the basis of assessed need. Eligibility for benefits is determined through means testing. Selective programs are distinct from *universal programs*.

Social assistance: An income security program that uses a "means" or "needs" test to determine eligibility.

Social insurance: An income security program in which eligibility for benefits is determined on the basis of a record of contribution and the occurrence of a foreseen contingency, such as injury, retirement, unemployment, or the death of an income-earning spouse.

Social policy: The statements of the selected social goals and objectives to which a group—be it professional, governmental, or private—is committed.

Social welfare: A complex network of personal relationships, institutions, policies, and services that a society creates in order to contribute to the well-being, or welfare, of its members.

Specific purpose grant: A cash transfer provided by one level of government to another. The amount of the transfer is tied to its intended purpose; an example would be a matched or shared-cost program. Its opposite is a *block grant*.

Standard of living: A term denoting the necessities and luxuries required for living in a particular circumstance.

Sustainability: An economic, political, and environmental world view that promotes present and future generations of stewardship of the physical world.

Universal programs: Social welfare programs based on national and categorical membership. These programs are available to all persons regardless of need. They are distinct from *selective programs*.

Vertical imbalance: An unequal relationship in fiscal capacity between the federal and a provincial government.

Welfare state: A term coined by the Archbishop of Canterbury during World War II to describe those governments, such as Canada's, that were committing themselves to the use of resources and to the development of social policies for the collective well-being of all.

Women's caring: A term coined by scholars to describe the social construction of women as principal caregivers in family and social relationships.

Women's domesticity: A term coined by scholars to describe the social construction of women in the domestic or home realm—daughters, mothers, wives, or widows. This term contrasts with the gendered social construction that encouraged men to take on economic, political, and social activities outside of the home. See also *breadwinner male*.

World view: An outlook drawn from religious, political, social, and physical information about humans and the societies they create.

References

Adams, R. (2002). *Social policy for social work*. Houndmills, Basingstoke, Hampshire UK: Palgrave Macmillan.

Allen, R. (1971). *The social passion. Religion and social reform in Canada, 1914–1928*. Toronto: University of Toronto Press.

Amernic, J., & Craig, R. (2006). *CEO speak*. Montreal: McGill-Queen's University Press.

Anderson, G., & Marr, W. (1987). Immigration and social policy. In S. Yelaga (Ed.), *Canadian social policy* (Rev. ed.) (pp. 88–114). Waterloo, ON: Wilfrid Laurier University Press.

Anderson, J.E. (1990). *Public policymaking*. Boston: Houghton Mifflin.

Armitage, A. (1996). *Social welfare in Canada revisited: Facing up to the future*. (3rd ed.). Don Mills, ON: Oxford University Press.

Armitage, A. (2003). *Social welfare in Canada*. (4th ed.). Oxford: Oxford University Press.

Aronowitz, S. (1992). *The politics of identity: Class, culture, social movements*. New York: Routledge.

Artibese, A.F.J., & Stelter, G.A. (1985). Urbanization. *The Canadian encyclopedia* (Vol. 3, p. 1887). Edmonton: Hurtig.

Babbie, E. (1977). *Society by agreement*. Belmont, CA: Wadsworth.

Babbie, E. (1986). *Observing ourselves: Essays in social research*. Belmont, CA: Wadsworth.

Bailey, R., & Brake, M. (Eds.). (1975). *Radical social work*. London: Edward Arnold.

Baines, C., Evans, P., & Neysmith, S. (1998). *Women's caring: Feminist perspectives on social welfare*. (2nd ed.). Toronto: Oxford University Press.

Bakan, J. (1997). *Just words: Constitutional rights and social wrongs*. Toronto: University of Toronto Press.

Bakan, J. (2004). *The corporation: The pathological pursuit of profit and power*. New York: Simon and Schuster.

Baker, M. (1995). *Canadian family policies: Cross national comparisons*. Toronto: University of Toronto Press.

Ball, O., & Gready, P. (2006). *The no-nonsense guide to human rights*. Toronto: New Internationalist Publications.

Banks, K., & Mangan, M. (1999). *The company of neighbours: Revitalizing community through action-research*. Toronto: University of Toronto Press.

Bannock, G., Baxter, R.E., & Davis, E. (Eds.). (1998a). *The Penguin dictionary of economics*. Retrieved June 6, 2007, from: http://www.xreferplus.com. ezproxy.lib.ucalgary.ca/entry/445411

Bannock, G., Baxter, R.E., & Davis, E. (1998b). In *The Penguin dictionary of economics*. Retrieved June 6, 2007, from: http://www.xreferplus.com. ezproxy.lib.ucalgary.ca/entry/445417

Banting, K.G. (1985). Institutional conservatism: Federalism and pension reform. In J.S. Ismael (Ed.), *Canadian social welfare policy: Federal and provincial dimensions* (pp. 48–74). Kingston/Montreal: McGill-Queen's University Press.

Barata, P. (2000). *Social exclusion in Europe: Survey of literature*. Unpublished paper. Toronto: Laidlaw Foundation.

Barker, J. (1999). *Street-level democracy: Political settings at the margins of global power*. Toronto: Between the Lines.

Barker, R.L. (1991). *The social work dictionary*. Washington, DC: National Association of Social Workers.

Barlow, M., & Clarke, T. (2001). *Global showdown: How the new activists are fighting global corporate rule*. Toronto: Stoddart.

Barter, K. (1996). Collaboration: A framework for northern practice. In R. Delaney, K. Brownlee, and K.M. Zapf (Eds.), *Issues in northern social work practice* (pp. 72–94). Thunder Bay: Centre for Northern Studies.

Battle, K. (1993). *Federal social programs: Setting the record straight.* Ottawa: Caledon Institute of Social Policy.

Battle, K. (2001). *Relentless incrementalism: Deconstructing and reconstructing Canadian income security policy.* Ottawa: Caledon Institute of Social Policy.

Battle, K. (2002). *Social policy that works: An agenda.* Ottawa: Caledon Institute of Social Policy.

Battle, K., & Mendelson, M. (1997). *Child benefit reform in Canada: An evaluative framework and future directions.* Ottawa: Caledon Institute of Social Policy.

Beach, C.M., Green, A.G., & Reitz, J.G. (Eds.) (2004). *Canadian immigration policy for the 21st century.* Montreal: McGill-Queen's University Press.

Beauchesne, E. (2004). Family tax burden at 47% and climbing. *Montreal Gazette,* February 5, B1.

Berkowitz, I. (1980). Social choice and policy formulation: Problems and considerations in the construction of the public interest. *Journal of Sociology and Social Welfare, 16*(2), 533–545.

Berman, M. (2000). *Wandering God: A study in nomadic spirituality.* Albany: State University of New York Press.

Bickenbach, J.E. (1993). *Physical disability and social policy.* Toronto: University of Toronto Press.

Bickenbach, J.E., Chatterji, S., Badley, E.M., & Ustün, T.B. (1999). Models of disablement, universalism and the international classification of impairments, disabilities and handicaps. *Social Science and Medicine, 48*(9), 1173–1187.

Bishop, A. (1994). *Becoming an ally: Breaking the cycle of oppression.* Halifax: Fernwood.

Bishop, A. (2002). *Becoming an ally: Breaking the cycle of oppression.* (2nd ed.). Halifax: Fernwood.

Bishop, A. (2005). *Beyond token change: Breaking the cycle of oppressive institutions.* Halifax: Fernwood.

Bissoondath, N. (1994). *Selling illusions: The cult of multiculturalism in Canada.* Toronto: Penguin.

Blackburn, R. (2002). *Banking on death, or investing in life: The history and future of pensions.* London: Verso.

Blake, R., Bryden, P., & Strain, F. (Eds.). (1997). *The welfare state in Canada: Past, present, and future.* Concord, ON: Irwin.

Bobbitt, P. (2002). *The Shield of Achilles: War, peace, and the course of history.* New York: Anchor Books.

Bopp, J., Bopp, M., Brown, L., & Lane, P. (1985). *The sacred tree.* Lethbridge: Four Worlds Development Press.

Bourgeault, R. (1988). Race and class under mercantilism: Indigenous people in nineteenth-century Canada. In B. Bolaria and P. Li (Eds.), *Racial oppression in Canada* (2nd ed.), 41–70. Toronto: Garamond Press.

Boychuk, G.W. (1998). *Patchworks of purpose: The development of provincial social assistance regimes in Canada.* Kingston/Montreal: McGill–Queen's University Press.

Brager, G., Specht, H., & Torczyner, J. (1987). *Community organizing.* New York: Columbia University Press.

Braybrooke, D., & Lindblom, C.E. (1963). *The strategy of decision.* New York: Free Press.

Broad, D., & Antony, W. (1999). *Citizens or consumers? Social policy in a market society.* Halifax: Fernwood.

Bruce, M. (1961). *The coming of the welfare state.* London: B.T. Batsford.

Burns, T.J., Batavia, A.I., & DeJong, G. (1994). The health insurance work disincentive for persons with disabilities. *Research in the Sociology of Health Care, 11,* 57–68.

Callahan, M. (2004). Chalk and cheese: Feminist thinking and policy-making. In B. Wharf and B. McKenzie (Eds.), *Connecting policy to practice in the human services* (2nd ed.), 128–140. Don Mills, ON: Oxford University Press.

Campaign 2000 (2007). *Raising the falling fortunes of young families of Canada.* Toronto: Family Service Association of Toronto.

Canada (1966). *Canada assistance plan.* Ottawa: Queen's Printer (Repealed in 1995).

Canada (1984). *The health act.* Ottawa: Queen's Printer.

Canada (1985, 1995). *Federal–provincial fiscal arrangements act.* Ottawa: Queen's Printer.

Canada (1997). *Canada health and social transfer regulations.* Ottawa: Queen's Printer.

Canadian Council on Social Development (1991). *Social policy in the 1990s: The challenge.* Ottawa/Montreal: CCSD.

Canadian Council on Social Development (2002). *2002 Poverty Lines.* Retrieved May 15, 2007, from: www.ccds.ca/factsheets/fs_lic02.htm

Cannadine, D. (2006). *Mellon: An American life.* New York: Allen Lane.

Caragata, L. (1997). How should social work respond? Deconstructing practice in mean times. *Canadian Social Work Review, 14*(2), 139–154.

Careless, J.M.S. (1954). Frontierism, metropolitanism, and Canadian history. *Canadian Historical Review, 35,* 1–21.

Carniol, B. (1987). *Case critical: Challenging social work in Canada.* (2nd ed.). Toronto: Between the Lines.

Carniol, B. (1995). *Case critical: Challenging social work in Canada.* (3rd ed.). Toronto: Between the Lines.

Carty, R.K., Cross, W., & Young, L. (2000). *Rebuilding Canadian party politics.* Vancouver: University of British Columbia Press.

Cassidy, F. (Ed.) (1991). *Aboriginal self-determination.* The Institute for Research on Public Policy and Oolichan Books.

CASSW (1996). *The manual of standards and procedures for the accreditation of Canadian programs of social work education.* Ottawa: Author.

Castellano, M. (2002). *Aboriginal family trends: Extended families, nuclear families, families of the heart.* The Vanier Institute of the Family.

Central Intelligence Agency (2007). *The world fact book, 2007.* Washington: Author. Retrieved June 5, 2007, from: https://www.cia.gov/library/publications/the-world-factbook/

Chamberlin, J. (1997). A working definition of empowerment. *Psychiatric Rehabilitation Journal, 20*(4), 43–46.

Chappell, R. (1997). *Social welfare in Canadian society.* Scarborough, ON: International Thomson Publishing.

Chappell, R. (2006). *Social welfare in Canadian society.* (3rd ed.). Toronto, ON: Nelson Thomson Learning.

Chapin, R.K. (1995). Social policy development: The strengths perspective. *Social Work, 40*(4), 506–514.

Cheal, D. (2002). (Ed.). *Aging and demographic change in Canadian context.* Toronto: University of Toronto Press.

Chomsky, N. (1991). *Deterring democracy.* London: Verso.

Chouinard, V., & Crooks, V. (2005). "Because *they* have all the power and I have none": State restructuring of income and employment supports and disabled women's lives in Ontario, Canada. *Disability and Society, 20*(1), 19–32.

Christensen, C. (1995). Immigrants and minorities in Canada. In J. Turner and F. Turner (Eds.). *Social welfare in Canada* (3rd ed.), 179–212. Scarborough, ON: Allyn and Bacon Canada.

Christian, W., & Campbell, C. (1990). *Political parties and ideologies in Canada.* (3rd ed.). Toronto: McGraw-Hill Ryerson Ltd.

Chui, T. (1996). *Canada's population: Charting into the 21st century.* Catalogue No: 11-008-XPE. Ottawa: Statistics Canada.

Citizenship and Immigration Canada (2005). *Facts and figures 2005.* Ottawa: Author. Retrieved from: www.cic.gc.ca/english/pub/facts2005

Clarke, T. (1997). *Silent coup: Confronting the big business takeover of Canada.* Ottawa: Canadian Centre for Policy Initiatives & Toronto: James Lorimer & Co.

Cohen, E. (2006). Why have children? *Commentary Magazine,* June, 44–49.

Commissioner of the Environment and Sustainable Development (2006). *2006 Report of the commissioner of the environment and sustainable development.* Ottawa: Office of the Auditor General of Canada. Retrieved May 15, 2007, from: http://www.oag-bvg.gc.ca/domino/reports.nsf/html/c2006menu_e.html

Cooke, M. (2003). The Canada Pension Plan goes to market. *Canadian Review of Social Policy, 51,* 126–131.

Copp, T. (1974). *The anatomy of poverty: The conditions of the working class in Montreal, 1897–1929.* Toronto: McClelland and Stewart.

Cossman, B. (1996). Same-sex couples and the politics of family status. In J. Brodie (Ed.). *Women and Canadian public policy.* Toronto: Harcourt Brace and Company.

Dare, B. (1997). Harris' first year: Attacks and resistance. In D. Ralph, A. Regimbald, and N. St-Amand (Eds.), *Open for business, closed to people.* (pp. 20–26). Halifax: Fernwood.

Davies, J.B., Sandstrom, S., Shorrocks, A., & Wolff, E.N. (2006). *The world distribution of household wealth.* Retrieved June 12, 2007, from: http://www.wider.unu.edu/research/2006-2007/2006-2007-1/wider-wdhw-launch-5-12-2006/wider-wdhw-press-release-5-12-2006.htm

Deffeyes, K.S. (2006). *Beyond oil: The view from Hubbert's Peek.* New York: Hill and Wang.

Delaney, R. (1995). The philosophical base. In J. Turner and F. Turner (Eds.), *Canadian social welfare* (3rd ed.) (pp. 12–27). Scarborough, ON: Allyn and Bacon Canada.

Delaney, R., & Brownlee, K. (Eds.). (1995). *Northern social work practice.* Thunder Bay: Lakehead University Centre for Northern Studies.

Delaney, R., Brownlee, K., & Graham, J.R. (Eds.). (1997). *Strategies in northern social work practice.* Thunder Bay: Centre for Northern Studies.

Delaney, R., Brownlee, K., & Sellick, M. (Eds.). (1999). *Social work with rural and northern communities.* Thunder Bay: Lakehead University Centre for Northern Studies.

Delaney, R., Brownlee, K., & Sellick, M. (2001). Surviving globalization: Empowering rural and remote communities in Canada's provincial norths. *Australian Rural Social Work, 6(3),* 4–11.

Delaney, R., Brownlee, K., & Zapf, K.M. (Eds.). (1996). *Issues in northern social work practice.* Thunder Bay: Centre for Northern Studies.

Department of Canadian Heritage. (August 9, 2000). *A graphic overview of diversity in Canada.* Retrieved from: www.pch.gc.ca/multi/assets/ ppt/jed-site_e.ppt

Department of Canadian Heritage. (2006). *Multiculturalism program: Annual report, 2005-06.* Ottawa: Author. Retrieved from: www.pch.gc.ca

Department of Finance Canada (2006). *The economic and fiscal update 2006.* Ottawa: Public Works and Government Services Canada. Retrieved: http://www.fin.gc.ca/budtoce/2006/ec06_e.html

Department of Finance Canada (2007a). *Federal transfer payments to provinces and territories.* Ottawa: Author. Retrieved on May 10, 2007, from: www.fin.gc.ca/FEDPROV/mtpe.html

Department of Finance Canada (2007b). *Restoring fiscal balance for a stronger federation.* Ottawa: Author. Retrieved May 10, 2007, from: http://www.budget.gc.ca/2007/bp/bpc4e.html# equalization

Department of Finance Canada (2007c). *Budget 2007: A stronger, safer, better Canada.* Ottawa: Author. Retrieved May 13, 2007, from: http://www.budget.gc.ca/2007/themes/bkrfbse.html

de Schweinitz, K. (1943). *England's road to social security.* Philadelphia: University of Pennsylvania Press.

Desert, G. (1976). Une source historique trop oublié: Les archives hospitaliers. *Gazette des Archives, 94,* 145–164.

Diamond, J. (2005). *Collapse: How societies choose to fail or succeed.* New York: Viking Books.

Doern, B., & Aucoin, P. (Eds.). (1971). *The structures of policy-making in Canada.* Toronto: Macmillan.

Dolgoff, R., & Feldstein, D. (1984). *Understanding social welfare.* (2nd ed.). London: Longman.

Dominelli, L. (1988). *Anti-racist social work*. London: Macmillan.

Dominelli, L. (1997). *Sociology for social work*. London: Macmillan.

Dominelli, L., & McLeod, E. (1989). *Feminist social work*. London: Macmillan.

Drover, G. (1988). Social work. In *The Canadian encyclopedia* (pp. 2034–2035). Edmonton: Hurtig.

Drover, G. (2000). Redefining social citizenship in a global era. *Canadian Social Work Review*, 17 (special issue on social work and globalization), 29–49.

Easterbrook, W.T., & Aitken, H.G.J. (1956). *Canadian economic history*. Toronto: Macmillan.

Egale. (2006). *Equal marriage backgrounder*. Retrieved May 4, 2007, from www.egale.ca

Eichler, M. (1987). Social policy concerning women. In S. Yelaga (Ed.), *Canadian social policy* (Rev. ed.) (pp.139–156). Waterloo, ON: Wilfrid Laurier University Press.

Ellwood, W. (2006). *The no-nonsense guide to globalization*. Toronto: New Internationalist Publications.

Emery, J.C.H. & Emery, G. (1999). *A young man's benefit: The Independent Order of Odd Fellows and sickness insurance in the United States and Canada, 1860–1929*. Montreal: McGill–Queen's University Press.

Esping-Anderson, G. (1990). *The three worlds of welfare capitalism*. Cambridge, UK: Polity Press.

Etzioni, A. (1968). *The active society*. New York: The Free Press.

Etzioni, A. (1975). *A comparative analysis of complex organizations*. (2nd ed.). New York: Free Press.

Evans, P. (1995). Women and social welfare: Exploring the connections. In J.C. Turner and F. Turner (Eds.), *Canadian social welfare* (3rd ed.) (pp.150–64). Scarborough, ON: Allyn and Bacon Canada.

Evans, P. (1997). Divided citizenship? Gender, income security, and the welfare state. In P. Evans and G. Wekerle (Eds.), *Women and the Canadian welfare state:*

Challenges and change (pp. 91–116). Toronto: University of Toronto Press.

Evans, P., Jacobs, L., Noel, A., & Reynolds, E. (1995). *Workfare: Does it work? Is it fair?* Montreal: Institute for Research on Public Policy.

Federal/Provincial/Territorial Ministerial Council on Social Policy Renewal (2003). *Three year review: Social union framework agreement*. Ottawa: Social Development Canada. Retrieved May 13, 2007, from: http://socialunion.gc.ca/menu_e.html

Federico, R. (1983). *The social welfare institution*. (4th ed.). Toronto: D.C. Heath.

Feehan, K., & Hannis, D. (Eds.). (1993). *From strength to strength: Social work education and Aboriginal people*. Edmonton: Grant MacEwan Community College.

Fingard, J. (1989). *The dark side of life in Victorian Halifax*. Porters Lake, NS: Pottersfield Press.

Finkel, A. (2006). *Social policy and practice in Canada: A history*. Waterloo: Wilfrid Laurier University Press.

Finlayson, A. (1996). *Naming Rumpelstiltskin: Who will profit and who will lose in the workplace of the 21st century*. Toronto: Key Porter Books.

Flannery, T. (2006). *The weather makers: The history and future impact of climate change*. Berkeley: Atlantic Monthly Press.

Florini, A.M. (2000). *Third force: The rise of transnational civil society*. Washington D.C.: Carnegie Endowment for International Peace.

Flynn, J.P. (1992). *Social agency policy*. (2nd ed.). Chicago: Nelson-Hall.

Forster, M. & d'Ercole, M.M. (2005). *Income distribution and poverty in OECD countries in the second half of the 1990's*. Paris: OECD Publications.

Foucault, M. (1972). *Power/knowledge: Selected interviews and other writings*. NY: Pantheon Books.

Frankl, V. (1969). *The will to meaning*. Scarborough: Plume.

Fraser, N. (1989). *Unruly practices: Power, discourse and gender in contemporary social theory*. Minneapolis: University of Minneapolis Press.

Fraser, N. (1995). From redistribution to recognition? Dilemmas of justice in a 'post-socialist' age. *New Left Review, 212,* 68–93.

Fraser, N., & Honneth, A. (2003). *From redistribution to recognition? A political-philosophical exchange.* London: Verso.

Freeman, H., & Sherwood, C. (1970). *Social research and social policy.* Englewood Cliffs, NJ: Prentice-Hall.

Freiler, C. (2000). *Social inclusion as a focus of well-being for children and families.* Unpublished paper. Toronto: Laidlaw Foundation.

Freiler, C., & Cerny, J. (1998). *Benefiting Canada's children: Perspectives on gender and social responsibility.* Ottawa: Status of Women Canada.

Freire, P. (1968). *Pedagogy of the oppressed.* New York: Seabury Press.

Freire, P. (1985). *The politics of education: Culture, power and liberation.* South Hadley, MA: Bergin and Garvey.

Freire, P. (1994). *Pedagogy of hope.* New York: Continuum.

Frideres, J. S., & Gadacz, R. R. (2005). Aboriginal peoples in Canada. (7th ed.). Toronto: Pearson Prentice Hall.

Fromm, E. (1955). *The sane society.* Greenwich: Fawcett.

Fromm, E. (1967). The psychological aspects of the guaranteed income. In R. Theobald (Ed.), *The guaranteed income* (pp. 183–193). Garden City: Anchor.

Fukuyama, F. (1992). *The end of history and the last man.* New York: Avon Books.

Galabuzi, G.E. (2006). *Canada's economic apartheid: The social exclusion of racialized groups in the new century.* Toronto: Canadian Scholars Press.

Galbraith, J.K. (1983). *The anatomy of power.* Boston: Houghton Mifflin.

Galper, J. (1975). *The politics of social services.* Englewood Cliffs, NJ: Prentice-Hall.

Galster, G. (1996). *Reality and research: Social science and U.S. urban policy since 1960.* Washington: Urban Institute Press.

George, U. (2006). Immigration and refugee policy in Canada: Past, present and future. In A. Westhughes (Ed.), *Canadian social policy: Issues and*

perspectives (4th ed.) (pp. 349–374). Waterloo ON: Wilfrid Laurier Press.

Germain, C., & Gitterman, A. (1980). *Social work practice, people and environments: An ecological perspective.* New York: Columbia University Press.

Germain, C., & Gitterman, A. (1996). *The life model of social work practice: Advances in theory and practice.* New York: Columbia University Press.

Gil, D. (1970). A systematic approach to social policy analysis. *Social Service Review, 44*(4), 411–426.

Gil, D. (1990). Implications for conservative tendencies for practice and education in social welfare. *Journal of Sociology and Social Welfare, XVII*(2). n.p.

Gil, D. (1992). *Unravelling social policy* (rev. 5th ed.). Rochester: Schenkman Books.

Gil, D. (1998). *Confronting injustice and oppression: Concepts and strategies for social workers.* New York: Columbia University Press.

Gilbert, N., & Specht, H. (1974). *Dimensions of social welfare policy.* Englewood Cliffs, NJ: Prentice Hall.

Giugni, M. (1999). Introduction: How social movements matter. Past research, present problems, future developments. In M. Giugni, D. McAdan, and C. Tilly (Eds.), *How social movements matter* (pp. iii–xxxiii). Minneapolis: University of Minnesota Press.

Globe and Mail, The (February 13, 1995). Fair taxes, not more taxes, A12.

Globe and Mail, The (February 10, 2005). A better way to share, A23.

Globe and Mail, The (July 4, 2006). Some provinces are more equal than others, A12.

Gonthier, N. (1978). Dans le Lyon medival: Vie et mort d'un pauvre. *Cahiers d'Histoire, 23*(3), 335–347.

Good-Gingrich, L. (2003). Theorizing social exclusion: Determinants, mechanisms, dimensions, forms and acts of resistance. In W. Shera (Ed.), *Emerging perspectives on anti-oppressive practice* (pp. 3–23). Toronto: Canadian Scholars' Press Inc.

Gordon, L. (1990). The new feminist scholarship on the welfare state. In L. Gordon (Ed.), *Women, the state and* welfare (pp. 9–35). Madison: University of Wisconsin Press.

Gormley. W.T. (2007). Public policy analysis: Ideas and impacts. *Annual Review of Political Science, 10,* 297–313.

Government of Alberta (2002). *A framework for reform: Report of the Premier's Advisory Council on Health.* Edmonton: Author.

Government of Alberta (2007a). Budget 2007: Managing our growth. Edmonton: Author. Retrieved on May 10, 2007, from: www.gov.ab.ca/budget2007/

Government of Alberta. (2007b). *Alberta Workers' Compensation Board.* Accessed at http://www.wcb.ab.ca/pdfs/wage_loss.pdf

Government of Canada. (2007). *Citizenship and Immigration Canada website.* Accessed at http://www.cic.gc.ca/english/refugees/asylum-1.html#convention

Government of Ontario. (2007a). *Ontario guaranteed annual income system (GAINS).* Accessed at www.trd.fin.gov.on.ca/English/tax/credit/gains

Government of Ontario. (2007b). *Ontario workplace safety and insurance board.* Accessed at http://www.wsib.on.ca/wsib/wsibsite.nsf/public/BenefitsLOE

Government of Saskatchewan. (2007). *Saskatchewan income plan.* Accessed at www.dcre.gov.sk.ca/financial/SIPoverview.html

Graham, J.R. (1992). The Haven, 1878–1930. A Toronto charity's transition from a religious to a professional ethos. *Histoire Sociale/Social History, 25*(50), 283–306.

Graham, J.R. (1995). Lessons for today: Canadian municipalities and Unemployment Relief during the 1930s Great Depression. *Canadian Review of Social Policy, 35,* 1–18.

Graham, J.R. (1996a). *A history of the University of Toronto School of Social Work, 1914–1970,* PhD dissertation, University of Toronto.

Graham, J.R. (1996b). A practical idealism: A theoretical values conception for northern social work practice. In R. Delaney, K. Brownlee, and J.R. Graham (Eds.), *Strategies in northern social work practice* (pp. 95–103). Thunder Bay: Centre for Northern Studies.

Graham, J.R. (1996c). An analysis of Canadian social welfare historical writing. *Social Service Review, 70*(1), 140–58.

Graham, J.R. (2008a). Canadian approaches to income security. In J.C. Turner and F.J. Turner (Eds.), *Canadian social welfare* (6th ed.) (pp. 276–293). Toronto: Prentice Hall.

Graham, J.R. (in press, 2008b). Who am I? An essay on inclusion and spiritual growth through community and mutual appreciation. *Journal of Religion, Spirituality, and Social Work, 27.*

Graham, J.R., & Barter, K. (1999). Collaboration: A social work practice method. *Families in Society: The Journal of Contemporary Human Services, 80*(1), 6–13.

Graham, J.R., Kline, T.J.B., Trew, J.L., & Schmidt, J.A. (in press, 2008). Influences on the subjective well-being of practicing social workers. *Canadian Social Work.*

Gramsci, A. (1971). *Prison notebooks.* New York: International Publishers.

Grant, G. (1965). *Lament for a nation: The defeat of Canadian nationalism.* Toronto: Anansi.

Grant, G. (1969). *Technology and empire: Perspectives on North America.* Toronto: Anansi.

Greenaway, N. (2004). Fewer Canadians on welfare: Study. *The Globe and Mail,* August 20, A9.

Grob, G. (1992). How policy is made and how evaluators can affect it. *Evaluation-Practice, 13*(3), 175–183.

Guest, D. (1997). *The emergence of social security in Canada.* (3rd ed.). Vancouver: University of British Columbia Press.

Guillemette, Y. (2003). Slowing down with age: The ominous implications of workforce aging for Canadian living standards. *C.D. Howe Institute Commentary, 182.* Retrieved May 15, 2007, from: www.cdhowe.org

Guillemette, Y., & Robson, W.B.P. (2006). *No elixir of youth: Immigration cannot keep Canada young.* C.D. Howe Institute Backgrounder 96. Toronto: CD Howe Institute.

Gwyn, R. (1995). *Nationalism without walls: The unbearable lightness of being Canadian*. Toronto: McClelland and Stewart.

Haber, A., & Runyon, R. (1986). *Fundamentals of psychology*. (4th ed.). New York: McGraw-Hill Company.

Hage, J., & Hollingsworth, J.R. (1977). The first steps toward the integration of social theory and social policy. *Annals of the American Academy of Political and Social Science, 434,* 1–23.

Hall, M.H., de Wit, M.L., Lasby, D., McIver, D., Evers, T., Johnston, C., et al. (2004). *Cornerstones of community: Highlights of the national survey of non-profit and voluntary organizations*. Ottawa: Minister of Industry.

Hamdad, M., Joyal, S., & Van Rompaey, C. (2004). *Satellite account of non-profit institutions and volunteering: 1997 to 1999*. Ottawa: Minister of Industry.

Handler, J. (1979). *Protecting the social service client: Legal and structural controls on official discretion*. New York: Academic Press.

Handler, J.F., & Hasenfeld, Y. (1991). *The moral construction of poverty: Welfare reform in America*. Newbury Park, CA: Sage.

Hansen, P. (1999). The welfare state as political community. In D. Broad and W. Antony (Eds.). *Citizens or consumers? Social policy in a market society* (pp. 314–321). Halifax: Fernwood Publishing.

Hargrove, B. (1999). Unions and social policy: Confronting a challenging future. In D. Broad and W. Antony (Eds.), *Citizens or consumers? Social policy in a market society* (pp. 73–82). Halifax: Fernwood Publishing.

Haskins, R., & Gallagher, J.J. (1981). *Models for analysis of social policy*. Norwood, NJ: ABLEX Publishing Corporation.

Heisz, A. (2007). *Income inequality and redistribution in Canada: 1976 to 2004*. Catalogue No. 11F0019MIE—No. 298. Ottawa: Ministry of Industry, Government of Canada.

Henry, F., Tator, C., Mattis, W., & Rees, T. (1995). *The colour of democracy: Racism in Canadian society*. Toronto: Harcourt Brace.

Herberg, D., & Herberg, E. (1995). Canada's ethno-racial diversity: Policies and programs for Canadian social welfare. In J. Turner and F. Turner (Eds.), *Social welfare in Canada* (3rd ed.) (pp. 179–212). Scarborough, ON: Allyn and Bacon Canada.

Hess, M. (1993). *An overview of Canadian social policy*. Ottawa: Canadian Council on Social Development.

Hick, S. (2007). *Social welfare in Canada: Understanding income security* (2nd ed.). Toronto: Thomson Educational Publishing.

Hobsbawm, E. (1995). *Age of extremes: The short twentieth century 1914–1991*. London: Abacus.

Hogwood, B., & Gunn, L. (1984). *Policy analysis for the real world*. Toronto: Oxford University Press.

Homan, M. (1994). *Promoting community change: Making it happen in the real world*. Pacific Grove, CA.: Brooks/Cole Publishing Company.

Hoover, K.R. (1992). Conservatism. In M. Hawkesworth and M. Kogan (Eds.), *Encyclopedia of government and politics* (Vol. I, pp. 139–154). New York: Routledge.

Horowitz, G. (1970). Red Tory. In W. Kilbourn (Ed.), *Canada: A guide to the peaceable kingdom* (pp. 254–260). Toronto: Macmillan of Canada.

Human Resources and Skills Development Canada. (2004). *Employment insurance and regular benefits*. Accessed at: www.hrsdc.ca

Human Resources and Social Development Canada. (2005). *Social Security Statistics Canada and Provinces 1978–79 to 2002–03* Tables. Retrieved May 15, 2007, from: http://www.hrsdc.gc.ca/en/cs/sp/sdc/socpol/tables/page02.shtml

Human Resources and Social Development Canada. (2006). *Low income in Canada: 2000–2002 using the market basket measure*. Ottawa: Author. Retrieved March 7, 2007, from: http://www.hrsdc.gc.ca/en/cs/sp/sdc/pkrf/publications/research/2002-000662/SP-628-05-06e.pdf

Human Resources and Social Development Canada. (2007a). *Employment Insurance*

Program Characteristics. Ottawa: Author. Retrieved March 29, 2007, from: http://srv200.services.gc.ca/iiws/eiregions/geocont.aspx

Human Resources and Social Development Canada (2007b). *Homelessness Partnering Strategy*. Retrieved May 15, 2007, from: www.homelessness.gc.ca

Ignatieff, M. (2000). *The rights revolution*. Toronto: Anansi.

Indian and Northern Affairs. (2007). *Annual reports, minister's message*. Retrieved from: www.tbs-sct.gc.ca

Inwood, G.J. (2000). Federalism, globalization, and the (anti-)social union. In Burke, M., Mooers, C., & Shields, J. (ed.). *Restructuring and resistance: Canadian public policy in an age of global capitalism* (pp. 124–144). Halifax: Fernwood Publishing.

Irving, A. (1987). Federal–provincial issues in social policy. In S.A. Yelaja (Ed.), *Canadian social policy* (pp. 326–349). Waterloo ON: Wilfrid Laurier University Press

Irving, A., Parsons, H., & Bellamy, D. (1995). *Neighbours: Three social settlements in downtown Toronto*. Toronto: Canadian Scholars Press.

Jackson, A., & Robinson, D. (2000). *Falling behind: The state of working Canada, 2000*. Ottawa: Canadian Centre for Policy Alternatives.

Jackson, A., & Sanger, M. (1998). *Dismantling democracy: The multilateral agreement on investment (MAI) and its impact*. Ottawa, ON: Canadian Centre for Policy Alternatives and James Lorimer & Co.

Jackson, A., & Sanger, M. (2003). *When worlds collide: Implications of international trade and investment agreements for non-profit social services*. Ottawa: Canadian Centre for Policy Alternatives.

Jansson, B. (1990). *Social welfare policy: From theory to practice*. Belmont, CA: Wadsworth Publishing Company.

Jenson, J. (1998). *Mapping social cohesion: The state of Canadian research*. Canadian Policy Research Network Study No. F103. Ottawa: Renouf Publishing Co.

Johnson, L. (1986). *Social policy: A generalist approach* (2nd ed.). Boston, MA: Allyn and Bacon, Inc.

Johnston, P. (1983). *Native children and the child welfare system*. Toronto: James Lorimer and Company.

Jones, A., & Rutman, L. (1981). *In the children's aid: J.J. Kelso and child welfare in Ontario*. Toronto: University of Toronto Press.

Kadushin, A., & Martin, J. (1988). *Child welfare services*. (4th ed.). New York: Macmillan.

Kahn, A.J., & Kamerman, S.B. (1998). *Big cities in the welfare transition*. New York: Columbia University School of Social Work.

Kallen, E. (1989). *Label me human: Minority rights of stigmatized Canadians*. Toronto: University of Toronto Press.

Kallen, E. (1995). *Ethnicity and human rights in Canada*. (2nd ed.). Toronto: Oxford University Press.

Kallen, E. (2004). *Social inequality and social injustice: A human rights perspective*. New York: Palgrave Macmillan.

Kealey, G.S. (1980). *The working class response to industrial capitalism in Toronto, 1867–1892*. Toronto: University of Toronto Press.

Kealey, L. (Ed.). (1979). *A not unreasonable claim: Women and reform in Canada, 1880s–1920s*. Toronto: The Women's Press.

Kent, M.M., & Haub, C. (2005). Global demographic divide. *Population Bulletin, 60*(4), 1-25. Accessed at www.prb.org

Kerans, P. (1994). Need and welfare: "Thin" and "thick" approaches. In A. Johnson, S. McBride, and P. Smith (Eds.), *Continuities and discontinuities: The political economy of social welfare and labour market policy in Canada* (pp. 44–59). Toronto: University of Toronto Press.

Kerstetter, S. (2002). *Rags and riches: Wealth inequality in Canada*. Toronto: Canadian Centre for Policy Alternatives.

Kingdom, J. (1995). *Agendas, alternatives, and public policies* (2nd ed.). New York: Harper/Collins.

Klasen, S. (1998). *Social exclusion and children in OECD countries*. Paris: OECD Publications.

Klein. N. (2000). *No logo: Taking aim at the brand bullies*. Toronto: Vintage Canada.

Krieger, J. (Ed.). (1993). *The Oxford companion to politics of the world*. New York: Oxford University Press.

Lafitte, F. (1962). *Social policy in a free society*. Birmingham: Birmingham University Press.

Lamarshe, L. (1999). New governing arrangements, women and social policy. In D. Broad and W. Antony (Eds.), *Citizens or consumers? Social policy in a market society* (pp. 5–72). Halifax: Fernwood Publishing.

Lapointe, M., Dunn, K., Tremblay-Cote, N., Bergeron, L.P., & Ignakzac, L. (2006). *Looking ahead: A ten year outlook for the Canadian labour market*. Ottawa: Human Resources and Social Development Canada Publications Centre.

Laxer, J. (1997). *In search of a new left: Canadian politics after the neoconservative assault*. Toronto: Penguin.

Lecomte, R. (1990). Connecting private troubles and public issues in social work education. In B. Wharf (Ed.), *Social work and social change in Canada* (pp. 31–51). Toronto, ON: McClelland and Stewart Inc.

Leiby, J. (1978). *A history of social welfare and social work in the United States*. New York: Columbia University Press.

Leonard, P. (1975). Towards a paradigm for radical practice. In R. Bailey and M. Brake (Eds.), *Radical social work* (pp. 46–61). London: Edward Arnold, Ltd.

Leonard, P. (1984). *Personality and ideology: Towards a materialist understanding of the individual*. Atlantic Highlands, NJ: Humanities Press.

Leonard, P. (1997). *Postmodern welfare: Reconstructing an emancipatory project*. London: Sage Publications.

Lerner, M. (1997). *The politics of meaning: Restoring hope and possibility in an age of cynicism*. Don Mills, Ontario: Addison–Wesley.

Lessard, H. (1997). Creative stories: Social rights and Canada's Constitution. In

P. Evans and C. Wekerle (Eds.), *Women and the Canadian welfare state: Challenges and change* (Ch. 3). Toronto: University of Toronto Press.

Lewin, A.C., & Hasenfeld, Y. (1995). AFDC and marital dissolution: Does welfare policy reduce the gains from marriage? *American Sociological Association Papers*.

L'Heureux-Dube, C. (2000). A conversation about equality. *Denver Journal of International Law and Policy, 29*(1), 65.

Lightman, E. (2003). *Social policy in Canada*. Don Mills: Oxford Press.

Lipsky, M. (1980). *Street-level bureaucracy: Dilemmas of the individual in public services*. New York: Russell Sage Foundation.

Little, B. (2001). Remarkable progress cutting federal debt. *Globe and Mail*, May 21, B7.

Little, M.M. (1999). The limits of Canadian democracy: The citizenship rights of poor women. *Canadian Review of Social Policy, 43*, 59–76.

Livesey, B. (2007). Moneybags. *The Walrus, 4*(6): 36–43.

Lonergan, A., & Richards, C. (Eds.) (1988). *Thomas Berry and the new cosmology*. Mystic, CT: Twenty-Third Publications.

Lovelock, J. (2006). *The revenge of Gaia: Earth's climate crisis and the fate of humanity*. New York: Basic Books.

Lower, A. (1958). *Canadians in the making. A social history of Canada*. Toronto: Longmans, Green, and Company.

Lubove, R. (1965). *The professional altruist: The emergence of social work as a career, 1880–1930*. Cambridge: Harvard University Press.

Lukes, S. (2005). *Power: A radical view*. (2nd ed.). New York: Palgrave-Macmillan.

Luttwak, E. (1999). *Turbo-capitalism: Winners and losers in the global economy*. New York: Harper Collins.

Macarov, D. (1995a). *The design of social welfare*. New York: Holt, Rinehart and Winston.

Macarov, D. (1995b). *Social welfare structure and practice*. Thousand Oaks, CA: Sage.

Mannheim, K. (1936). *Ideology and utopia*. New York: Harcourt, Brace & World.

Marchak, M.P. (1988). *Ideological perspectives on Canada*. (3rd ed.). Toronto: McGraw-Hill Ryerson Ltd.

Marfleet, P. (1998). Against the globalist paradigm. *International conference on globalization: political, social, and economic perspectives*, held at Eastern Mediterranean University (TRNC), November 19–21, 1998.

Marno, P. (1997). Empowerment in the social work literature. *Unpublished Master's thesis*, School of Social Work, York University.

Marshall, T.H. (1949). Citizenship and social class. Reprinted in D. Held et al., *States and societies* (1983). London: Open University.

Marshall, T.H. (1965). *Social policy*. London: Hutchinson, 1965.

Marumba, S.K.I. (1998). Cross-cultural dimensions of human rights in the twenty-first century. In A. Anghie and G. Sturgess (Eds.), *Legal visions of the 21st century: Essays in honour of Judge Christopher Weeramantry* (pp. 201–240). The Hague: Kluwer Law International.

Marx, K., & Engels, F. (1846, trans. 1947). *The German ideology* (parts 1 and 3). New York: International Publishers.

Maslow, A.H. (1954). *Motivation and personality*. New York: Harper.

Mason, D., Talbott, S., & Leavitt, J. (1993). *Policy and politics for nurses*. (2nd ed.). Toronto: W. B. Saunders Co.

Mawhiney, A. (1995). The First Nations in Canada. In J. Turner and F. Turner (Eds.), *Canadian social welfare* (3rd ed.) (pp. 213–230). Scarborough, ON: Allyn and Bacon Canada.

McGilly, F. (1998). *An introduction to Canada's public social services*. Don Mills, ON: Oxford University Press.

McInnis-Dittrich, K. (1994). *Integrating social welfare policy and social work practice*. Pacific Grove, CA: Brooks/Cole Publishing Company.

McKenzie, B. (1997). Connecting policy and practice in First Nations child and family services: A Manitoba case study. In J. Pulkingham and G. Ternowetsky (Eds.), *Child and family policies: Struggles,*

strategies and options (pp.100–114). Halifax: Fernwood Publishing.

McMenemy, J. (1995). *The language of Canadian politics: A guide to important terms and concepts*. Waterloo ON: Wilfrid Laurier University Press.

McNally, D. (2006). *Another world is possible: Globalization and anti-capitalism*. (Rev. ed.). Winnipeg: Arbeiter Ring Publishing.

McPherson, D., & Rabb, D. (1994). *Indian from the inside: A study in ethno-metaphysics*. Thunder Bay: Centre for Northern Studies.

McQuaig, L. (1993). *The wealthy banker's wife*. Toronto: Penguin Books.

McQuaig, L. (1995). *Shooting the hippo: Death by deficit and other Canadian myths*. Toronto: Viking.

McQuaig, L. (1998). *The cult of impotence: Selling the myth of powerlessness in the global economy*. Toronto: Viking.

Meyer, S.M. (2006). *The end of the wild*. Cambridge MA: MIT Press.

Mills, C.W. (1959). *The sociological imagination*. Oxford: Oxford University Press.

Mills, C.W. (1963). *Power, politics and people*. New York: Ballantine Books.

Minoto, H., & Cross, P. (1991). The growth of the federal debt. *Canadian Economic Observer* (June). 3.1–3.17.

Mishra, R. (1981). *Society and social policy: Theories and practice of welfare*. (2nd ed.). London: Macmillan.

Mishra, R. (1995). The political bases of Canadian social welfare. In J. Turner and F. Turner (Eds.), *Canadian social welfare* (3rd ed.) (pp. 59–74). Scarborough, ON: Allyn and Bacon Canada.

Mishra, R. (1999). *Globalization and the welfare state*. Cheltenham UK: Edward Elgar.

Mittlestaedt, M. (2001). Commission throws water on Ottawa's lakes cleanup. *Globe and Mail*, October 3, A13.

Mittlestaedt, M. (2006). Drug residue tainting water, report warns. *The Globe and Mail*, March 6, A5.

Moreau, M. (1989). *Empowerment through a structural approach to social work*. Ottawa: Carleton University School of Social Work.

Morgan, S.P. & Taylor, M.G. (2006). Low fertility at the turn of the twenty-first century. *Annual Review of Sociology, 32,* 375–90.

Morissette, R., & Zhangi, X. (2006). Revisiting wealth inequality. *Perspectives on Labour and Income,* 7(12), December. Statistics Canada—Catalogue no. 75-001-XIE.

Morissette, R., Schellenberg, G., & Johnson, A. (2005). Diverging trends in unionization. *Statistics Canada's Perspectives on Labour and Income,* 17(2), n.p. Retrieved June 10, 2007, from: http://www.statcan.ca/bsolc/english/bsolc?catno=75-001-X20050027827

Morris, M., & Gonsalves, T. (2005). *Fact sheets: Women and poverty.* (3rd ed.). Canadian Research Institute for the Advancement of Women. Retrieved from: www.criaw.ca

Morrison, I. (1997). Rights and the right: Ending social citizenship in Tory Ontario. In D. Ralph, A. Regimbald, and N. St-Amand (Eds.), *Open for business, closed to people* (pp. 68–79). Halifax: Fernwood.

Morton, W.L. (1969). *The kingdom of Canada.* Toronto: McClelland and Stewart.

Mulé, N. (2005). Equality's limitations, liberation's challenges: Considerations for queer movement strategizing. *Canadian Online Journal of Queer Studies in Education,* 2(1).

Mullaly, R. (1993). *Structural social work.* Toronto: McClelland and Stewart.

Mullaly, R. (2002). *Challenging oppression: A critical social work approach.* Don Mills, ON: Oxford University Press.

Mullaly, R. (2007). *The new structural social work.* Don Mills, ON: Oxford University Press.

Mulvale, J.P. (2001). *Reimagining social welfare: Beyond the Keynesian welfare state.* Toronto: Garamond.

Muszynski, L. (1987). *Is it fair? What tax reform will do to you.* Ottawa: Canadian Centre for Policy Alternatives.

Myers, R., & Worm, B. (2003). Rapid world-wide depletion of predatory fish communities. *Nature, 423* (May 15), 280–283.

National Council of Welfare. (1993). *Incentives and disincentives to work.* Ottawa: Ministry of Supply and Services Canada.

National Council of Welfare. (1995). *The 1995 budget and block funding.* Ottawa: National Council of Welfare.

National Council of Welfare. (2001). *Child poverty profile 1998.* Ottawa: National Council of Welfare.

National Council of Welfare. (2004). *Income for living?* Vol. 120. Ottawa: National Council of Welfare.

National Council of Welfare. (2006a). *Poverty profile 2002 and 2003.* Catalogue No.SDZ5-1/2003E. Ottawa: Minister of Public Works and Government Services Canada.

National Council of Welfare. (2006b). *Welfare incomes 2005.* Ottawa: Minister of Public Works and Government Services Canada. Retrieved May 13, 2007, from: www.ncwcnbes.net/en/research/welfare-bienetre.html

National Council of Welfare. (2007). *Solving poverty: Four cornerstones of a workable national strategy for Canada.* Ottawa: National Council of Welfare.

Naylor, C.D. (1986). *Private practice, public payment.* Montreal/Kingston: McGill-Queen's University Press.

Naylor, D., & Martin, R. (2005). A better way to share. *Globe and Mail,* February 10, A23.

Nelles, H.V. (1974). *The politics of development: Forests, mines, and hydro-electric power in Ontario, 1849–1941.* Toronto: Macmillan.

Neysmith, S. (Ed.). (2000). *Restructuring caring labour: Discourse, state practice and everyday life.* Don Mills, ON: Oxford University Press.

Neysmith, S., Bezanson, K., & O'Connell, A. (2005). *Telling tales: Living the effects of public policy.* Halifax: Fernwood.

Nikiforuk, A. (2007). Is Canada the latest emerging petro-tyranny? *The Globe and Mail*, June 11, 2007, p. A13.

Notes from Nowhere (Ed.). (2003). *We are everywhere: The irresistible rise of global anti-capitalism.* New York: Verso.

Nova Scotia Finance. (2007). *Nova Scotia budget documents for the fiscal year 2007–2008.* Halifax: Author. Retrieved on May 10, 2007, from: http://www.gov.ns.ca/finance/budget07/

Obituaries. (April 26, 1997). *Globe and Mail.*

O'Brien, C. (1998). *Sexual regulation and Ontario social policies in the 1990s.* Doctoral dissertation. Faculty of Social Work, University of Toronto.

O'Brien, C., & Weir, L. (1995). Lesbians and gay men inside and outside families. In N. Mandell and A. Duffy (Eds.), *Canadian families: Diversity, conflict and change* (pp. 111–139). Toronto: Harcourt Brace and Company

Offe, C. (1984). *Contradictions of the welfare state.* Cambridge: MIT Press.

O'Neill, B. (2006). Toward inclusion of gay and lesbian people: Social policy changes in relation to sexual orientation. In A. Westhues (Ed.), *Canadian social policy: Issues and perspectives* (4th Edition). Waterloo: Wilfrid Laurier University Press.

Ontario (1997). *Ontario Works Act.* Government of Ontario: Queen's Printer for Ontario.

Palmer, B.D. (1979). *A culture in conflict: Skilled workers and industrial capitalism in Hamilton, Ontario, 1860–1914.* Montreal/Kingston: McGill-Queen's University Press.

Parkinson, R. (2004). *Declining voter turnout in Canada: What can be done?* Retrieved May 28, 2007, from: www. mapleleafweb.com

Pascal, G. (1993). Citizenship—A feminist analysis. In G. Drover and P. Kerans (Eds.), *Welfare theory.* Aldershot UK: Edward Elgar Publishing.

Pateman, C. (1992). Equality, difference, and insubordination: The politics of motherhood and women's citizenship. In G. Bock and S. James (Eds.), *Beyond equality and difference: Citizenship, feminist politics, and female subjectivity* (pp. 17–31). New York: Routledge.

Patterson, E. (1987). Native peoples and social policy. In S. Yelaja (Ed.), *Canadian social policy* (Rev. ed.) (pp. 175–194). Waterloo ON: Wilfrid Laurier University Press.

Pay Equity Task Force. (2004). *Pay equity: A new approach to a fundamental right.* Ottawa: Minister of Justice and Attorney General of Canada, and the Minister of Labour.

Payne, J. (1998). *Overcoming welfare: Expecting more from the poor—and from ourselves.* New York: Basic Books.

Pearson, G. (1975). Making social workers: Bad promises and good omens. In R. Bailey and M. Brake (Eds.), *Radical social work* (pp. 13–45). London: Edward Arnold, Ltd.

Penner, N. (1992). *From protest to power: Social democracy in Canada 1900–present.* Toronto: Lorimer.

Picot, G., Hou, F., & Coulombe, S. (2007). *Chronic low income and low-income dynamics among recent immigrants.* Catalogue no. 11F0019MIE—No. 294. Ottawa: Statistics Canada.

Pierce, D. (1984). *Policy for the social work practitioner.* New York: Longman.

Polese, M. (1998). Regional economics. *The 1998 Canadian and World encyclopedia.* CD–ROM. Toronto: McClelland and Stewart.

Popple, P., & Leighninger, L. (2001). *The policy-based profession: An introduction to social welfare policy for social workers* (2nd ed.). Boston: Allyn and Bacon.

Pratt, C. (2007). New big thing could put brakes on CEO pay. *Globe and Mail*, June 11, 2007, B2.

Prentice, A., Bourne, P., Cuthbert Brandt, G., Light, B., Mitchinson, W., & Black, N. (1988). *Canadian women: A history.* Toronto: Harcourt, Brace, Jovanovich.

Putnam, R.D. (2000). *Bowling alone: The collapse and revival of American community.* New York: Simon and Schuster.

Raphael, D. (Ed.). (2004). *Social determinants of health: Canadian perspectives.* Toronto: Canadian Scholars' Press.

Reamer, F. (1993). *The philosophical foundations of social work.* New York: Columbia University Press.

Rebick, J. (2000). *Imagine democracy.* Toronto: Stoddart.

Rein, M. (1974). Social policy analysis and the interpretation of beliefs. *The American Institute for Planners Journal,* September, 297–310.

Rein, M. (1983). *From policy to practice.* Armonk NY: M. E. Sharpe Inc.

Report for the Interprovincial Conference of Ministers Responsible for Social Services (1980). *The income security system in Canada.* Ottawa: Canadian Intergovernmental Conference Secretariat.

Ricciutelli, L., Larkin, J., & O'Neill, E. (1998). *Confronting the cuts: A sourcebook for women in Ontario.* Toronto: Inanna Publications and Education Inc.

Rice, J.J., & Prince, M.J. (2000). *Changing politics of Canadian social policy.* Toronto: University of Toronto Press.

Richmond, M. (1930). *The long view.* New York: Russell Sage Foundation.

Rioux, M. (1997). Disability: The place of judgment in a world of fact. *Journal of Intellectual Disability Research, 41*(2), 102–111.

Roeher Institute. (1996). *Disability, community and society.* Toronto: Roeher Institute.

Rooke, P.T., & Schnell, R.L. (1987). *No bleeding heart: Charlotte Whitton, a feminist on the right.* Montreal/Kingston: McGill-Queen's University Press.

Rose, N. (1996). Psychiatry as a political science: Advanced liberalism and the administration of risk. *History of the Human Sciences, 9*(2), 1–23.

Ross, D.P., Scott, K.J., & Smith, P.J. (2000). *The Canadian fact book on poverty.* Ottawa: The Canadian Council on Social Development.

Runnals, D., & Matn, H. (2001). From shield to sword. *The Gazette,* Montreal, Que., April 28, B5.

Ryan, B., Brotman, S., & Roe, B. (2000). *Access to care: Exploring the health and well-being of gay, lesbian, bisexual and two-spirit people in Canada.* Montréal: McGill Universiity, McGill Centre for Applied Family Studies.

Sachs, J. (2005). *The end of poverty: Economic possibilities for our time.* New York: Penguin.

Sachs, W., Loske, R., Linz, M., et al. (1998). *Greening the North: A post-industrial blueprint for ecology and equity.* New York: Zed.

Sale, K. (2006). *After Eden: The evolution of human domination.* Durham NC: Duke University Press.

Saul, J.R. (1995). *The unconscious civilization.* Concord, ON: House of Anansi Press.

Sayeed, A. (2002). *The 1997 Canada Pension Plan changes: Implications for women and men.* Ottawa: Status of Women Canada.

Schansberg, D.E. (1996). *Poor policy: How government harms the poor.* Boulder, CO: Westview Press.

Schorr, A. (1985). Professional practice as policy. *Social Service Review, 59*(June), 185–86.

Schragge, E. (Ed.). (1997). *Workfare: Ideology for a new under-class.* Toronto: Garamond Press.

Schragge, E., & Deniger, M. (1997). Workfare in Quebec. In E. Schragge (Ed.), *Workfare: Ideology for a new under-class* (pp. 59–84). Toronto: Garamond Press.

Schumacher, E.F. (1973). *Small is beautiful: Economics as if people mattered.* New York: Harper and Row.

Schwartz, W. (1969). Private troubles and public issues: One social work job or two? *Social Welfare Forum,* 22–43.

Schwartz, W. (1974). Private troubles and public issues: One social work job or two? In Weinberger, P.E. (Ed.). *Perspectives on social welfare* (2nd edition). New York: Macmillan.

Scott, K. (1998). *Women and the CHST: A profile of women receiving social assistance in 1994.* Ottawa: Status of Women, Canada.

Seidman, S. (1997). *Difference troubles: Queering social theory and sexual politics*. Cambridge: Cambridge University Press.

Sen, A. (1992). *Inequality reexamined*. New York: Harvard University Press.

Senate Committee on Poverty. (1971). *Poverty in Canada*. Ottawa: Canadian Government Publishing Centre.

Service Canada (2007). *Employment Insurance and regular benefits*. Ottawa: Author. Retrieved on March 7, 2007, from: http://www1.servicecanada.gc.ca/en/ei/types/regular.shtml#Qualifying

Shah, P.J., & Smith, P.K. (1995). Do welfare benefits cause the welfare caseload? *Public Choice, 85*(1–2), 91–105.

Shewell, H. (2007). *Gathering strength or just more welfare? The socio-economic situation of First Nations before and since the Royal Commission on Aboriginal Peoples*. Unpublished paper.

Shewell, H., & Spagnut, A. (1995). The First Nations of Canada: Social welfare and the quest for self-government. In J. Dixon and R. Scheurell (Eds.), *Social welfare with indigenous peoples* (pp. 1–15). London: Routledge.

Silver, H. (1994). Social exclusion and social solidarity: Three paradigms. *International Labour Review, 1333*(5–6), 531–578.

Simon, H. (1957). *Administrative behavior: A study of decision-making processes in administrative organization* (3rd ed.). New York: Free Press.

Sirico, R.A. (1997, July 27). Work is moral and so is workfare. *New York Times*, E15.

Smiley, D. (1976). *Canada in question: Federalism in the seventies* (2nd ed.). Toronto: McGraw-Hill Ryerson.

Smith, P.K. (1993). Welfare as a cause of poverty: A time series analysis. *Public Choice, 75*(2), 157–170.

Soros, G. (1997). *The crisis of global capitalism: Open society endangered*. New York: Public Affairs.

Splane, R.B. (1965). *Social welfare in Ontario 1791–1893: A study of public welfare administration*. Toronto: University of Toronto Press.

Stainton, T. (1994). *Autonomy and social policy*. Aldershot: Avebury.

Stainton, T. (2005). Empowerment and the architecture of rights based social policy. *Journal of Intellectual Disabilities, 9*, 289–298.

Statistics Canada. (2001). Census Data 2001, 97F003XCB2001002.

Statistics Canada. (October 29, 2003). Charitable donors: 2002. *The Daily*. Retrieved May 1, 2007, from: http://www.statcan.ca/Daily/English/031029/d031029b.htm

Statistics Canada. (December 16, 2003). *Total income groups in constant (2000) dollars*, file no. 97F0020XCB2001073. Ottawa: Author. Retrieved March 29, 2007, from: http://www12.statcan.ca/english/census01/products/standard/themes/RetrieveProductTable.cfm?Temporal=2001&PID=60960&APATH=3&GID=355313&METH=1&PTYPE=55496&THEME=54&FOCUS=0&AID=0&PLACENAME=0&PROVINCE=0&SEARCH=0&GC=99&GK=NA&VID=0&VNAME=&VNAMEF=&FL=0&RL=0&FREE=0

Statistics Canada. (2005a). *Population: Urban and rural, by province and territory*. Ottawa: Author.

Statistics Canada. (2005b). *The Daily* (March 22, 2005). www.statscan.ca/Daily/English/050322/do50322b.htm.

Statistics Canada. (March 7, 2006). Women in Canada. *The Daily*. Retrieved from: http://www.statcan.ca/Daily/English/060307/d060307a.htm

Statistics Canada. (June 15, 2006). Government finance: Revenue, expenditure, and surplus. *The Daily*, Catalogue No. 11-001-XIE, 2–5. Retrieved May 13, 2007, from: http://www.statcan.ca/Daily/English/060615/d060615a.htm

Statistics Canada. (2006). *Low wage and low income*. Catalogue no. 75F0002MIE. Ottawa: Statistics Canada.

Statistics Canada. (2007a). *Income in Canada*. Retrieved May 1, 2007, from: http://dsp-psd.tpsgc.gc.ca/Collection/Statcan/75-202-XIE/75-202-XIE2004000.pdf

Statistics Canada. (2007b). *Table 282.0002*. Labour force survey estimates (LFS), by sex and detailed age group, annual (persons), 1976 to 2006. Ottawa: Author. Retrieved June 5, 2007 from:

http://cansim2.statcan.ca/cgi-win/
cnsmcgi.pgm?regtkt=&C2Sub=
&ARRAYID=2820002&C2DB=PRD&
VEC=&LANG=E&SrchVer=&ChunkSize
=&SDDSLOC=&ROOTDIR=CII/&
RESULTTEMPLARTE=CII/CII_PICK&
ARRAY_PICK=1&SDDSID=&
SDDSDESC=

Statistics Canada, Health Statistics Division.
(2006). *Deaths, 2004*. Ottawa: Minister
of Industry. Retrieved June 10, 2007 from:
http://www.statcan.ca/english/freepub/
84F0211XIE/84F0211XIE2004000.htm

Statistics Canada, Income Statistics Division.
(2006). *Low income cut-offs for 2005 and
low income measures for 2004.* Catalogue
no. 75F0003MIE. Ottawa: Statistics
Canada.

Statistics Canada, Income Statistics
Division. (2007). *Low-income cutoffs for
2006 and low income measures for 2005.*
Income Research Paper Series,
Catalogue No. 75 F0002MIE. Ottawa:
Minister of Industry.

Statistics Canada Pensions and Wealth
Surveys Section (2005). *The wealth of
Canadians: An overview of the results of
the survey of financial wealth.* Ottawa:
Author. Catalogue No. 13F0026MIE.

Status of Women Canada, (2007). *Status
Report.* Retrieved from: http://www.swc-
cfc.gc.ca/index_e.html

Stelter, G.A., & Artibese, A.FJ. (Eds.).
(1977). *The Canadian city: Essays in urban
history.* Toronto: McClelland and Stewart.

Stroman, D. (1989). *Mental retardation in
social context.* Lanham, MD: University
Press of America, Inc.

Strong-Boag, V. (1976). *The parliament of
women: The National Council of Women
of Canada, 1893–1929.* Ottawa: National
Museum of Man.

Struthers, J. (1983). *No fault of their own:
Unemployment and the Canadian welfare
state 1914–1941.* Toronto: University of
Toronto Press.

Struthers, J. (1994). *Limits to affluence:
Welfare in Ontario, 1920–1970.* Toronto:
University of Toronto Press.

Swift, K. (1995). *Manufacturing bad mothers:
A critical perspective on child neglect.*
Toronto: University of Toronto Press.

Swift, K. (2001). The case for opposition:
Challenging contemporary child welfare policy directions. *Canadian Review
of Social Policy, 47,* 59–76.

Swift, K., & Birmingham, M. (1999).
Caring in a globalizing economy: Single
mothers on assistance. In D. Durst
(Ed.), *Canada's new National Child
Benefit: Phoenix or fizzle?* (pp. 84–102).
Halifax: Fernwood Publishing.

Teilhard de Chardin, P. (1955). *The phenomenon of man.* New York: Harper &
Brothers.

Tertzakian, P. (2006). *A thousand barrels a
second: The coming oil point and the
challenges facing an energy dependent
world.* Toronto: McGraw-Hill.

Thompson, N. (1993). *Anti-discriminatory
practice.* London: Macmillan.

Thomlison, R., & Bradshaw, C. (1999).
Canadian political processes and social
work practice. In F. Turner (Ed.), *Social
work practice: A Canadian perspective*
(pp. 264–275). Scarborough, ON:
Prentice Hall Canada.

Tilly, C. (1999). From interactions to out-
comes in social movements. In M.
Giugni, D. McAdan, and C. Tilly (Eds.),
How social movements matter (pp.
253–270.). Minneapolis: University of
Minnesota Press.

Titmuss, R.M. (1958). *Essays on the welfare
state.* London: George Allen & Unwin
Ltd.

Titmuss, R.M. (1970). *The gift relationship:
From human blood to social policy.*
London: George Allen & Unwin Ltd.

Titmuss, R.M. (1974). *Social policy: An introduction.* London: George Allen &
Unwin Ltd.

Titmuss, R.M. (1987). *Selected writings of
Richard M. Titmuss: The philosophy of
welfare.* London: Allen and Unwin.

Torjman, S. (1996a). *Workfare: A poor law.*
Ottawa: Caledon Institute of Social Policy.

Torjman, S. (1996b). *History/hysteria.*
Ottawa: Caledon Institute of Social Policy.

Torjman, S. (1997). *Welfare warfare.* Ottawa:
Caledon Institute of Social Policy.

Torjman, S. (1998a). *Community-based
poverty reduction.* Ottawa: Caledon
Institute of Social Policy.

Torjman, S. (1998b). *Welfare reform through tailor-made training*. Ottawa: Caledon Institute of Social Policy.

Torjman, S. (1999). *Dumb and dumber governments*. Ottawa: Caledon Institute of Social Policy.

Torjman, S. (2005). *Disability tax: The budget's quiet little secret*. Caledon Institute of Social Policy. ISBN#1-55382-134-3.

Torjman, S. (2007). *Repairing Canada's social safety net*. Ottawa: Caledon Institute of social policy.

Torjman, S., & Battle, K. (1995a). *Can we have national standards?* Ottawa: Caledon Institute of Social Policy.

Torjman, S., & Battle, K. (1995b). *The dangers of block funding*. Ottawa: Caledon Institute of Social Policy.

Torrie, R. (2000, May 19). A clear and present danger. *Globe and Mail*, A13.

Townson, M. (2006). *Growing older, working longer: The new face of retirement*. Ottawa: Canadian Centre for Policy Alternatives.

Trudeau, P.E. (1990). The values of a just society. In T. Axworthy and P.E. Trudeau (Eds.), *Towards a just society* (pp. 357–385). Markham: Viking.

Turk, J., & Wilson, G. (1996). *Unfair shares: Corporations and taxation in Canada*. Don Mills: Ontario Coalition for Social Justice and Ontario Federation of Labour.

Turner, F. (1995). Social welfare in Canada. In J. Turner and F. Turner (Eds.), *Canadian social welfare* (3rd ed.) (pp. 1–11). Scarborough, ON: Allyn and Bacon Canada.

United Nations, Department of Economic and Social Affairs, Population Division. (2002). *World population ageing 1950–2050*. New York: United Nations Publications.

United Nations Development Programme. (2006). *Human development report 2006. Beyond scarcity: Power, poverty, and the global water crisis*. New York: Author.

United Nations Statistics Division. (2007). *Environmental indicators: CO₂ emissions, 2003*. Retrieved May 15, 2007, from: http://unstats.un.org/unsd/environment/air_co2_emissions.htm

Ursel, J. (1992). *Private lives, public policy: One hundred years of state intervention in the family*. Toronto: Women's Press.

Valentine, F. (2001). *Enabling citizenship: Full inclusion of children with disabilities and their parents*. Discussion paper No. F/13. Ottawa: Canadian Policy Research Network.

Van Wormer, K. (1997). *Social welfare: A world view*. New York: Nelson Hall.

Vosko, L.F. (2006). Precarious employment: Towards an improved understanding of labour market insecurity. In L.F. Vosko (Ed.), *Precarious employment: Understanding labour market insecurity in Canada* (pp. 3–39). Montreal & Kingston: McGill-Queen's University Press.

Waldi, P. (2006). Canadian firms and charity: Are they scrooges? *Globe and Mail*, November 16, p. B2.

Webb, D. (1981). Radical and traditional social work. *British Journal of Social Work, 11*, 143–158.

Weber, M. (1930, trans. 1958). *The Protestant ethic and the spirit of capitalism*. New York: Charles Scribner's Sons.

Wein, F. (1991). *The role of social policy in economic restructuring*. Halifax, NS: The Institute for Research on Public Policy.

Westhues, A. (Ed.) (2003). *Canadian social policy: Issues and perspectives*. Waterloo, ON: Wilfrid Laurier Press.

Wharf, B. (1986). Social welfare and the political system. In J. Turner and F. Turner (Eds.), *Canadian social welfare* (2nd ed.) (pp. 103–120). Don Mills: Collier Macmillan.

Wharf, B. (Ed.). (1990). *Social work and social change in Canada*. Toronto: McClelland and Stewart.

Wharf, B. (1992). *Community and social policy in Canada*. Toronto: McClelland and Stewart.

Wharf, B., & Cossom, J. (1987). Citizen participation and social welfare policy. In S. Yelaja (Ed.), *Canadian social policy* (Rev. ed.) (pp. 266–287). Waterloo, ON: Wilfrid Laurier University Press.

Wharf, B., & McKenzie, B. (1998). *Connecting policy to practice in the human services*. Toronto: Oxford University Press.

Wharf, B., & McKenzie B. (2004). *Connecting policy to practice in the human services* (2nd ed.). Don Mills: Oxford University Press.

Wilensky, H.L., & Lebeaux, C.N. (1958). *Industrial society and social welfare*. New York: Russell Sage Foundation.

Williams, F. (1989). *Social policy: A critical introduction*. Cambridge: Polity Press.

Wintemute, R. (1995). *Sexual orientation and human rights*. Oxford: Clarendon Press.

Woodsworth, D. (1986). Canadian realities. In J. Turner and F. Turner (Eds.), *Canadian social welfare* (2nd ed.). Don Mills: Collier Macmillan.

World Wildlife Fund. (2006). *Living planet report: 2006*. Gland, Switzerland: Author.

Wright, R. (2004). *A short history of progress*. Toronto: Anansi.

Yelaja, S. (Ed.) (1987). *Canadian Social Policy* (Rev. ed.). Waterloo ON: Wilfrid Laurier University Press.

Young, C. (1994). Taxing times for lesbians and gay men: Equality at what cost? *Dalhousie Law Journal, 17*(2), 534–559.

Zapf, M.K. (1999). Geographic factors. In F. Turner (Ed.), *Social work practice: A Canadian perspective* (pp. 344–358). Scarborough ON: Allyn and Bacon Canada.

Index

Note: Entries for figures and tables are followed by "*f*" and "*t*," respectively.